Hunting the Golden Lion
a cycle safari through France

Having recklessly declared in a previous book
that it must be possible to cross all of France
staying only in hotels called the
HOTEL DU LION D'OR,
Martin Lloyd is challenged by his
critics to prove his assertion in the only
way possible – by doing it.

ely it will be a straightforward and leisurely
ride through France? As long as the hotels are
no more than a day's cycle ride apart, of course.
And if your bicycle has been constructed this
century, and if you remember to take with you
all that you need... and if your name isn't
Martin Lloyd.

Is this why, on the the first day of his safari,
he is standing in his pyjamas on a pavement
a thousand miles from home,
clutching a broken bicycle
with a bleeding hand?

also by Martin Lloyd

The Passport
The Trouble with France
The Trouble with Spain
The Chinese Transfer
Every Picture
(further details at end of book)

Hunting the Golden Lion

a cycle safari through France

Martin Lloyd

Queen Anne's Fan

First published in 2009 by Queen Anne's Fan
PO Box 883 • Canterbury • Kent • CT1 3WJ

ISBN 9780 9547 1506 9

A CIP record of this book can be obtained from the British Library.

Cover photograph by Andrew Lloyd-Cook

Set in New Baskerville 11 on 12pt.

Printed in England

Queen Anne's Fan

List of Chapters

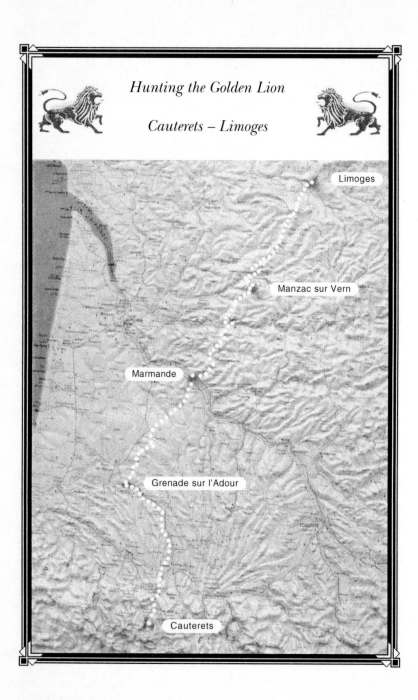

Hunting the Golden Lion

Cauterets – Limoges

Limoges

Manzac sur Vern

Marmande

Grenade sur l'Adour

Cauterets

CHAPTER ONE – PREPARATION

'And that, ladies and gentlemen, is the end of my talk.'

Quick, whilst the audience is applauding, nip down the aisle, switch off the projector lamp, keep the fan running and wheel the projector up to the front otherwise it will waltz to the hatch with the vanguard of tea drinkers.

'I am sure you have thousands of questions ladies and gentlemen. Fire away!'

They probably have but they have also been sitting in plastic buckets for over an hour and are gasping for a cuppa and a bit of abdominal massage. Ah, there's always one.

'Mr Lloyd, I know I speak for everybody here when I say that we have enjoyed immensely the fascinating slides of your bicycle travels. The question I think that must be on everybody's mind is: England, France, Spain, the Far East; where are you going next?'

'I am glad you asked me that, madam. The answer is: France, but with a difference. For my next book I am going to try to cycle through France and stay only in hotels called, 'Hotel du Lion d'Or'. And the title of the book will be something like, *Hunting the Golden Lion – a cycle safari through France.*'

That was all very well but a few weeks later, at the end of another talk, when I had been asked the same question my reply had been: I am glad you asked me that sir, I shall be writing another book about passports but this one will be

7

designed for family historians and the title will be something like, '*How to Read a Passport*'.

And all that had happened eighteen months ago. The slot that I had earmarked in my busy timetable to undertake the Golden Lion Safari was fast approaching. I would be setting off in about five weeks from now. I really ought to do something about it. Like, find out how many such hotels existed and where they were.

The telephone rang. I turned away from my computer screen. The text I was working on was neither Golden Lions nor passports, it was a cracking good dialogue for the sequel to the thriller romance that my readers were demanding.

It was John on the phone. MyMateJohn. One of those people whose brain is so remarkably agile that he can give a conversation only half his attention. So whilst you are talking to him about the carrots in your garden, he will pick up the magazine on your kitchen table, leaf through it and say, 'Have you ever been to the Isle of Skye?' A telephone conversation with him is like an excerpt from an absurd play by Eugene Ionescu. The magazine on your kitchen table is replaced by his broadband internet connection. Whilst talking to you he will be simultaneously surfing the ether on a totally unrelated subject to the one you think you are discussing and of course, you are hampered by not having his computer screen before you. At least with the magazine he does give you a clue by turning it around and showing you the photograph.

'How did the talk go last night?' he asked.

'OK. I need to try to find a new mains lead for my projector though. That won't be easy.'

'It's not standard then?'

'No, it's a thirty year old Rollei. They have a special three pin socket a bit like a kettle, but not quite. How was the cycle ride on Sunday? I'm sorry I could not make it, I just was too busy.'

'And of course it was raining.' I hear his fingers on the keyboard. *Chock, chock, chock, chock.*

'Well that was a factor I took into consideration. My waterproof jacket has failed. It's about five years old now. They don't last much longer.'

Chock, chock, beep, chock, chock.

'There's one here, complete, for a hundred and twenty five pounds.' *Chock, chock, chock.*

'One "what" for a hundred and twenty five pounds?'

'Rollei 35mm projector and screen. It's in the States.'

'That's no good, and anyway, my slides are not 35mm, they are six by six. You know they are, you've seen them.'

Chock, chock, chock, chock.

'John.'

'Is it a Dual 66 your projector?'

'John.'

'Cos there's one here in Ireland.'

'John.'

'It's without its lens.'

'John.'

'What?' *Chock, chock, chock, beep.*

'John, what did you ring for?'

'I wondered how you were getting on with your golden lion safari thing.'

'Oh that. Well I should be doing it now instead of writing another novel.'

'What have you got left to do?'

'Not much. Find the hotels, work out an itinerary, work out a budget. The lot, really.'

'How long will the journey take?'

'I don't know till I've found the hotels. What I do know is that I will be paying for a hotel every night, so that will be expensive.'

'How many have you found so far?'

'About fifty six. I've been scanning through the Michelin and the Logis guides.'

Chock, chock, chock.

'There's one here, *Hotel du Lion d'Or, Amboise.*'

'Yeah, I've got that one, John.'

'And Marmande, where the tomatoes come from?'

'Yeah, I know about that one as well.'

'There's one here. Looks very nice. Oh it's in Montreal. Do you fancy Whitstable on Thursday?'

'Yes, let's ride to Whitstable. It will give me an incentive to tune up the bicycle ready for my expedition.'

FOUR WEEKS TO GO

My bicycle does not need any tuning or maintenance. I use it all the year round and so have to keep it in running order. MyMateJohn displays an unhealthy fanaticism with regard to bicycle cleanliness, proudly washing down his bicycle after a rainy ride and polishing the spokes and vacuum cleaning the handlebar grips. Of course, he can do this because he has taken the precaution of buying two identical bicycles, both painted blue, so that he can ride one whilst the other is in the wash and nobody will know. Unless, of course, he thinks it will be really muddy in which case he uses his third machine, the mountain bike with knobbly tyres. He puts that through the car wash.

I clean my bicycle once a year and for a few weeks it is sparkling green. I even wax it. For the rest of the year it is a drab muddy colour with a frosting of powdered dust from the trails in the Peak District.

'All you need,' John says, 'is a bowl of warm soapy water and a paintbrush. It doesn't take five minutes.'

'I keep my bicycle clean right where it matters – on the transmission. I regularly wipe the chain and oil it. That is what counts.'

'But if you cleaned your bicycle regularly you would find all the things that were wrong with it and adjust them before they developed into big problems.'

'But I don't get big problems with my bicycle. I designed

it to be problem free. Why are you slowing down?'

'Something wrong with my gears.' He fiddles with the lever, tugging at the cable with his fingers. 'The lever keeps slipping a cog.'

'You've probably cleaned it too much. A good dollop of clag in the mechanism is what you need. Why are you on your mountain bike anyway? It's not muddy.'

'The blue bike's got a puncture.'

'And the other blue bike.'

'It's in the wash.'

That is the trouble when you have more than one bike. You can postpone the required remedial maintenance by picking another machine off the pile. If, like me, you have only one machine for overseas touring, pootling about and shopping, then as soon as it goes wrong you have to fix it. Or walk.

So what does my bicycle need? This set of tyres has only done about a thousand miles, it will be good for another couple of thousand with no problem. I will put a new cable on the rear brake because it is beginning to feel a bit spongey and I might have some mountain work to do. What else? Squirt a drop of oil on the chassis of the saddle to get rid of that creaking noise. That's it. I apologise if it sounds smug but that is the reward for having only one bicycle and keeping it in tip top condition.

THREE WEEKS TO GO

I start to do some serious map work. I take a map of France and mark on it in ink all the Lion d'Ors that I can find. Some are in the middle of nowhere and I need a large scale map to locate them on the small scale map. Some are in one guide book and not in the other. MyMateJohn gives me some that he has plucked from the ether. MyMateMargaret prints out reams from her computer, details of Golden Lions with photographs and rates and opening dates. The map begins to fill up but not evenly.

If I am to go from one Lion to another I need the hotels to be within a day's cycling distance of each other and for me that means about fifty miles. They are not. Some gaps are two hundred and fifty kilometres.

My eyes are going funny as I try to decipher the town names on the map. At the opticians they admit that they have given me the wrong prescription so I have to order a new set of lenses.

'No problem,' the helpful girl says. Everything to her is 'no problem'.

'I'm going to France in three weeks and I will need them by then.'

'No problem. Come back here in an hour and they will be ready,'

'No they won't. I ordered glass lenses. They said it would take two weeks for glass.'

'No problem. Come back in two weeks. We will ring you when they are ready.'

'And then I will want to have the pair that I am wearing now, to be tinted to use as sunglasses.'

'We can do that. No problem.'

MyMateMargaret rings up with some additions and amendments to the list. We compare notes. This hotel is closed for the first two weeks of August, this one is closed for the last two weeks. Only a French hotelier would think of going away on holiday during the holiday period. This one has no restaurant in July, this one is closed on Mondays.

'Of course,' she says, 'it's the worse possible time to go. You will be there for the first of August when they all get in their cars and head for the sun and for the fifteenth of August holiday when everything will probably be shut.' I agree with her. I have to keep her sweet. She will become my lifeline when I am on safari. 'Have you thought about booking hotels?' she adds.

'I don't want to book. When you are cycling you never know how far you can get in a day. In my twenty years of cycletouring, on only one occasion did I ever phone ahead and book a hotel, and then I never reached it which I thought was dreadfully unfair so I don't do it.'

I got a 'humph'.

Two things become apparent. One, if I do a complete circuit of France it will take me over a month and cost thousands of pounds and, two, I have a peculiar tingling sensation in my mouth.

'Go to the doctor,' says MyMateMargaret.

I go to the chemists.

'Fungal infection,' he says, and gives me some nice gel to rub inside my mouth four times a day.

TWO WEEKS TO GO

MyMateJohn rings up. He is jubilant because he has got seats in the grandstand for the finish of the first stage of the Tour de France in Canterbury... in five days time. Are we there already? Time is squeezing past me in the doorway without so much as an elbow in the ribs. The Tour de France this weekend? All those people? I phone up MyMateMargaret and explain the situation. She offers me two days asylum in a Tour-free zone. I grab my maps and notes and leave my front drive free for spectators to park on. For two days I make marks and annotations on the maps whilst Margaret coaxes Golden Lions out of dark undergrowth. Over in Canterbury a four hour caterpiller of obscene, fume-belching publicity vehicles crawls through the countryside, followed hours later by a ninety second burst of drug fuelled lycra. It has nothing to do with cycling.

A buff envelope is waiting for me upon my return. I had forgotten my income tax return. I need to do my year's accounts, not this stupid itinerary. Two days of scribing and calculating, checking and cross checking piles of dockets and receipts. In the middle of it, the typescript of the next novel comes back from Sylvia, one of my readers. She loved it but, and this is why I use her, she has some pertinent observations to make. I find myself browsing through it. It wouldn't take a minute just to put it up on the screen and make the amendments. Then of course, I need to change the title because the working title I had discovered had been used about thirty times already. I start to doodle a cover. Hmm, that's not bad. In no time at all I have slipped across to my Macintosh computer and am plunged into Photoshop humming along with the Beatles as the book cover evolves through version after version until at about midnight I have a fairly presentable first hard copy. But I should be looking for Golden Lions.

On the way home from my talk at Orpington I suddenly have a thought.

'You know this Golden Lion thing?' Margaret nods, her mouth is full of chocolate. My chocolate. 'Well, the challenge is not to perform a circumnavigation of France.'

'Isn't it?' Crumbs of sticky chocolate splatter onto the windscreen. Some people have tinted windscreens; I have speckled.

'No it's not. The original observation was, if I remember correctly, that it was probably possible to cross all of France staying only in hotels called "Hotel du Lion d'Or".'

'Well that makes a difference.'

'Yes. The first is the uncertainty. It is "probably" possible. So if I fail it will not matter.'

'And the second is that you only have to cross France, not go all around it.'

'Exactly. I could go from Calais down to Bordeaux or somewhere. That would be crossing France.'

'How long would that take you?'

'I could probably do it in ten days. If the hotels are in the right place.'

They are not. I decide that the best chance of success would be to land in France at Dieppe and start at the Lion d'Or at Neufchatel en Bray. It is only thirty five kilometres inland on a good cycle track and it has the advantage that I know the hotel, having stayed there before.

'How will you get back?' Margaret wants to know.

'I suppose I could carry on into Spain and visit Alan and Raquel in Bilbao and come home by ship.'

'And miss my birthday.'

'I don't fancy trying to get back on a French train. I have bad memories of my scuffles with the SNCF.'

'Well what was that coach thing that you used last time?'

'Yes, of course, that's the answer. Clever of me to think of it. The Bike Express. I could do it the other way around. I could go right down to Lourdes on the coach and then cycle back up.'

'That would be more sensible. It would mean that as the weather got hotter, you would be moving northwards.'

Cauterets is the southernmost Lion d'Or in France. That is where I will start. Once I have decided to go down by coach then the date of depature is chosen for me by the coach timetable and seat availability. Things are beginning to fit together at last. But I still have that tingling in my mouth. I have to go and see the doctor. He prescribes a different kind of gel and books me a blood test for the Friday before I am due to leave. I will not have the results before departure. I hope they don't discover something awkward. I imagine myself dozing comfortably on an air conditioned coach as I speed southwards into La Belle France, generously dispensing bubonic plague.

I don't bother to tell the doctor about my athlete's foot; one thing at a time. I just dig out the half empty tube of ointment that I had bought for the previous outbreak a couple of years earlier and apply it assiduously to my toe, morn and night. Margaret wants to know where I caught it from. I can only offer up my thirty year old wellington boots with the mouse-chewed lining that I had worn without socks to mow the lawn. I get another 'humph' and a sad shake of the head. I have now got fungus top and toe. I am rotting at both ends.

'Have you booked any hotels yet?' she asks.

'I told you, I do not do that sort of thing. It never works.'

'You're a twit.'

'OK. When I get near a hotel I will ring up the day before.'

'What on? You don't have a mobile.'

'They have public telephones in France.'

'My mum will lend you her mobile.'

'I don't want it. I don't use them. I don't know how to use them.'

'Have you got any further with the itinerary?'

'No, not really.'

'What have you been doing today then?'

'Well I had to deliver a book to Broadstairs.'

'You could have posted it.'

'I went by bike. It's only forty two miles return. It was a lovely ride.'

'But you haven't got the time, Martin. You should be concentrating on this trip.'

'Wait till you see the cover I've designed for my next novel.'

'Oh yes, and when did you do that?'

'Oh a couple of nights ago.'

'When you should have been sorting out your itinerary. Have you thought how you are going to pay for all this?'

'I'll use my debit card.'

'Make sure you have enough in your account then.'

Good point. I transfer a huge sum of money from my deposit account to my cheque account. It is all that I can afford so it had better be sufficient.

ONE WEEK TO GO

The service on my van is due. I take it into the garage so that my six months pregnant daughter can use the vehicle with complete peace of mind whilst I am away.

The opticians ring. I collect my spectacles and hand in the others to have them tinted to make prescription-lens sunglasses. I hope that where I am going it will be bright and sunny.

'I've got a bit of shopping to do. I'll call back in an hour,' says I, knowing the patter.

'No problem.'

An hour later, Miss No Problem is explaining to me that they cannot tint glass lenses.

'But... but...' Why am I such a wimp? 'Can you make me a pair of plastic subscription sunspecs then?'

'No problem. Be ready next Thursday.'

'I need them on Tuesday. I am going on holiday on Wednesday.'

'No problem. We'll ring you when they are ready.'

Time to think about clothes. When I was in Help the Aged in Bexhill I bought a brand new cycling fleece in fluorescent yellow with reflective stripes. I have given it a few road tests in varied weather conditions and discovered that if worn with a thin layer underneath, then it has the magical property of keeping me cool in the heat and warm in the cold. I decide that this garment will be the kingpin of my wardrobe. I will take my cycling shorts, one pair of pyjamas, a cotton tee shirt, three pairs of pants and one pair of socks. For the hotel dining room I will take a pair of dark coloured, thin trousers and a hideously patterned silk shirt. The hideous pattern is essential. It means that I don't have to iron the shirt after washing because the creases won't show. On the bike I will keep a pair of waterproof overtrousers and my waterproof-jacket-that-isn't. I really ought to get another before I leave.

I do not need variety in my clothing because I shall be moving each day and only I will know that I am wearing the same clothes. It does not matter if I get bored with them.

So... think this thing through. I cycle in shorts, tee-shirt and fleece. When I get to the hotel the first thing I do is put up my washing line and wash pants, socks and tee shirt. I then wash myself, put on black trousers, clean pants and silk shirt; no socks but use those cheap very lightweight sandals that I got from the market, and then go down for dinner. At bedtime, pyjamas on and into bed. I can wash the silk shirt when needed just before getting into bed because it dries in about four hours. In the morning, if tee shirt is still damp I can wear my pyjama top under my fleece instead. If the socks are still wet I can go without. As long as I have got rid of my athlete's foot, that is. I keep putting the stuff on my toe but it is not having much effect. When my pyjamas need washing I can wear the tee shirt. Or sleep in the nuddy.

Fine. Now where did I get to on my novel?

SIX DAYS TO GO

I am having trouble with the Loire. I need to cross it from south to north but the gap between Golden Lions in this direction is too great for my frail legs. If I wanted to travel east-west it would be no problem, the Golden Lions are positively prowling nose to tail along the river bank down to the sea. Perhaps if I veered eastwards towards Burgundy and then came westwards down the Loire valley, from Lion to Lion, to the Atlantic coast then I could turn northwards into Brittany and tack back eastwards towards Dieppe? The giant zigzag would add a week to my itinerary but it would solve the problem. I pull out some more maps from my box. The floor of my lounge is a battlefield of contorted maps, twisted in torture and pinned down by blood red slabs of Michelin guides, one of which is so old that it tells you where you can get the accumulators charged to power the magneto on your car.

MyMateMargaret has found a cycle track on an old railway line and it goes from Lourdes to Cauterets. Brilliant! That will be my first day, from the coach stop, nineteen miles up into the Pyrenees. The cycle track on the railway line is a bonus because it will be a gentle gradient and I will have to do it twice: up to the first Lion d'Or and then back down again in the morning for the mad dash to the next, eighty six miles away. If nearly twenty of those miles in each direction are on an old railway line, the job will be easier.

The garage is on the telephone about the van. It has had its service and it is ready for collection. I am only half listening as I tot up mileages on the maps. Twelve hundred? Is that kilometres or miles? Suddenly it clicks in. Twelve hundred pounds.

'Did you say twelve hundred pounds?' My voice is faint with dread and incredulity.

'Twelve hundred and thirty four, sir.' I suppose you get a 'sir' if it is over a grand. But he is still talking. 'And there is some work that needs doing on it.' How could there be anything more that needs doing? 'You need a new pedal box. It needs replacing urgently, it could fail at any moment and that will cost two hundred and sixty pounds, fitted. You also need a new clutch, that will be five hundred and forty and a new catalyser which is five hundred and twenty.'

I collect the hated car and the rest of the day passes in a cotton wool haze. In the space of a few seconds I have spent more than all the money I had put in my account to cover my expedition. What do I do now?

MyMateJohn phones up and I cry on his shoulder.

'You could buy a good bike for twelve hundred pounds.'

'I've got a good bike and I've just spent twelve hundred pounds, not earned it. What I haven't got is the money to pay for the hotels.'

'Put it on your credit card,' he says.

'I don't have a credit card.'

'What? Not any?'

'No. Never have had.'

'You could camp. Nobody would know that you had not stayed at the hotels. You could still visit them.'

'It would be cheating and I would know. If I was going to do it that way I could sit at home in my garden and write the book.'

'Like H.V. Morton used to.'

'Did he used to sit in my garden? I never knew that. Perhaps I could get a blue plaque put up.'

'Or you could do it from the internet. Oh, I forgot. You haven't got the internet either have you?'

To cheer me up I shall go into town and buy a new waterproof jacket and a pair of thin trousers. I jump on my bike. It goes like a bird. All the waterproof jackets are midnight black or camouflage green. I don't want to blend in, I want to stand out. The light coloured and fluorescent jackets are not waterproof. No we will not be getting in any more stock before next Tuesday, sir.

I screw up my courage and go into one of those shops designed for the generation that transferred directly from pushchair to skateboard. Shoes have velcro straps and the trousers are held up by elastic string. Skateboarders can neither tie laces nor buckle belts – they never had to learn how. I find the pair of least unsuitable black trousers and am nonplussed to discover that the lining seems to have been fashioned from those net bags that oranges are sold in and attached to the elastic string is a toy plastic compass. Whilst I am standing in the queue, stoically waiting for the waif at the till to finish her dance, a Chinaman inspects the trousers folded over my arm. He pulls at the cloth and reads the price ticket. Perhaps he recognises them. Or maybe he's looking for directions.

MyMateMargaret phones up. She dictates to me a list of addresses and telephone numbers of Lion d'Ors. We check and cross check our lists. I explain my Loire zigzag.

'If I cut north east from Bourges I can stay at the Lion at a village called Léré just above Cosne sur Loire. I can then pedal either down the towpath alongside the canal or on the minor road alongside the Loire to Sandillon near Orleans; then Candé sur Beuvron or Amboise – both have Lion d'Ors.'

'I still think you should be reserving hotels. This is the holiday season. That hotel at Léré has only got six rooms.'

'Well, I might ring them up and ask them if they have room at the moment. I mean, if they are already full for the day in question then there is no point going there at all.'

'And what about the closing days? Some of them close one day a week. You need to think about that.'

Everything she says makes sense but I am still reluctant. MyMateMargaret says that it is not reluctance, it is stupidity, but she will look for the numbers for the extra hotels.

That evening I decide that she is right. I ruminate over my first hotel, Cauterets. I am sure to get to that one; the coach will be dropping me off less than twenty miles away. I phone up and book the hotel but don't tell Margaret. Tension is good for her.

FRIDAY. FIVE DAYS TO GO

Nothing to eat from midnight and then I cycle down to the doctor's. The nurse wants to take blood from my left arm. I tell her to take it from my right; they can never find the vein on the left arm. She fills up two pots full of blood and then I wobble faintly back up the hill for breakfast.

MyMateJohn is worried because I don't have a mobile phone; he offers me one from his stable. I say that I will use the public phones so he offers me a French phone card. My pride forbids me from accepting it. Is there nothing he has not got?

There is something I have not got. I need large scale maps of the area north of the Loire in Brittany and Normandy. The two maps I am using still have marked on them the sunken river ferries and blown up bridges from 1944. I ask my friends who travel daily to Calais to get the required maps but those maps are not stocked because they are not local to Calais. Eventually I discover that I can buy them in Canterbury so I pedal off down the hill again. I would use the car but I am a little worried about that clutch pedal that the garage said might fail and which I cannot afford to fix before I go.

'And what are you going to do about the freezer?' MyMateMargaret wants to know. 'It would be best to empty it and clean it.' Why does she have to be so practical?

'I can empty it but have you got any spare room in your freezer for my stuff?'

'I can let you have one drawer. Will that be enough?'

'It will have to be. I dare not ask John to store the stuff, he would eat it all.'

My freezer is full of fruit. Every September, our monthly ride takes us to the north Kent coast, into a network of hedged lanes. There, our cartographic trustee reverently unfolds the Treasure Chart upon which is marked with an X, the hedge full of wild cherry plums, Victoria plums and damsons. For this day in the year I put pannier bags on the front carriers of my bicycle as well as the back. We go down that lane on both sides like a vacuum cleaner. Polythene bags bulge with plums; damsons dribble down sleeves and are squashed under foot. Last year I returned with forty three pounds of fruit. Then I made jam. It takes hours. Mashing the stewed damsons to extract the stones makes me reflect that perhaps this is why nobody else bothers to pick them. The fruit that I can't jam, I freeze for another day. That day has just arrived. I cannot, by any stretch of friendship, unload this lot on MyMateMargaret.

I have no time for refinement; put the whole lot in together. It will be mixed fruit jam: damson, apple, plum, blackberry. I empty the bags into saucepans for the fruit to thaw and pedal off into town to buy sugar. I abandon Golden Lions and for the rest of that day I make jam. I stew, I stone, I stir, I skim, I pour, I seal. At eleven o'clock at night I am proudly surveying fourteen beautiful jars of jam.

As I clear away the empty bags I read the labels. I discover that what I had thought was apple was stewed parsnip. I have fourteen jars of mixed damson, blackberry, plum and parsnip jam. Oh well, MyMateJohn will eat it.

SATURDAY. FOUR DAYS TO GO

MyMateMargaret rings up early. She has found another cycle track railway line, a *voie verte*, the French call them, and it runs for the last ten miles of my eighty seven mile day from Cauterets. This impossible stage is beginning to look more and more realisable if the route starts and finishes on smooth cycle track. My spirits begin to rise. Perhaps I will not fail at this second Lion.

'And you had better do a set of back up disks to give me in case your house burns down. I'll be over this afternoon to collect them. How many hotels have you booked?'

'Er... one. Cauterets.'

'You're hard work sometimes. Book the rest.'

I would do but I have not actually fixed the itinerary further than the third day. I avoid the issue by starting the process of backing up my hard disk to floppies. If you don't know what that expression means it is not important. It just took me the rest of the morning, that's all.

As threatened, MyMateMargaret turns up later in the afternoon. We go down to the town and try to buy me a waterproof cycling jacket. I can find nothing suitable.

'It doesn't matter. I can use my present one.'

'You mean the jacket that you packed away when it was still wet and which then grew blue mould on the collar?'

'Yes, but it still keeps out some of the rain.'

'But your neck came up in a rash of spots.'

She has a habit of remembering trifling details and then resurrecting them at inappropriate moments. I turn and squint through the window of the building society.

'Come on, three o'clock. I'll buy you coffee.' I thought

that was generous of me.

'Why did you look in there?'

'To read the time. Building societies and estate agents are the only high street shops which display clocks; all the others want you to forget the time and keep spending so, no clocks.'

'What will you do in your hotel room in France? How will you know when it is time for breakfast or dinner if you have got no watch?'

'I always have that problem. About twenty years ago you could walk down a street and read the time from a dozen digital dashboard clocks, but they don't make them that bright any more.'

She steers me towards the jewellers. I start to panic.

'Look in that window. There is a watch there for fifteen pounds,' she says.

Am I relieved!

'I'm not spending fifteen pounds on a watch.'

'You don't want breakfast then? What about that one? Eleven pounds.'

'I haven't worn a watch for ten years.'

'How do you know it's ten years?'

'I still buy calendars. Do you want coffee or not?'

After coffee we visit that old stalwart, the Help the Aged shop. There, in a glass display case, I see an electronic watch which I buy for three pounds. And the money is going to a good cause – I hope to be aged one day.

Back home on my kitchen table, Margaret lays out the survival pack that she insists I take with me. What price peace? I can always sort through it after she has gone and discard anything I do not want to take.

I try booking hotels. My telephone seems not to want to communicate with France. Every number has to be dialled three times. I discover that you must not pause for breath whilst dialling otherwise the exchange doggedly goes back to its knitting. This is rather ironic when I remember the trouble everybody in our office used to experience thirty years earlier when trying to telephone Paris from London. It regularly took three hours to find a line and then it had the audio quality of two baked bean cans and a length of taut string.

My idea of a zigzag down the Loire is aiming for success but I cannot contact the hotel at the western end until Monday night because it is closed and the hotel at the eastern end does not open until the morning of the day I leave the UK. But then, as I explain to a tooth-sucking Margaret; it does not matter because they are a week into the safari and I will be able to phone them from France.

'You ought to book La Fresnaye because they have only three rooms. And try Tourny – it should make your crossing of the Seine easier.'

I ring La Fresnaye and speak to a bemused *patronne* who assures me that there is no need to book, they will have space even if they have only three rooms. It is only later that I discover the import of that assurance. I am less successful with Tourny.

'Is that the Lion d'Or at Tourny?'

'Just a minute.' There is a scuffling noise followed by the yelping of a dog. *'Allo?'* another voice says.

'Is that the Lion d'Or at Tourny?'

'Yes... Probably. What do you want?' The voice is heavy and lugubrious.

'Have you got room in August?'

'No, not really. We stopped doing the hotel months ago.'

SUNDAY. THREE DAYS TO GO

I give up trying to talk to French hoteliers and instead I concentrate on practical things. I weed the carrots and beetroot and mow the lawns. I start to cut the hedge but the electric hedgetrimmer is blunt and worn out. I should have replaced it but I was probably writing a book instead.

MyMateJohn comes around for a cup of tea.

'You are not allowed to eat cake are you?' I ask as I cut two thick slices of Mrs Baker's fruit cake.

'No,' he admits as he takes a bite from the thicker slice. 'Have you done your bike?'

'Nothing to do on it.'

'What about those pads on your handlebars?'

'What about them?'

'Well you could get some handlebar tape. You know, the proper stuff and wind it around neatly.'

'What I've got works all right.'

'But it's pipe lagging.'

'I know. The plumber left it behind.'

'Well it's not the right stuff for handlebars. It will break up and fall off.'

'That's all right. I can easily replace it. I've got a shed full of it.'

He sighs and rubs his forehead with his hand.

'You could clean your bike,' he suggests.

'Oh don't start that again. By the way, I shan't be at the Manciple's Garden Party on Wednesday. Can you give my excuses?'

'Where will you be?' He licks the cake crumbs from his fingers.

'If all goes according to plan; in darkest France.'

'Are you sure you don't want one of my mobile phones? Or a phone card?'

I am touched by his concern and generosity but don't show it. I'm a man. We are tough, us men.

'There is something you can do for me if you want to.'

'What is that?' he asks, eyeing my portion of cake.

'Do you want to read another of my novels? It's just come back from a reader and I thought it would be interesting to have it read by a man.'

'Yes, I'll do that. I enjoyed the other one.'

'You might not enjoy this one. It's more romance and

less thrill. So far it has been read by five ladies.'

'I don't see why I should not like it. It was written by the same bloke. I think you've hit on a new genre – the jolly good read. It's traditional story telling.'

'I hope so. Anyway, do your best but don't struggle. I mean, if you can just get to the end of it, that would be an achievement.'

'Have you got it there? Shall I take it with me?'

'I'll bring it round. I need to revise it first and put the corrections in from my last reader.'

It is one hundred and thirty five thousand words long. I finish working on it at one o'clock in the morning. No time for Golden Lions, and anyway, this is more fun. I fall into bed. Tomorrow is another day.

MONDAY. TWO DAYS TO GO

I wake up with the idea that I have some jobs to do. Just as I am working out what they are the postman drops a letter through my door. It is from the RNIB. I recorded *The Passport* as a talking book for them some months earlier. It was hard work but fun. Now they want me to do *The Trouble with France* and *The Trouble with Spain*. Those two will be a challenge. I start to practise voices for the characters.

Stop! Focus! Golden Lions are on the menu today. But I could do with a bit of exercise. I jump on my bike and cycle the corrected typescript around to MyMateJohn's house. Nobody at home so I leave it in a polythene bag on his doorstep. As I cycle back I notice that it is the day for the recycling paper collection in his part of town. I have a feeling of dread but do nothing about it.

The secretary of the Marden Society rings up to remind me that I am giving them a talk tomorrow night. As if I had forgotten! I take a quick look in my diary. It's a forty five minute dramatic presentation which I do straight from my head. It is not written down anywhere. If I dry up, or lose the thread, nobody can help me. I have nothing to fall back on. I have always found abject terror to be a great stimulant for concentrating the mind. Perhaps I should run through it once before I go.

Margaret has found me a couple more Golden Lions around the Loire. This will be a piece of cake. I try phoning Sandillon which is now the kingpin of the Loire zigzag but all I get is the answerphone. I think this idea of booking hotels is daft. Why don't I just ask them if they will be open during the period in which I think that I will be in their area? Then I can book them the night before. I speak to the hotel at Ingrandes and they happily agree that they will be open for me and will have no problem providing me with a room whenever I turn up. Now that was easier, wasn't it? I should have thought of this way of doing it earlier.

MyMateMargaret phones up to enquire progress and to remind me to empty the fridge and freezer tomorrow and bring the stuff to her on the way to do the talk at Marden. I tell her about my new hotel system. The silence at her end of the line is cathedral-like. She must have fainted.

TUESDAY. ONE DAY TO GO

At last, I get through to Sandillon.

'Is that the Hotel du Lion d'Or at Sandillon?' The line is atrocious but I think she gives me a qualified 'yes'. 'Will you be open in the first two weeks of August?' I enquire.

'Yes, monsieur.'

'I cannot say exactly which day I will arrive but it will be some time during early August.' I decide spontaneously that this lady should share the excitement of my great adventure. 'I have chosen your hotel because I am cycling right across France, from the Pyrenees to the Channel coast and I am going to stay only in Hotels du Lion d'Or.' When put like that it makes my choice sound quite gracious.

'En effet!' she responds magnificently. 'That, monsieur, is an incredible undertaking and I wish you every success.'

'Thank you mademoiselle.' This is rather forward of me but she sounds quite young.

'It is such a shame that we will not be able to take a part in your success.'

I am trying to think of the French term for 'reflected glory' in order to make an appropriate conciliatory remark when her words suddenly hit home.

'What do you mean?'

'Well, firstly, we are full for the month of August.'

'What, for the entire month?'

'Yes monsieur and if we were not, we would be of no use to you.'

'Why not?'

'We're not called the *"Lion d'Or"* anymore. We changed our name over two years ago.'

The French have a word that begins with M. I use it on every pedal beat as I pound down the road to Otterstone's. I urgently need some large scale maps of the area north of the Loire. Will I have to thread my way through the *bocage* of Normandy? What are the hills like in Brittany? I recall the labouring groan from the French coach on our school trip to St Malo forty years earlier. On my bicycle, I am the motor.

The great advantage with these enormous bookshops is that you are not really expected to purchase books in them. Proper book buyers go to a shop where the assistants are polysyllabic and can do joined-up handwriting. But here, you can drink coffee and lounge about on a sofa to read the newspapers. In my childhood summers I loved to get around a book and curl up in the sun; now I can sit and watch the cheap covers on the 'three for two' offers do the same.

I make a beeline for the maps and pull out several that I need. I am not going to buy them of course, just consult them. I don't like the look of Brittany and Normandy. Oh yes, there are some beautiful cycle tracks where there had formerly been railway lines but they are all going the wrong way. Some of my day mileages are easily stretching into the seventies.

What's the time? I look about me. Of course, no clock. I must remember to take that confounded watch with me. Pedal home. Lunch from the fridge and then empty it. Leave milk for breakfast tomorrow, oh and the bread. Get my stuff together for my talk tonight, load the van. Perhaps I should put my bike in the van now? Yes, good idea – it will save messing about in rain in the morning. Dump the cycle bags in the hall ready for packing tomorrow.

I run off a couple of copies of my itinerary. One for MyMateMargaret and another for her mother to show her friend Pat down the road. It is a beautiful piece of work, listing towns and roads with mileages and names and addresses of the hotels and the dates that I will be reaching them. It is a greater work of fiction that the typescript of my novel that MyMateJohn is reading for me.

The freezer! I pad a cardboard box with newspaper and stack bricks of frozen food into it. Choc ices? Am I really going to save nine choc ices? I eat one and throw the remainder in the rubbish. Funny, I've still got that fungus in my mouth; and my athlete's foot is still raging. Sort of foot and mouth disease.

I drive straight to MyMateMargaret's house and fill up her freezer. I really appreciate the generosity of her gesture considering that the last time I opened her freezer I forgot to close the door and when she came home she had to throw everything away. But good can come of ill – at least it means she has now got room for my stuff. Must make sure I close the door properly.

'How is the fungus in your mouth?' Margaret asks.

Why are women so morbid?

'Still there, but going down. I am more concerned about my foot. I keep putting the stuff on but it doesn't seem to make any difference.'

'What did the doctor say about it?'

'I didn't tell him.'

'Where did you get the stuff from to put on your foot then?'

'It was some I had left over from last time.'

'That was two years ago. It must be out of date. Show me the tube.'

I fish in my bag and hand her a twist of ointment tube. She straightens it out to read the notices on the side of it.

'Those expiry dates don't mean anything really,' I assure her. 'Nothing to worry about. They often use Roman numerals – it isn't that old. And in any case, medecine does not suddenly lose its effectiveness overnight.'

She looks at me with one of her exasperated expressions picked from the top shelf.

'And how have you been applying this stuff?'

'Rubbing it into my toe morning and evening.'

'Since when?'

'Every day for the last couple of weeks. I might just as well not have bothered for all the effect it has had.'

'I agree.' I am thunderstruck by her quick concurrence. Her idea of health control is to stuff me full of vitamin pills so that I rattle like a set of maraccas. She waggles the tube dangerously at me. 'This ointment is not for treating athlete's foot.'

'Oh,' says I, a little bemused, 'no wonder it didn't work. What is it for then?'

'Haemorrhoids.'

'I'll give it to MyMateJohn then. He's got piles.'

'You're not going to put that in the book are you?'

'Of course not.'

'I don't understand why you had to get yourself booked to give a talk on the evening before your departure,' she continues as we trundle through the Wealden lanes. 'You ought to be resting.'

'They booked the talk over a year ago. That was before I had sorted out this safari.'

'So it is sorted out then?'

'You've got the itinerary.'

'And the hotels are booked?'

'Yeah, most of them... Some of them... Well, those that matter.'

'And your maps are all prepared?'

'I can do that when I get home tonight.'

'At midnight? After a talk?'

'Oh look, there's the village hall. We've arrived.'

I do the talk. I have spoken to them before and they remember me. I can remember some of them. They are a lively group – interested and interesting.

'And that, ladies and gentlemen, is the end of my talk. I'm sure you have thousands of questions, so fire away.'

'Martin, what is your next book about?'

'I'm glad you asked me that Edith. Outside in my van is my bicycle and tomorrow morning I will be setting off on a...'

OH MY GOD, IT'S TODAY.

Breakfast. Any left overs, put in box to give daughter to feed her children with. Ring daughter.

'Izzi?'

'Hi Dad.'

'If I bring my van down then you can try it out. If you are OK with it then I will unload my bike and you can use the van whilst I am away. Is that OK?'

'Yes. Brilliant.

'I've got to be at Dover for half past one so I'll be with you at about twelve.'

'That's fine. I'll work around what you want.'

'I'll ring you before I leave.'

Clean the fridge and the freezer. Bowls of steaming soapy water, towels everywhere. That bundle on the table I must remember to take with me, it is three meals' worth of sandwiches that MyMateMargaret has made for me. It weighs about fourteen hundredweight.

Right, sort the clothes and pack the bags. This cotton tee shirt is really thick and it is heavier than my pyjama top. Do I really need to take it? Why don't I just take two pyjama tops? Clever idea. Nobody will know that I am wearing my pyjamas as the layer under my fleece. Fling the tee shirt back in the drawer. Don't like the stupid lining in those trousers. Get the scissors and cut it out. Weigh it on kitchen scales. Seventy five grams saved. Every little bit helps.

Do the maps, no, wait a minute, what about your bloody sunglasses? Can't take the bike as it is already loaded so jump in the van and go to opticians. Ugh. Grey glass to match the silver frame – as if colour coordination mattered! Grey sunglasses is life trapped inside a black and white television. Brown would have been better, it's warmer. You've just driven past the chemist's. Get another tube of that stuff to put in your mouth. Turn at the lights. Sorry mate, thought you were picking your nose, not waving me across.

'Mr Chemist, can I stick my tongue out at you?'
'Go ahead. Hmm. It's not clearing up much is it?'
'Can I have some more of that stuff?'
'Not without a prescription.'
'Bum. What can I have?'
'This. It tastes of orange.'
'Great.'

What is this packet on the kitchen table? Oh it's MyMateMargaret's survival pack. Well I'm not taking all that with me. Let's sort it out. Butterscotch sweets? You can't suck a sweet whilst pedalling, you need all the space in your mouth for breathing. Discard. Rehydration sachets? *'Mix with half a cupful of....'* Where am I going to find a cup in the middle of the desert? And if I've got water to put in the cup why don't I just drink more water to rehydrate myself? Discard. Immodium, *'for diarrhoea'*. Well I don't want diarrhoea. Discard. Nail scissors? Oh come on! Discard. What is this sheet of aluminium foil? Am I going to roast a turkey? Oh it's an emergency survival blanket. It's France I'm going to, not the North Pole. Discard. Cough lozenges for a sore throat. In summer? Discard. That was easy. What am I left with? A small tube of Savlon. I'll take that.

The maps! I can't carry that lot. Do a scissors job on them. Just cut out the bits I need. *Snip, snip, snip.* Wait a minute. Number the bits for each day so that I know where I am. That's planning for you. What's the time? TEN TO TWELVE? I'm late. Leave the rubbish on the floor.

Stuff maps in bags. Change into cycling shorts and pyjamas. Lay out fluorescent fleece and bright orange scarf ready on bed. Better ring Izzi.

'Dad?'

'I'm running a bit late.'

'That's alright. Why don't I drive you to Dover rather than you cycle? It will save time.'

'Good idea. I'm leaving in five minutes.'

'See yer.'

Lock the back door. Check all the taps are off. Switch off boiler and timing clock on water softener. Put bags in van with bicycle. Lock front door. Sandwiches! You've left them on the kitchen table. Go back and get them. Lock door again.

I'm off.

 ★ ★ Lion D'Or

2 – CAUTERETS

Gently rocking in a reclining seat, swaying sleepily in pyjamas, drifting down through night-darkened France with no effort and no worries; my cycle bags nodding on the empty seat at the side of me, keeping all my food and drink to hand for when I need it. Everybody else doing the work; all the smooth driving, the passing silently along the coach to tap cyclists on their shoulders as dropping off points are reached, the whispered unloading of bicycles from the trailer. This is the worthy reward for my intensive and inspired good planning.

We were well south of Bordeaux and droning across the flat boredom of the Landes before I was fully awake. The rising sun was still low, a yellow ball peeping over the banks of white mist. It looked like a fried egg seen from the bacon. The next stop was Bayonne. All the remaining passengers on the coach, except me, were getting off there. I would be going around the corner to Lourdes. The cyclists who boarded at Bayonne to start on their way home via Lourdes and Toulouse were suntanned and happy. Would I look the same after my safari?

On the approach to Lourdes I sat up and began to take notice. Working from map number two, I began to tick off landmarks for my journey back this way tomorrow. I was particularly pleased to identify the difficult left turn that I would have to make from the main road.

At the coach park, after unloading my bicycle from the trailer, Jason and his team locked up the coach and strolled off into town. My task now was to strap on my cycle bags and realign my handlebars. It had been necessary to turn the latter so that the bicycle would fit in the trailer. I had kept my adjustable wrench in the pocket of my shorts especially for this purpose. The significance of the nudge and grin that one passing backpacking young lady had given to her companion did not filter through to me until much later.

A bicycle, underneath its chrome and hi-tech finish, is, to my mind, still a very primitive mechanical machine. This must be true since I blithely undertake maintenance operations with remarkable success and my mechanical expertise does not extend much further than knowing which way to turn a nut. As it transpired, that was the only skill needed. The handlebars are held in place by an enormously long bolt, it must be about twelve inches from end to end. The head of the bolt sits in the middle of the bars, the nut on the other end is utterly inaccessible and buried way down inside the upright steering tube of the frame. But the clever bit is that this nut is wedge shaped. When you tighten the bolt at the top, way down in the depths of the bicycle the nut creeps up the thread on the other end and splays out the bottom end of the handlebars which is split to serve that purpose. The more you turn, the wider they split and the harder they wedge into the steering tube. Primitive but effective.

The first operation is to wrench the bars into alignment. You remember doing this as a child. It's the game where you stand facing the bike, grip the front wheel between your knees, and jerk the bars from side to side until they are at right angles to the frame. I remember a dance in the 1960s called the Twist. I think it was inspired by a bicycle mechanic. At the first grab my hand slipped and I gashed my knuckles on a sharp edge. I had never been any good at the Twist either.

I sucked my wound and straddled the wheel again. With several hefty jerks, I succeeded in aligning the bars. Now to the bolt. It was quicker to turn it with my fingers to start with, reserving the wrench for when it began to tighten up. But it never did tighten up. It just turned in the void. I experimentally lifted it and it emerged happily from the top of the tube to have a good look around its new horizons. A twelve inch long shiny chromium bolt with nothing on the end. I should not be able to do that. I stared at it for a while, not understanding the conjuring trick that I had performed. The truth hit me like a sledgehammer. The vibration of the journey had shaken the nut from the end of the bolt and it had dropped to the unreachable bottom of the tube. Like a dead owl in a hollow tree.

I did not know what to do. I slumped on the stone wall to think it out. To retrieve the nut I would have to take the handlebars completely out of the upright tube. To do that, I would have to disconnect my trip computer and remove the mounting, unscrew my gear change lever and remove its bracket and then cut off my rubber handlebar grips so that I could unbolt my brake levers and slide them over the ends of the bars. It was not an operation to be undertaken lightly or on the pavement. If I entrusted it to a cycle shop there was little chance that they would be able to do it today and I was already booked into a hotel for tonight, and another the night after. And another the night after that. I had told MyMateMargaret on several occasions that it was stupid to book hotels!

I sat in the sun and thought. What could I do? Well, I could start by getting dressed. I couldn't sit here forever in my pyjamas. Three frantically incredulous minutes later I was back on the wall, revising that assertion. I went over my final preparations in my head. I distinctly recalled laying out ready on the bed, the kingpin of my wardrobe: the fluorescent fleece and my orange scarf. And that was where I had left them – on the bed.

So I was going to cycle back to England staying only in hotels called the 'Lion d'Or' was I? I had made a good start. I was a thousand miles from home with a broken bicycle, a bleeding hand and only my pyjamas to wear.

It's all in the preparation, you know.

I suppose a certain feeling of despair came over me. I think it was understandable. Then my immensely fertile brain clicked into overdrive and I began to consider the contingencies. That coach, for example, I knew was leaving for England in an hour's time and I was sure they had spare seats. I could simply get back on it and go home. By this time tomorrow morning I could be sitting in my front room saying what a jolly jape it had all been. It would be the end of my Golden Lion Safari though. The next coach down would be too late. I would be back into my talks season. Would it matter if I didn't do this silly ride? After all, the people challenging me to do it had not provided the money. I was having to pay for it all.

But I knew deep within me that I was procrastinating. I was trying to put off the moment when I would inevitably make the insane decision to try to cycle back to the UK in my pyjamas on a broken bicycle. I mean, the sun was shining. It was not as if I was cold in my pyjamas. And they were not striped, rather a discreet grey. What about the handlebars though? You cannot ride a bicycle if the handlebars are loose. But are they loose? Of course they are not. Look at the effort that you had to make; all that wrenching and swearing, to get them straight. They are definitely not loose; merely unsecured. Well that's settled then. It didn't take long. Now where is this old railway track that I am supposed to take to get to my first Golden Lion?

I cycled off gingerly towards the station, fearing that at any minute my handlebars would turn in one direction and the wheel in the other. The young lady at the information desk in the station showed me on a map where the track that I was seeking left the town. It was not far. And she did not even say one word about my pyjamas.

I sat on the bench outside to eat some sandwiches from my mountain and watch the varied and various travellers arriving and leaving. Whether they were young, tee-shirted and backpacked or mature, coutured and suitcased they were all of them going about their business with a happy and confident purpose. Was it the religious antecedents of Lourdes that invested them with this conviction?

Whilst I was eating, three sisters of religion walked slowly by. Each wore an enormous silver cross chained from their neck to swing before them as if cutting a swathe through the infidels. They bowed their heads to me in greeting. I automatically nodded a response, fighting the urge to look behind me to see whom they were really saluting. They were almost reverential to me. I mentally shrugged and returned to my sandwich pack. Staring up at me from the nest of crumpled aluminium foil in my lap were two of MyMateMargaret's special bombproof food nuggets: a chunk of cheddar cheese rammed into a hot cross bun. Was it these anaemic pastry crosses that they had seen? Had they mistaken my earthly engorgement for some fanatical religious ritual? I would never know. Nor would the buns.

Cauterets is a small town in the Pyrenees. It owes its prosperity to the thermal springs whose development in the nineteenth century encouraged the building of a tramway from Lourdes up the valley to Pierrefitte. From this latter town the track veers into the mountains proper and tackles seriously the problems of gradient.

The enterprises in this era were not restricted by laws protecting the consumer nor, apparently, hindered by the complications that always accompany a single-minded search for veracity. Reading the 1897 prospectus of the Cauterets Thermal Springs Company, not only could one find a medical name for that annoying little condition which one was certain one suffered from but, miraculously, bubbling away within the limpid effusions of the source one would find the trace element which would effect a certain cure. The latest claim was that two professors of the Académie des Sciences had discovered the water to be rich in argon and helium. This was lively marketing, considering that the two gases had only been discovered on earth two years earlier. New as they were, these gases came without medical testimonials and so their beneficial effect was implied to be their mere existence in the water. It was not until later that their full qualities would be exploited for the benefit of mankind: argon to fill light bulbs and helium to inflate birthday balloons.

The tramway was opened in 1897 and was an instant success but it eventually succumbed to the motor car as everything in today's world seems to do. The trackbed now serves the cyclists, walkers and roller bladers as a smoothly surfaced, gently graded climb towards the mountains. I was pleased with this configuration. Not only for the small effort that was required to assure a steady progress but for the lack of frightening obstacles to be negotiated at speed. I feared that an emergency wrench on my handlebars would break their grip at the very moment when I would appreciate most the maintenance of the status quo. Merely thinking of this scenario frightened me so I did the only sensible thing – I stopped thinking about it.

When I reached the intermediate station at Pierrefitte Nestalas, I stopped in a square to sit on a red hot stone bench and eat some more of my rations. I was not hungry but I had to lighten my bags somehow. The sun was now beating out from a clear blue sky. The only other inhabitant of the square was a teenage girl. She was sitting on the steps opposite me, talking on her mobile phone. She was wearing jeans and a thin sweater. Perhaps the locals did not feel this weather to be hot.

The track now left the settlements and began to climb the side of the valley, edging its way into a position from which it could dominate the road from above. I stopped at the entrance to a short tunnel and looked back. I could see down onto the plain where Lourdes lay shimmering in the haze. Unfortunately the track surface was no longer the beautiful smooth tarmac but a spread of loose stones and gravel with the occasional hole thrown in for variety. Then I came to a section where houses had been built on the alignment. A diversion around the two metre high chain link boundary fence had been provided for the cyclists. It was a path wide enough for two contradirectional under-nourished mountain goats to rub ribs and it plunged in a tortuous wriggle down the valley side almost to the level of the road and then clawed its route skywards over tree roots and rocks back to its original height. To climb, I had to jerk my bicycle forwards and upwards and then hold it in that position on both brakes whilst I pulled myself up to it. Always assuming, of course, that there was enough space on the path for both of us.

I decided that the notice board in Pierrefitte had allowed enthusiasm to displace accuracy when it had proudly claimed that this track was suitable for cyclists. I needed to get onto the road as soon as possible. At the next opportunity, I slid down a farm track and continued my ascent into the Pyrenees the easy way – on tarmac.

The 'easy way' was a classification containing a heavy component of relativity for it was still a gradient of 1 in 6. These mountain passes tend to throw up the same problem. Maps are flat. Where they go into the mountains, they become pretty with greens and browns and wiggly blue bits. At home, in front of a roaring log fire of a winter's evening and prospecting routes for an expedition, I suddenly feel capable of feats of endurance to make your eyes bulge. I sign up for death-defying descents and muscle-splitting climbs with a simple stroke of the pen; then I stir my my

Horlicks, chuck another log on the fire and curl up in the wingback and dream of sunshine.

Well, I had got the sunshine, but it came with the gradient. Perhaps I should have flattened the creases in my map. It was always the same. When I got to the road I could never believe that the hill could possibly be that steep – and it was always steeper. And every time I swore not to commit the same mistake again... but those pretty north light shadings on the contours seduced me every time.

When I reached the hotel I was a little confused for the image that I had retained in my mind was one that MyMateMargaret had provided from her internet gleanings and which I had registered as a sort of two storey chalet with mountains in the background yet this hotel was a five storey block in a town street. But it was definitely the Lion d'Or so I went in. The mystery was solved when I was shown where to lodge my bicycle, for the other door of the hotel was two floors up on the street which ran behind and from this point the hotel appeared as it had in the photograph.

Madame allotted me a room complete with wooden rocking chair and second bed. The former was a charming irrelevance; the latter I felt was overkill. I quickly changed out of my pyjamas, did my washing and stretched out my line. Thirty minutes later I was sitting on a café terrace in my revolting silk shirt and black trousers with the lining cut out and sipping a coffee as I tried to ignore the brain numbing 'music' blasting from the huge disco installation outside the Town Hall. It eventually beat me and I had to move on but not before I had observed a walker with a three foot long ice pick strapped to his back and a girl wearing only shorts, tee shirt and compass. It must be something to do with the mountains.

I moved to a bench by the Casino and sat gazing at the blue craggy summits with a mixture of emotions. I was pleased that I had bagged my first Golden Lion but was full of misgivings as to the likelihood of a successful conclusion to the safari. I had only cycled nineteen miles today. I still had free-thinking handlebars and an embarrassing lacuna in the wardrobe department. To cover the eighty five miles tomorrow to the next Golden Lion I would have to pedal at an improbably high average speed. When dreaming at home with the map on my knees I had convinced myself that I would come down the mountain at thirty five mph. That speed would have been reckless on a fault-free machine; it would now be suicide on mine. I would have to do some serious thinking. But not yet.

Dinner was uncomplicated and good: home made vegetable soup, stuffed tomatoes, trout with almonds and *crème brulé*.

Then I phoned Mission Control.

'So, where are you?'

'Where I am supposed to be, Cauterets.'

'In the Lion d'Or?'

'The very same.'

'Everything OK?'

How should I put it?

'Well...'

'Come on, let's hear it.'

'I seem to have forgotten to bring my clothes.'

'What, all your clothes?'

'No. I've got my cycling shorts but no fleece. I've only got my pyjamas.'

'You can't cycle in your pyjamas.'

'I did today.' Silence. 'I said, "I did today".'

'I heard you. You can buy clothes tomorrow. They have shops in France.'

'And I need a slight adjustment to my handlebars.'

'How slight?'

'Fairly slight... ish. Well, there's a bit that has dropped off.'

'They have bicycle shops in France too.'

'I know. I passed one today.'

'Why?'

'What do you mean?'

'Why did you go past it? You should have gone in and got your bike adjusted.'

'Well I was worried I might not reach the hotel.'

'So you can go in to the shop on your way back down tomorrow then, can't you?'

Things always seem simple when you are far away.

3 – Grenade sur l'Adour

I must have eaten breakfast but I did not notice it. I was running through in my mind the problems that would present themselves that day and then trying to find solutions to them. I needed to cover about eighty five miles. If I managed to average ten mph that would require eight and a half hours' pedalling. With meal breaks and rest stops the journey would take me at least ten hours. I would be exhausted. But it would be sensible to get my handlebars fixed and that would take time. It would make me even later. And more tired. What would I do if the cycle shop took the bike to pieces and then found that they needed to order a part? I would lose a day and my whole itinerary would fall like a row of dominoes.

I suppose I could go straight to the railway station in Lourdes and see if there was a train to get me to Grenade sur l'Adour? Or even part of the way. Yes, that seemed like a sensible course of action. I paid my bill and took the opportunity to ask madame how the hotel got its name.

'Oh it's always been called that. It's a name that was very popular for coaching inns. But I don't know why they chose "Lion d'Or". There are lots of them about.'

'Yes, about fifty six in France that I have found.'

'Well there you are then.'

Quite.

Over my pyjamas I pulled on my waterproof-that-isn't, and pedalled into town. Before leaving Cauterets I stocked up on food for the day; individual quiches, croissants and tomatoes and then launched myself down the mountain. For the first few kilometres I took the curves and hairpins gingerly, wincing each time that my front wheel hit a bump and then breathing a sigh of relief when I found myself still at the tiller. My speed crept up to twenty five mph and I held it at that until the gradient flattened out.

At the bottom I made what I hoped would be a quick stop at the supermarket to purchase a toothbrush which I had unaccountably omitted to pack, and an extra water bottle which I now realised that I needed for my bicycle. It did not take me long to discover that they had no water bottles for sale but my choice of toothbrush was delayed whilst I pondered the concept of a 'professional toothbrush'. Did this really mean that I could be paid for cleaning my teeth? Or was I supposed to telephone for an appointment with a professional teethbrusher and sit in a waiting room until I was called in by the teethbrusher's assistant? He would surely have an assistant.

I chose a brush at random and made for the till. There was only one customer before me and she had about half a dozen items. That wouldn't take long. I had forgotten that I was in the south of France. Very near Spain. In Spain you always buy a day's extra provisions because it will take you a day to get through the till. It is only slightly better on the French side of the border.

The cashier laid a heavy fist on the first item and dragged it through the scanner as if it weighed fifty kilos. It was a small bag of pasta. It beeped. She seemed bitterly disappointed with her success and frowned fiercely at the bag, gripping it as if she wanted to strangle the life from it. Eventually she let it go and it began to crawl lethargically down the chute towards the customer. In a Parisian super-market, the goods zing down the ramp like children on a helter-skelter. But this is southern France. The pasta stopped halfway to look at the view. Next item was a tin of skinned tomatoes. This also disgusted her by beeping immediately.

'Peeled plum tomatoes,' she read from the label. 'What do you use those for?' With a hoary hand she clamped the tin to the top of the chute, refusing to release it until the customer had made a full declaration of its intended use. It was to make a sauce for the pasta. And what were the other ingredients? Which herbs did she use? How much oil?

Had the woman been purchasing a couple of sticks of gelignite and a box of detonators I could have seen the point of the cross examination, but pasta? Has any terrorist ever managed to sow chaos and disorder with five hundred grams of tortellini and a couple of skinned tomatoes?

The next few items ambled through the till more or less successfully but then we hit the jackpot. The carton of UHT milk would not beep. The cashier turned it one way, she turned it the other. She demonstrated to the customer in several and varied manners that the customer had been stupidly deficient in picking out a non-scannable item. Just to prove the point, she waved it again at the reader. Still no beep. She shrugged her shoulders, pursed her lips and sighed heavily. She would have to 'go manual'. She began to unbutton the top of her tunic. When she got to the point where I thought it would be prudent for me to avert my eyes, she thrust an arm down her bosom and pulled out a pair of pince-nez spectacles which had been hanging around her neck on a chain. These she pressed onto her face, once she had unravelled the chain, of course. Then she wrinkled up her nose and peered at the bar code.

'Oh, they always print these numbers so small!' She was in ecstasy. 'You need a microscope to read them.'

I did a rapid mental audit of my cycle bags. No, I did not have a microscope in them. Pity. Must remember to bring one for next time.

'Three,' she said and stabbed a podgy finger at the keypad. 'Four.' Stab. 'Zero.' Stab. 'Four' Stab.

And so on. What are the chances that she will make a mistake? No matter how much care I take, I often misdial a telephone number. It is straining the tenets of probability that she might read every number correctly and then stab the corresponding button.

'Oh look. It's come up as stuffed olives. That's funny.' Hilarious. She cleared the till screen and started again. 'Three.' Stab. 'Four.' Stab. 'Zero.' Stab. The steel girders supporting the roof were painted grey. 'Zero again.' Stab. 'Eight.' Stab. A car had come up the wrong entrance to the car park and was causing chaos as it tried to negotiate an acute turn. 'Five.' Stab. 'Five.' Stab. One of the floor tiles by the door had worn through to the concrete.

Did I really want this toothbrush? Was dental hygiene more important to me than my sanity? What? Oh, she's talking to me.

'Is this your newspaper, monsieur?'

But before I can reply, I hear the dreaded contradiction from the lady customer.

'No, no, it's mine.'

The cashier paused with her podgy finger hovering over the '*total*' button.

'You just told me in time,' she accused. She looked quite upset. 'I would have had to total it separately.' She held up the newspaper before her to jiggle the barcode onto the scanner. 'Well!' she announced in a scandalised tone. 'That is just what I would have expected from him.' She laid the paper flat on the desk and continued to read the headline article. 'He's not a mayor, he's a charlatan. He always was.' We stood quietly whilst she read some more. 'Oh that really is too much!' She looked up at the customer and tapped the article. 'Have you seen this?' she asked.

Without a trace of irony the lady replied, 'Not yet.'

'An absolute charlatan!' the cashier affirmed as she

lifted the paper towards the chute. 'Oh, looks as if it will be another fine day,' she added, digesting the weather forecast on the back. 'Rain in the mountains though.'

Right. Fine. You've scanned the goods, you've pressed the buttons, you've read the newspaper. Will you please take this woman's money and let me get out whilst I still have some teeth left to brush?

'Five euros, fifty two.'

That's about one euro per minute of queue. But I have miscalculated. The customer unclasps her handbag, delves within and pulls out a large purse. From this she extracts a small wallet and flips it open to reveal her identity card. What on earth for? Oh no, I don't believe this. She's not going to write a cheque for five euros fifty two is she?

Oh yes she is.

I pounded down the smooth tarmac towards Lourdes. It had taken me eighteen minutes to purchase a toothbrush. In a surge of annoyance I pressed harder and the figure on my trip computer notched up to fifteen mph. If I could pedal like this all day long it would take me less than six hours to get to Grenade. Six hours! I could purchase twenty toothbrushes in that time.

As I hurled myself down the main street of Lourdes, I saw a bicycle shop; not the one that I had noticed yesterday. I screeched to a halt by the kerb and went in. Passing along the rows of filigree cycle frames and skinny saddles I knew that I was on a forlorn quest. He would not have a cheap plastic water bottle. It was like going in to a Jaguar showroom and asking for a floor mat for a van. He did not quite eject me but I don't think he put me on his Christmas card list.

It was now eleven o'clock and, ironically, I was in the same place at the same time as I had been yesterday. And still in my pyjamas. I made for the railway station to see if I could get a train to help me along the way. After a serious study of the departures board which I complemented as best I could by examining those portions of the maps that I had brought with me, I had managed to identify the destinations and directions of the trains for the day. There were six trains, none of them went anywhere near Grenade and three of those trains were buses anyway and would not have taken bicycles. Things were not looking good. I still had sixty six miles to cover.

Then I saw the car rental office. Just by chance I had brought my driving licence with me. No, it was not by chance, it was an intelligent part of the comprehensive preparations that I had made for this expedition. Surely I could hire a van or an estate car to transport my bicycle?

The man looked up from the computer screen as I entered and then pressed the sequence of keys necessary to hide the game that he had been playing and replace it with his work schedule.

'If I hired a car here, could I leave it in Grenade?'

'Where is Grenade?'

'Grenade sur l'Adour.'

'That must be in the Gers mustn't it? A small town is it?'

Why do Frenchmen apparently believe that every foreigner carries in his head a map of their country, complete with departmental numbers and population totals?

'I don't know which *département* it is in. Is it important?'

'Well we're in the Hautes Pyrenees here.'

'Yes I know that, but I don't know which *département* Grenade is in. I do know it is near Mont de Marsan. At the edge of the flat bit,' I added, my cyclist's memory instantly latching onto the important data.

'That will be the Landes then.'

'Probably. So, can I hire a car or a van? A van would be better.'

'A van is more expensive.'

'The price is no object,' I announced grandly. I just had to get to Grenade. I could not face failure so early in my

Golden Lion Safari.

'I don't have any vans. I only do cars.'

'Do you have a car in which I could put my bicycle? It's a big bicycle.'

'You could put it in a car like that grey hatchback out there, couldn't you? The seats fold down.'

I looked doubtfully at it. When I said my bicycle was big, I meant it. A friend had once pooh poohed my prophecies and tried to squeeze my bicycle into his enormous Citroen estate car. The same vehicle in which he claimed to have transported a baby grand piano. With the tailgate up and all the rows of seats prostrate like the faithful at Mecca, he had still failed to accommodate my bicycle. I chose to gloss over the matter of size until later in the negotiations.

'OK. If I hire a car here can I leave it at Mont de Marsan?'

'You can leave it at Bordeaux.'

'I don't want to go to Bordeaux. I want to go to Grenade.'

'Well, you would need to bring it back here then.'

'That's no good to me. I thought you could hire in one place and leave it in another.'

'Well in theory you can, but we have to move them back again by lorry. It depends where the lorry is when you leave the car.'

'Where will it be tomorrow?'

'When do you want the car?'

'Now.'

'Not possible. I don't have any. It's the Tour de France you see. It's been like it all week. When a car breaks down they need a replacement straight away, you see. And the team that got sent home for using drugs, they all took cars.'

So I was being scotched by the drug-fuelled lycra brigade was I? I looked out of the window and pondered whether, if I unbolted both my wheels, I would manage to get my bicycle into the hatchback.

'I could take that one out there,' I suggested.

'Which one?'

'The grey hatchback you showed me.'

'Oh that's not for hire.'

'But you said that I could get my bike into it.'

'Yes. I was just using it as an illustration. We have cars like that but that's not one of our cars. It belongs to the hairdresser.'

'So, do you have any vehicles that I can hire today?'

'No. Do you want me to work out a price for you?'

'Not a lot of point if you've got no cars.'

'No, I suppose not.'

I was disappointed that he did not ask me to fill in a customer satisfaction questionnaire.

I went outside, straddled my bike and smacked its bags.

'Well Dobbin, me ol' pal, it's sixty six miles to Grenade. 'Looks like it's just you an' me. Giddy-up.'

On the exit northwards from Lourdes I noticed the cycle shop that I had seen when I had been coming in on the coach on the previous day. But this time I did not go past it. MyMateMargaret had insisted that I go in, so I did. I bought a plastic water bottle. I even asked the lady to fill it up with water for me which she did with no fuss and much great humour. Mission Control would be proud of me, I was sure. Then I put my head down and pedalled like a demon to Grenade sur l'Adour. I averaged over twelve miles per hour for seven hours and arrived at the Lion d'Or at seven thirty.

How had I managed it? I had no idea. Some luck, some skill. At one point on the journey I had come across the inevitable *'road closed – diversion'* sign. The motorcyclist and I had weighed up the odds. Was it worth taking the risk and ignoring the sign? Roads are rarely completely closed to cyclists. He had taken the diversion, I had pedalled straight ahead. After two hundred yards I had lifted my bike over the trench and crept around the sleeping excavator and carried on. After five miles I had stopped for my lunch by the war memorial in a village. Five minutes into my lunch, the motor cyclist had rattled past. He had raised a gloved hand to me in ironic salute.

Reading the war memorial reminded me that the first world war had made a tragically greater impression on the populace than the second. This village had lost seventeen men in 1914-18 and two in 39-45. And what about that for a name? – Vital Orsin. And then on I had pedalled.

When I had reached Aire, the town before Grenade, I had decided to indulge a little luxury. The luscious, fresh fruit in France bears no resemblance to the stuff that we get in England which is picked unripe and then transported across Europe in a chilled lorry to appear bright and pretty and uneatable on a supermarket shelf, so I purchased two peaches and carried them to a bench to enjoy them. They were as hard as iron, tasteless and had cost me as much as the fruit did in England. I obviously needed to do some more homework.

By this time I was feeling pretty weary and was ready for the final twelve miles to Grenade on the cycle track which MyMateMargaret had promised me. Unfortunately she had not told the SNCF who had obstinately declined to lift their railway lines for me and had compounded the insolence by running trains on them which, obviously, had not been anywhere near Lourdes.

But here I was standing outside the Lion d'Or in Grenade sur l'Adour. I knew that it was not a real hotel. It had been in the past but it had fallen into disuse and had been abandoned. The present owners had seen it advertised for sale on the internet and had bought it a couple of years ago. They were busy renovating it and repairing it and to help finance this, they had just started to do bed and breakfast.

I peered through the iron grill into the sunlight and shade of the courtyard beyond. A man was sitting at a table.

He saw me and came to the gate.

'Monsieur Lloyd?'

'It's me.'

'Good morning,' he announced proudly in English. 'I am José.'

'Bonsoir,' I replied and shook hands. I wheeled in my bicycle.

'Would you like a drink?'

'I'd love a glass of water.'

I sat at the table under the green glinting shade of leaves. A wisteria was pressing itself against the ancient wall of the main building, its twisted trunk writhing skywards from the ground like a plume of smoke from a volcano, the branches spreading out along the wires as if billowing below a ceiling.

The jug of water arrived with two young children; Mélodie and Jeff and their mother, Eliane. The latter appeared a little embarrassed. The problem was that they had not had time to finish the work in the room that I had reserved, and so if I was prepared to stay, then they would give me a reduction. She assured me that it had a bed, a table and a chair but nothing else.

I readily agreed without even inspecting my lodgings. The cost was immaterial; I did not want to cycle another mile. Eliane, José and the children adopted me as a new member of the family. Soon I was dragged, not altogether reluctantly, into a game of *'touché coulé'*. This was a modern version of the 'battleships' which, as a child, I had played with a pencil and a sheet of graph paper. At that time it was unashamedly employed as a means of teaching children the principle of co-ordinates. Today's child had individual peg boards, differing coloured pegs for shell hits and a comprehensive fleet of plastic vessels to distribute across the grid.

I introduced them to the concept of the soundtrack accompaniment. Every cannon, I explained, made this noise when it fired, then the shell made this noise as it travelled to its target and this noise when it exploded. Of course, if you hit the magazine then it sounded like this; and in any case the diesel engines were always roaring, and the sirens whooping and when a boat sank all the air bubbled up like this...

Eliane took me on a short tour of the house. It was built around a courtyard with the stables below and the living accommodation above. The corridor which served the rooms had been built wide enough so that the guests could dine on the landing outside their rooms, as was the custom of the time. She was pleased that the village had reacted positively to their trying to resuscitate this Golden Lion. Several neighbours had complimented them on the traditional golden lion sign which they had ordered to be made for the facade. One old man had told them how, every year, he used to undertake a transhumanse with his cattle which took three weeks and the Golden Lion was always one of his stops. The cattle were lodged downstairs and he slept above them.

'And this is your room.'

She threw open the door and grimaced. It was as she had said. A bed, a chair and a table. The floor was bare boards, the walls were mostly stripped, the electrical wiring was crocheted across the ceiling. A mattress was leaning against one wall; two bags of plaster and other building materials lurked by the window.

'It's lovely,' I said, and we both laughed.

After I had taken a shower, we all went out to dinner at the local pizzeria. I was already paying peanuts for my bed and breakfast; they now insisted against my many protests, on paying for my meal. I was unable to stop them. Then we ambled down to the square and drank coffee and ate ice creams at the café where they were known. Eliane told me how she had met José. He had come to help when she was recording her songs in studio. We chatted professionally about microphone technique and exchanged experiences about radio broadcasts we had done. Inevitably, as parents do, we decried the behaviour of youth who get drunk and have no respect and who cannot be disciplined at school because they are not disciplined at home. In the space of one conversation we aged a generation. We had started out with adolescent jokes and now we were delving deep into the pail of philosophical hindsight. Oh but it did me good!

'What is the significance of those branches of fir tree strapped to the door posts of that house?' I pointed across the square.

'Ah that is somebody's birthday.'

José gave the name and they discussed the family for a while.

'But why do they decorate the house like that?' I asked.

'It's an ancient and local tradition. It used to be a festival of spring, or more likely summer. It's called *'Maiy'* – like the month but not spelled the same. You're supposed to do it for the first of May. All the householders would decorate their doors with a branch, or a fir tree, or bamboo they sometimes use nowadays.'

'But we're in July.'

'Exactly. Now they do it for birthdays and weddings and such like.'

I looked up at the slowly darkening summer sky.

'I like it here.'

'It's a pity you're leaving tomorrow. You'll have to come back.'

HÔTEL du Lion d'Or

4 – Marmande

It was the mother-in-law's jam that did it. Not my mother-in-law: Eliane's. The jam was so nice that I ate a lot of bread and now as I waved goodbye I could feel it in my legs. Next stop Marmande, seventy five miles to the north.

Seated at the family table with the children dipping in and out of the breakfast option as they pleased, I had asked Eliane why the hotel was called the Lion d'Or.

'Ah,' she said, 'it dates back to the time of the stage coaches. People would put up a sign at their door to say that they had beds for the night: *"lit – on dort"*, bed – one can sleep. It sounded like "golden lion" in French and so they shortened it to a picture of a golden lion which anybody could recognise, whether or not they could read.'

I was too polite to express doubts and in any case, Eliane believed what she was telling me, but I did find it just a little too convenient. But as I had no better explanation, I decided to accept this one temporarily. I remembered somebody trying to convince me once that the llama owed its name to the Spanish Conquistadors in South America. Every time they had seen one of these animals they had asked the natives what it was called. What is its name? – *'como se llama?'* I had not believed that explanation either.

I turned out of the village and crossed the railway line which was still not a cycle track and headed off on the gentle climb towards the village of Maurrin. It was here that I would pass onto map number three and another expired section of my cartographic archive would wing its way into the nearest litter bin, lightening my baggage by an infinitessimally small amount but lightening it nonetheless. I had parted company with map number one just after Lourdes. Today's journey would be undulating for the first fifteen miles, then I would do about twenty five miles on another *voie verte* – a converted railway line. I was gambling on this being well surfaced so that I could push up my average speed. After the *voie verte* I would reach the eastern edges of the Landes and the roads would become mostly flat, mostly straight, mostly busy and mostly boring.

Yesterday, after the first few hours of riding, I had come to accept the state of my handlebars. It did not, and was unlikely to, affect my safety unless I was intending to do something rash or stupid. And this, of course, was just not my style. What impinged more upon my life was the noise that the loose bolt generated as it rattled in the tube. Sometimes it jingled like a horse harness, sometimes it rattled like a machine gun; on occasions, it was silent. I baptised it my 'clinkometer' and used it to gauge the smoothness of the road upon which I was travelling. Today it was accompanying my efforts with a gentle but insistent tintinnabulation, reminding me that a proportion of my pedalling effort was being absorbed in just getting the tyres to roll over the rough surface rather than moving me along the road.

The weather had not woken up yet. The sky was white, the air was warm but there was no indication of its ultimate intentions apart from the suggestion that the wind might be a headwind. I could feel a gentle breeze slipping down the neck of my pyjamas. Now, if I had been wearing that fleece, I would have simply pulled up the zip, snug to the scarf which would have been wrapped around my neck. But I was not. This was not a matter for despair. I thought that I had done rather well, despite the problems that vindictive fate had thrown at me. I was coping with the handlebars and the pyjamas. Yes, I was quite adaptable really.

When I reached the crossroads at Maurrin, I was offered the opportunity to extend this adaptablility to encompass deep memory recall. Map number three was not on the bike and map number four started three miles south of my destination, Marmande. Map number two stopped in one hundred yards. There was a slight gap of sixty seven miles in between. I suppose I could have held a court of enquiry or even a court martial but it would have been a waste of time and effort. Whatever the defence, the finger of accusation pointed only at me and the facts were indisputable and real. There was no map. Or if there was, it was screwed up on my kitchen floor.

I read the road sign. *'Villeneuve de Marsan'*. That sounded familiar. In fact, wasn't that where I was supposed to join the *voie verte?* I am sure it was. Half an hour later I was not so sure. I had followed the sign to Villeneuve railway station but could see no evidence of a track. The trackbed here was part of the garden of the former station. I circled around the car park a couple of times and then noticed a lady sitting on the steps of the station house.

'Bonjour madame.'

'Monsieur?'

'Do you live here?' She nodded. 'Ah then you must know where the *voie verte* is,' I assured her. She looked blankly at me. 'You know, the cycle track that has been made on the old railway line.' I nodded encouragingly.

She pulled at her flowered pinafore and shook her head slowly.

'What did you say it was called?'

'It's a *voie verte*. The converted railway line. It's for cyclists. And walkers,' I added graciously.

She shook her head again. I was worried. I needed to find that track because I was actually going out of my way to get on it in the hope that the surface and gradient would be so good that I would be able to notch up a considerable number of kilometres to more than offset the diversion that I had made.

At that moment arrived in a swirl of loose gravel the very person I needed – the post lady, and she was riding a bicycle. She was doubly qualified to know the answer – as a professional repository of addresses and as a cyclist. She hopped from her bike and handed a bundle of envelopes to the lady on the step. I was pleased to see that the French receive just as much rubbish through the mail as we do.

The *voie verte?* Oh it was down that way. It went to Mont de Marsan. It was really good. No, no, I explained, I wanted the other direction. The bit that went north east. She knew nothing about it. She questioned the station lady who shook her head as she inspected her junk mail. They shrugged their shoulders in harmony.

Oh dear. I was now off my map and sixty miles from the next map. The time that I had hoped I would be saving was slipping away like checkout girls for a fag. I would have to take the main road. But when I reached it I gazed at it in dismay. It was busy. Very busy. This was the Saturday that MyMateMargaret had said would be the silly one to be cycling on. Like an enormous football match at half time, the whole of France was changing ends. The homeward bound traffic was as frantic as the holiday bound; cars, caravans, cars with trailers, motor caravans, anonymous vans stuffed with chairs and mattresses, converted buses, huge motorbikes also towing trailers. No bicycles.

I could see that if I did not do something soon, I would be drawing my old age pension somewhere in the Landes. I dismounted and, after a couple of heart-thumping false starts, I ran my bicycle through the traffic, straight across the road and onto the grass verge opposite. I then had to try to slot myself in to the stream of vehicles but it was like trying to board a railway train which would not stop.

I closed my eyes and launched off. This was madness. I cycled four hundred yards and then veered off onto... the *voie verte*. It was there, complete with gates, signposts, map boards and it was going the correct way. Why was it that nobody in Villeneuve knew about it? Or was it merely that the two people whom you could expect to be clued up were the ones whom the rest of the commune had kept in the dark? Don't tell the post lady or the woman who lives at the station – they might tell the English.

As I rattled and bumped along its roughly grassed, uneven, stony surface I realised that, actually, I preferred my *voie vertes* not to be *verte* at all but a lovely shade of tarmacadam grey. Fortuitously I had managed to latch onto another place name – Gabarret. I had seen it on the map board and I remembered it as being the village where I had to leave the track.

But I never reached Gabarret. The bone shaking, nerve jarring ride had reduced my speed to five mph. Thirty miles would take me six hours (or twenty toothbrushes if you prefer). I stopped at a picnic site and chatted to a young French couple who had caught me up and who had cycled out from Mont de Marsan on the 'beautiful smooth tarmac' which stopped just before I joined the track. They were riding bikes with fat comfortable tyres but even they decided to turn around.

So when I reached the next road crossing I left the *voie verte*. I was still off my map and by doing this I had now abandoned the only track whose route had been drawn out for me. Stupid or what? I would have to do the rest of the day from memory. And then I thought about my evening wardrobe. I burrowed in my cycle bags and pulled out the trousers with the toy compass attached. That's the skill of efficient expedition planning; knowing what equipment to take with you. Drawing my directions from the gyrating needle I charged along the lanes until I came to the *route nationale*, and there I turned right. The original plan, back in the days when I had possessed the relevant maps, had been to approach Marmande on the minor roads and thus defuse MyMateMargaret's censure for travelling on such a busy day. When all you have got is a little plastic bubble and fifty miles of monsters and dragons, these intentions tend to get swept aside.

Now I definitely had a head wind. It was blowing down the v-neck of my pyjamas and onto my chest. The cooling effect was quite pleasant; I just wished that it would not make pedalling so arduous. For its part, the road lived up to my predictions. It was straighter than a Quaker, more boring than chess and as flat as my singing.

When I find I have a monotonous ride to undertake, I occupy my mind with other things. This is a great and underrated health advantage of cycling as compared with motoring. When the forty foot artic thunders down the road towards you, you try not to believe that the driver is racking his brains to think up ten words which begin with the letter Q and end with the letter Y but if that wobbling cyclist is performing such abstruse mental exercises it does not worry you in the slightest and quite rightly so. Regularly I set myself problems in mental arithmetic and then find incorrect answers; I design book jackets in my head; I run and re-run lines of dialogue and unravel twists in the plot of the novel that I might be currently writing.

Today I decided that as the exchange rate of the euro to the pound sterling was roughly the same ratio as the kilometre to the mile then I would convert all my expenses into miles and furlongs and all my distances into pounds and pence. My electronic trip computer gave me my speed so I calculated how many pounds per hour I was travelling and then multiplied that up to give me an annual salary of over twenty one thousand pounds. I was engrossed in trying to calculate my pension rights when I was brought back to the real world by the rich sound of an overtaking car suddenly flatulating behind me. *'Brrrp, brrrp.'*

I stared after it as it swished by and hurtled up the road towards Casteljaloux. '*Brrrrrp, brrrrrrp,*' the next car repeated. By the time that the third car had flatulated its way past me I had discovered the cause: the white line down the middle of the road which they were crossing in order to overtake me had been laid in a castellated form like a line of miniature battlements. The purpose of this was not to repel invaders but to wake up drivers. The roads in these parts tend to be straight and monotonous and drivers aware of these characteristics use them to their advantage by getting their heads down for a snooze as they belt along. There is no danger in this, of course, because if they slide off the road on their right side then they either come to a gentle halt in the sandy soil, thankfully not disturbing their slumbers, or they come to an abrupt halt against a conifer tree, in which case they are past caring about the comfort of life. The only danger that one could perceive would be if they wandered across the lanes and woke up a driver travelling in the opposite direction by selfishly colliding with his car. These bumpy white lines are designed to bring them to a form of consciousness just sufficient to enable them to redirect the car without actually waking up.

At first, I used the pitch and the length of the flatulence to estimate the speed of the car overtaking me but then I inevitably began to categorise the farts in the only way possible: *brrrrp,* brussels sprouts; *brrp, brrp, brrp,* cucumber; *brrrp, brrrrrp,* a pint of Guinness, *brrrrrrrrrrrrrrrrrp,* last night's curry; and so forth.

It may sound an utterly puerile pursuit but if car drivers travelling at eighty miles per hour feel that ten miles of straight and level road is tedious, imagine what a cyclist who is crawling along at ten miles per hour thinks of it.

I ate my lunch at the café hotel *Chez Mary* which, by chance, appeared alongside the main road at lunchtime. The establishment was closed for the holidays, of course, and although they had affixed chains across the entrances to the car parks to emphasise this closure, they had left their plastic chairs and tables stacked on the terrace overlooking the main road. So I took me a chair from the stack and arranged a table upon which I laid out my tomatoes, bread and cheese and nectarines. I passed an enjoyable thirty minutes eating my lunch and watching the traffic drone past in a continuous stream in both directions.

This entertainment was enlivened by an occasional enterprising Frenchman suddenly spotting that rarest of creatures – a restaurant apparently open on a French holiday route in the holiday season. The sequence of noises would be; *uurrrrr,* as he braked at the first sight of me eating on the terrace; *brrrp, brrrp,* as he farted his way across the road; *cockerbockerbocker* as he bounced over the rough verge; *kerrwhiiiickkk tinkle tinkle* as he skidded to a stop in a cloud of dust and rattling gravel three centimetres from the chain; *raaark,* as he slammed the gearstick into reverse; *rerrerrrerrrerr,* as he spun his tyres back onto the tarmac and then he would throw me a final farewell fart as he crossed back over the road to continue his journey. And that journey would be a fast one in two senses of the word.

For the remaining forty miles to Marmande I decided to count bicycles. The total eventually reached three hundred and sixty seven. But mine was the only bicycle being ridden, all the others were strapped to the backs or roofs of cars.

Marmande was heaving with people and music. It was the Week of the Tomato. At the busy stands in the main square you could sample sixty different varieties of tomato and I did not find one which was called *'Marmande'.*

I checked in to the Lion d'Or and booked dinner for the evening. I rushed up to my room and showered away sixty five miles of road dust and washed my clothes. Then I phoned Mission Control.

'Where are you?' MyMateMargaret asked.

'In Marmande, of course.'

'Where were you last night?'

'I got to Grenade OK.'

'You did not report in.'

I thought of the relaxed evening, playing with the children, eating pizza, laughing and joking at the café.

'It was hectic. I was cycling for over eight hours and then I was too tired to do anything.'

'All right, I understand. Did you buy some clothes?'

'I don't need more clothes. I already have clothes, it is just that I don't happen to have them with me. There's no point in buying any extra.'

'Does that mean that you have cycled for three days in your pyjamas? You'll get arrested. Did you go to a bicycle shop at least?'

'Yes. I promise you I did.'

'And you got your handlebars fixed?'

I try a non committal, 'Mmmm.'

'I'll ask that question again. Did you get your handlebars fixed?'

'I bought a water bottle for the bike. I am drinking litres in this heat.' Try and distract her. 'We need to talk about the itinerary.'

'Go on then.'

'That cycle track you gave me yesterday did not exist. It still had trains on it. The one you gave me for today was an awful surface, I had to abandon it and then navigate from my head across country.'

'Why were you navigating from your head? Didn't you have a map?'

'Well if I did, it was at home.'

'With your clothes. Is there anything else you have left behind?'

I decided to ignore that question. Answering it might have vexed her.

'Tomorrow I go to Manzac sur Vern and the day after that I cycle from there to the railway station at Périgueux.

I need absolutely to know whether I can take my bike on the train from Périgueux to Limoges. I could never do the road, it is sixty miles of switchback.'

'Right, I'll find out for you but I thought you had the itinerary sorted out?'

'Well, almost.'

'Ring me tomorrow night without fail.'

'Thank you.' Well that wasn't too bad was it?

My other pyjama top which I had put in Eliane's washing machine last night was still damp. I needed to dry it so that I could sleep in it tonight. I put it on and walked out into the baking hot streets and strutted about the town, steaming like a race horse in the paddocks after the Grand National. It did cause a few people to look, but they did not know they were looking at my pyjamas.

In the restaurant that night, the chef was offering a special tomato menu. Tomato at every course, including the dessert. I had to have that. When the first dish arrived I looked at the glass and the pots and spoons and had to ask the waitress what it was. She turned to me with a beautiful smile and pointed at the glass of red.

'That, monsieur, is a tomato juice.' And with a cheeky grin she added, 'And that is a dandelion leaf.'

I thanked her. She was very pretty. The tomato juice was such as I had never tasted before in my life. The evening was hot, the juice was cool, not cold. It had flavour and bouquet. It was pure crushed tomato and I drank it as slowly as I could because I did not want it to end. I have vowed that I will never write a book with a recipe in it but allow me to reproduce the menu:

jus de tomate de marmande
croustillant pomme d'amour à la tomate et aux anchois
supreme de pintadeau roti et sa tomate farcie
chèvre frais aromatisé à la tomate
douceur au chocolat et son sorbet à la tomate.

As I savoured my tomato sorbet with chocolate, I found myself listening to a conversation between an elderly English mother and her son. I always have my notebook with me and they were talking slowly. Out came my pen.

He was reading the label on the wine bottle.

'That can't be right, fifteen per cent. That's too much for wine.'

'Hasn't it been glorious? You look tired. What time did you get up?'

'Half six or half seven, French time. I can't understand this label, not fifteen per cent. It was presented to the salon de Paris in 1988.'

'It's very nice. Not Mouton Rothschild.'

'Don't talk to me of that. Angela gave my only bottle of Mouton Rothschild to charity.'

'She did not, she sold it.'

'Yeah but she took it to a bottle stall. I bet the bloke who bought it thought it was Christmas three times over. Probably got it for thirty pence.'

'It was for charity, dear.'

'That's not the point. I'd rather give them a five pound note and drink the stuff myself.'

'Why don't you go back to Angela?'

'I live with her now.'

'Only in the same village.'

'It can't be fifteen per cent. Not for wine.'

'You didn't have any Mouton Rothschild. It was a bottle of port.'

'That reminds me, Jean Claude owes me twelve euros.'

'Why?'

'I dont know. I said, "how much do I owe you?" because I thought I needed to give him some more but he said, "No, I owe you some, if anything".'

'I don't understand how George can mow the lawns every week and you can't.'

'His mower is self propelled. I have to push mine.'

'It has always been a thing, though, to keep the lawns nice.'

'But George has a self propelled mower, Mother. He doesn't have to push it unless it breaks down.'

'I suppose you've got no time. You could do it in the morning.'

'Seven o'clock, Radio Cambridge comes on. I have a shower, breakfast, out of the house at eight and I'm in the office by ten to nine. And I still get there before most of the others.'

'Yes dear.'

'Have you tried our shower?'

'Did you have one when you were there?'

'Yes, but we've got a new one.'

'Cheese. Of course you have to come to France to eat cheese.'

'Nonsense! We've got all the cheeses of the world in our country.'

'Yes but if you want them you have to eat at the Savoy.'

'No you don't Mother. The thing is, the French only have French cheese. We have English, French, German, Dutch, Australian, New Zealand and every bloody country's cheese.'

'I didn't know the Germans made cheese.'

'Emmenthal; they make that.'

'That's what I mean. It's not cheese is it?'

So next time you are chatting in a French restaurant and there is a chap at the corner table apparently doodling in a notebook, beware! It could be me.

Le Lion d'Or

5 – MANZAC SUR VERN

Sunday morning. Marmande is sleeping off Saturday night's rock concert and I have a sore throat. That is not good news. More intriguing is the answer to the question: where did I get it from? 'v-neck pyjamas,' I hear you shout. If you are wearing v-neck pyjamas and you cycle for four hours into a head wind then that engaging little breeze that you thought was rippling teasingly down your chest to cool you in your efforts was actually sand papering your larynx.

I swallow hard a couple of times and hope that the action will clear it. It doesn't, it just makes it more obvious. What I could really benefit from is a couple of those throat lozenges that I derisively ejected from MyMateMargaret's survival pack. I bet they are lying on my kitchen table right now and guffawing into their blister sheets.

I go down for breakfast and find a different world to the previous day. No pretty waitress and haute cuisine; this is France at its most impersonal. Everything I need for breakfast is on the buffet. There is even a hot water machine that dispenses one's chosen beverage at the push of a button. All I lack is a dish cloth and a bowl of soapy water and then I could do the washing up as well.

I pedal along the empty boulevard to the patisserie to buy my lunch and then I take the road northwards to Bergerac. As I cross the valley towards the higher lands I ponder upon this river which flows past Marmande on its way to the sea. The Garonne really is a remarkable concatenation; it collects watercourses which have given their names to *départements*. It rises far up in the Pyrenees, further east than my starting point. Flowing northwards out of the mountains, before it has reached Toulouse it has scooped up the Ariège. From Toulouse it turns westwards towards the Atlantic and adds the Tarn, the Gers and the Lot to its corporation before it arrives at Marmande. Continuing on through Bordeaux it effects a merger with the Dordogne which has brought its water from the Massif Central and has already bought out the Corrèze en route. At this point, rather like an overstretched multinational conglomerate, the Garonne loses all sense of purpose and identity and relaunches itself upon the riparian stock exchange as a holding company in the form of the Estuary of the Gironde. It will only last fifty miles in that form so sell your shares quickly.

I don't know where the word 'Gironde' comes from. It is perhaps a locality; or is it descriptive? For *'gironde'* when applied as an adjective to the charms of a woman evokes a broad comeliness and there is no doubt that the river at this point is broad. Or was it the other way around? Was it an entirely different womanly quality which was identified in the behaviour of the river? After all, whether you believe it to be the Gers, the Ariège, the Tarn, the Lot, the Corrèze, the Dordogne or the Garonne – it does not matter what you call the water; it is the Gironde that has the last word.

I'll leave you to ponder the full ramifications of that observation whilst I cycle to Bergerac. I have other things on my mind. I am worried about tomorrow. In theory tomorrow should be a relaxing day. All I have planned is a short twelve mile ride to Périgueux where I take the train for the one hundred kilometre ride to Limoges. What could be easier than that? I'll give you a clue. When did YOU last take a bicycle on a French train?

I remember vividly the last such occasion in my life. It started well with the station master conducting me to the train and helping me up with the bicycle and explaining where I would have to change. He could not have been more kind. I obviously met his *alter ego* when I changed trains. I hurried my bicycle up to the front of the rake where the guard gazed down upon me from his empty van.

'What do you want?' he asked.

'Can you help me up with my bike?'

'It's not coming in here. Take it down to the proper guard's van at the other end.'

'But this is the guard's van,' I said in surprise. That was my mistake. He waved his hand towards the nether end of the platform to where the end of the train was invisible in the obscurity of the night lit station.

'The other end.'

You don't argue with French petty officialdom, it only encourages them to extend themselves to commit some greater outrage. Under the stony eyes of the guard I hauled my bicycle around and started to force my way against the tide of travellers. And when I reached the third coach, he blew his whistle. He had timed it beautifully. It was a bit like musical chairs. Which way do I run? Back to the guard and force my way onto the train or down to the other end and the, as yet, unseen guard's van? I did neither. I opened the nearest door, tucked my bicycle under my arm like a newspaper, and climbed on.

When I was a train spotter I used to know all kinds of technical data. For example, the width of a British Railways passenger carriage was nine feet three inches; the three inches representing the sum of the thickness of the outside door handles on both sides. I expect some anorak will write to the publisher and say that I am wrong. I never studied foreign rolling stock but I can now tell you that the width of that particular carriage where I entered it, was exactly the length of my bicycle. I slammed the door and I was wedged, dividing the train in half. I rather hoped that the guard would want to come down the train and I would be able to obstruct him but the chances were pretty small; I was only travelling the five stations up to the end of the line.

When I reached that station, which had already closed and was in utter darkness, I could not get out because my door on that side of the train had not been unlocked. I banged on the window as the guard walked down the platform and he ignored me. The lights were extinguished in the train and it was only when I began to howl like a wolf that the driver came and let me out. I noticed as I left the platform via the wicket gate that there was no guard's van at the other end of the train.

So here I am cycling to Manzac and worrying that this might be as far as I get because although the French timetable might assure me that the train takes bicycles, and although the board in the station might do likewise, it only needs one Frenchman....

My throat is really niggling me now. I stop at a pretty little place called Eymet and buy myself a tube of those butterscotch sweets that MyMateMargaret had given me and which are rolling around with the other rejects on my kitchen table. They cost me five times more than they would have done in the UK. The wind is still blowing down my pyjama top so I bunch the neck up and pin it together with a blue plastic clothes peg from my laundry bag.

After Eymet I pull into a picnic layby and eat a *chausson aux pommes* whilst I inspect the white clouds for any sign of grey. It is still Sunday morning and the traffic is sparse. A lone car stops. The driver gets out, looks at me, frowns at my blue clothes peg and then turns to the hedge and urinates on the nettles. He drives off.

It occurs to me that I did not see one tomato growing in Marmande. I saw lettuces, tobacco, maize, fruit but no tomatoes. I suppose they do come from Marmande and are not imported from Turkey or Spain? You can never tell.

As I am pondering on the provenance of tomatoes another car drives in to the layby. The man gets out, nods at me and pees into the hedge, then he drives off. I am still worrying about that train tomorrow. A third car stops. The man wees into the hedge, blows his nose and drives away. I look at the end of the pastry in my hand. I toss it over my shoulder and take to the road again.

My mind turns back to trains. French officialdom has not always had its own way. I was coming back from the Massif Central by train one summer. I waited at Clermont Ferrand for the first train of the day upon which I could book my bicycle to travel with me. This is important because the French railway luggage people love to take your bicycle and then hang on to it and send it on a train of their choice later in the week. This has serious implications if you are starting out on a cycling trip. Can you imagine driving to a cross channel ferry to start your holidays on the Monday and being told that you can travel but they'll bring your car over some time on Thursday? That is the kind of argument that the cyclist is expected to swallow on French railways.

So I made sure that this train had my bike on board before I got on. I had forgotten about Paris. It suddenly dawned on me that I had booked the bike through to Calais and that when I changed trains in Paris, they would pounce on my poor machine gleefully and lock it up until the Beuajolais Nouveau had arrived or France had won the Eurovision Song Contest. So when we pulled in to Paris I legged it down the platform and, guessing that they would not read the label, I reclaimed my bicycle. I then cycled across the city and presented my bicycle to the guard of my train at the Gare du Nord.

'What's this?' he said. I felt sure that he knew that it was a bicycle – mine was not the only example in France. However, I had to play the game.

'My bicycle.'

'What do you expect me to do with it?'

'Hang it on that hook. It's going to Calais.'

'Have you got a ticket?'

'Yes, look.'

'You need to check the bike in. It won't go on this train.'

'It is checked in. The label is on the seat pillar.'

He studied it.

'This says, *"Clermont Ferrand"*.'

'That's where I've come from.'

'But how did you get to the Gare du Nord?'

'By bicycle.'

'But you can't do that. You took it outside SNCF custody. It's up to us to get it to the connecting station.'

'Well I've saved you the trouble.'

'But it doesn't work like that.'

'It's booked through to Calais. This train is going to Calais. I have a ticket for Calais. This is the guard's van and it is empty. Now explain to me what the problem is?'

He scowled and took my bicycle.

'It doesn't work like that,' he grumbled.

But it did.

And then of course there was that time I went by Motorail. 'You only go by Motorail once in your lifetime,' a friend had warned me. It was when I had wanted to do the Pyrenees. I found a train that went from Boulogne to Biarritz and another that came back from Narbonne to Boulogne. Opposite ends of the Pyrenees. Gettit?

I decided to travel first class as I had never been on a couchette train before. Leaving Boulogne, the only other occupant of my compartment was a Spanish mini-cab driver who had made his fortune in London and was now returning to retire in Spain. Parenthetically I could say that this was at a time before the entry of Spain into the European Community; an event which would have given him the right to work in the UK, and at that time there was no way that the British Home Office would have authorised a work permit for a Spaniard to drive a mini-cab. However, I digress.

The Motorail train has a line of wagons upon which the cars are loaded and this rake is coupled onto the end of the train of couchette carriages. This particular train had an additional wagon for bicycles. It was the classic brown goods van with sliding doors. The kind that Thomas the Tank Engine was always having trouble with.

The journey was interesting. For the the first mile out of Boulogne I thought that it was snowing but it was only the passengers unpacking their pre-ordered railway dinners and throwing the polystyrene cases out of the windows. This was soon followed by cans of red beans, packets of biscottes and any other of the contents that were considered to be unappetising. And yes, there was a notice saying, *'do not throw anything out of the window.'* At about ten o' clock, by mutual agreement we got into our bunks and this is where the dangerous seed was sown. As a cyclist, I had all my bags with me so, once on my bunk, I stripped off, got into my pyjamas and settled down. Nobody saw me so nobody told me that you were not supposed to undress.

At about one in the morning we were shunted into a siding somewhere outside Paris and all the ventilation was shut off. I could hear the family next door sniping at each other as the train got hotter and hotter. There was no water in the toilets and no water in the washbasins. When I questioned the SNCF staff about this afterwards they dismissed it as not being their responsibility.

'We do not own the train, it belongs to Motorail. We just pull it.'

'But surely you service the train? Put water in the tanks and all that kind of thing?'

'Only if they ask us.'

We eventually got to Biarritz and off I cycled into the mountains.

Ten days later I presented myself at Narbonne for the

return journey and was instructed to put my bicycle in the goods van. This was not the easy operation that it had been in Boulogne for here, the van was a solitary wagon loitering in the siding as if it wanted to have nothing to do with Motorail. I sympathised with it but have you any idea how high the floor of a railway truck is when you are standing on the ground? I am over six feet tall and I could only just reach it. How was I supposed to lift a bicycle up there?

'Is there somebody to help me with my bicycle?'

'I regret, monsieur, I am Motorail. The truck is SNCF.'

'Is there somebody here from the SNCF then?'

'No monsieur, they drive the locomotive.'

I did not really want to continue this investigation into the partition of responsibilities; I was afraid that he might start drawing me an organigram. It was obvious that nobody was going to help me so I waited until a snappy little lady cyclist turned up, but the gallantry for which the French are famous was not forthcoming. However, she was a plucky Brit and gave me a leg up. I scrabbled my way onto the dirty, straw strewn floor of the truck and then I squatted and stretched whilst she tried to lift the bikes high enough for me to grab a bit and haul them up.

Just get out and push your motor car up the ramp onto the ferry would you sir? It's all part of the service.

But worse was to come. The homeward train was all second class, which meant six bunks per compartment. It was heaving with campers rushing back from the south of France before their suntan faded. When I reached my compartment, I could hardly get in. Everybody seemed to know everybody else; husbands, wives, children, they were popping in and out of the doors like a Whitehall farce. I could not work out which of the men were in my compartment. I was fairly sure that the sixteen stone, bald headed, tattooed gentleman was married to the woman with ginger hair and black eyeshadow but whose the children were was anybody's guess.

There was obviously not going to be that moment of mutual agreement when everybody decided to go to bed and all the ladies returned to their compartment and all the gentlemen settled down in ours so I clambered up to my bunk with my cycle bags and started to arrange my sheet sleeping bag. Eventually things began to get quieter below me and I took no further interest. As I had done on the journey down, I stripped off, put my pyjamas on and slipped into the sheets.

We rumbled through the night, sometimes hearing the *ting, ting, ting,* of a level crossing bell, sometimes the grumbling of the tattoo lying somewhere below me. We got hotter and hotter and at one point in the night I pulled my pyjamas off and slept on in the buff. Everything was set for the drama which was to follow.

It had never occurred to me that I could be in a mixed compartment. There had been just us two men on the way down and I had supposed that there was segregation according to sex. How mistaken I was in this supposition, I and the entire carriage were about to discover. Piecing the events together from the inquest which occurred afterwards was not easy since most of it was conducted at ninety decibels in Estuary English but it would appear that the lady with ginger hair and black eyeshadow had been sleeping below me at some level and at about five in the morning, she had arisen and stretched. The first thing she had seen was a stark naked Martin lying on his side with an intimate and, thankfully, floppy part of his anatomy dangling before her eyes.

As is their wont on occasions such as this, the dame screeched.

'Oh my Gawd!'

I awoke to find a woman in the compartment and my sheet sleeping bag twisted around my feet like cat's cradle.

'There's a woman in here! There's a woman in here!' I shouted a warning as I clawed frantically at my sheets.

'What the **** do you fink you're ****ing well doing to my ****ing wife?' Tattoo demanded.

'Marm, Marm, what's the sharting abart?'

I won't go on. I am sure you can continue the scenario better than me. You must have seen it on every soap opera that has ever sudsed. Do you understand now why I have misgivings about my proposed train trip tomorrow?

I pedalled my way around Bergerac and descended the valley of the Dordogne for a couple of kilometres before turning up the next valley northwards. By not thinking about my cycling and worrying about everything else instead, I had made very good time. Bergerac is on the Dordogne and its valley is known as the preferred region of the English. Nearly every house along this road had a British car parked outside it.

I went into a country bar to fill up my water bottles. The money from the previous customer was still lying on the counter.

'There's a lot of English people in this area,' I said to the barman by way of conversation

'Not as many as there was,' he said as he filled my second bottle. 'It's beginning to stablilise.'

The money was still on the counter when I left.

At the disrespectfully early time of half past three I arrived at the Lion d'Or at Manzac. The lady asked me where I had come from and when she learned that it was fifty eight miles away she exclaimed, *'Oh punaise!'* It is a charmingly retro oath that I had not heard for thirty years. A *'punaise'* is a flea. It is also a drawing pin. Why either should become the focus of such an exclamation I cannot say. I suspect that it might be to avoid saying *'Oh putain!'* which is a more common and less polite oath, meaning, 'Oh prostitute!' I can't see the reason for employing that word either unless it is for its expressive and explosive use of the syllable *'pu.'*

I find 'Wednesday' is jolly useful in French; the word being *'mercredi.'* Just when the maiden aunt is reaching for the smelling salts because she thinks you are saying, *'merde'* you can recover yourself by stretching it into *'mercredi'* thus maintaining an angelic innocence and, of course, mortally embarrassing the maiden aunt for having revealed that she was familiar with the other word.

The hotel was not put out by my early arrival. My room was ready and what a room it was! The doors closed like air locks, the plumbing operated with the efficiency of medical engineering, the bathroom tiles were grouted and the beds had the correct number of legs. I wondered for the minute which country I was in. It scored eventually as the best appointed room of the entire trip.

But I had four hours to kill in Manzac on a Sunday afternoon. Manzac has a tile works, an automotive body repair shop strategically sited on a dangerous crossroads and a public weighbridge. Many years ago they planted trees in the pavement and these have now grown so big that they occupy the entire width of the sidewalk so that pedestrians are obliged to walk in the street. There is a shop which has a venetian blind hanging down the outside of its window. Manzac.

Ten minutes before dinner I rang in to Mission Control.

'I am at Manzac sur Vern,' I announced proudly. 'I got here at half past three.'

'Wow that's good. You've had plenty of time in the pool then?'

'The what?'

'The swimming pool. The hotel has a swimming pool, don't you remember? I wrote it on your itinerary.'

Ah yes, the pool. Now I remember. Bum!

'So what news on the train tomorrow?'

'According to the website...' (I wish she would not try to confuse me with jargon) '...you can take your bike on the trains to Limoges.'

'And are there any trains?' Don't you forget that I've had experience of French Railways.

'Yes, plenty of trains. How far are you booked ahead?'

'Two days. Limoges, Aubusson and then I must ring and reserve Montluçon.'

'I've found another Lion d'Or just north of Montluçon at a place called Estivareilles. If you book that you could avoid Montluçon altogether.'

'I'll try from Limoges tomorrow. If I get there.'

The sun came out and I dined on the terrace. By the swimming pool. The waitress bobbed along and plonked an *amuse bouche* in front of me. Do I ask what it is? Yesterday I had made a fool of myself by demanding to see the pedigree of a tomato juice. Well, here goes.

'And what is this, mademoiselle?'

'It is mousse of beetroot with a cucumber cream.'

Of course it is, silly me.

6 – LIMOGES

There were only three of us for breakfast. Singletons. We sat at the three points of a tricorn hat and ignored each other. I soon got rid of the other two.

The breakfast was unitary. Portioned into a basket for each guest; pastry, bread, jam, butter. I tested the bread. The baskets had been prepared the night before.

I remarked to the *patron* upon the blocked doorway in the ancient outside wall of the hotel and he explained that the hotel had originally been a shop.

'My grandmother had a grocery shop in here. Of course, in those days the commerce was in the village. We had everything here: milk, eggs, bread, the grocery, a butcher's. We had a clog maker for the *sabots* that all the workmen wore in those days. Then the motor car came along and grandmother opened a garage across the way there, so we had petrol. It was in cans at first. Nobody needed to leave the village for anything. All the commerce was here.

'When you opened your shutters in the morning you would look across to see if the neighbours were up and you would wave and say "good morning" and pass the time of day with them. Not now. We've got new people across the street there. Been there three years and I have hardly spoken to them.'

'What was the weighbridge used for?' I had inspected it

on my visit of the village yesterday afternoon. It was a cast iron balanced bed set into the surface of one corner of the village square. At the side of it officiated a quaintly imposing brick cabin which housed the mechanism and the dial to indicate the weight.

'The farmers would put their carts on it to weigh the forage and hay that they were selling. The stone at the side was for weighing pigs. I can remember them doing that.'

'When I was walking about yesterday I was surprised to see that there are two hotels in the village.'

'There used to be three.'

'Where do all the customers come from?'

He shrugged. I could not tell if that signified ignorance or an unwillingness to divulge what might be commercially sensitive information.

'It's no fun being a hotelier. Look at those lights for example.' I did so. They were the round bright things that fit flush to the ceiling. 'We are not supposed to have those, I've been told. They are a fire hazard in an old building like this. And the beams. All the beams have to be covered now to stop fire.'

'That's daft. They build modern hotels nowadays and put beams in to make them look old.'

'Ah, they are new beams. New beams are OK. They are not a fire problem. It's the old, genuine beams that are against the law. Regulations, regulations, regulations; that's all it is now.' He waved a hand at the front door. 'We've had to put in a disabled access for wheelchairs. It cost a fortune and we've not had one cripple yet. And then there's the famous thirty five hour week. Nobody takes on temporary workers any more because they all have rights and they are all entitled to holidays. So the hotels save on staffing by not opening their restaurants at midday. I know some restaurants who lose four lunchtimes per week because of that. Several of my colleagues have stopped doing hotel altogether. They have converted to bed and breakfast.

The regulations there are not so strict and you don't need the staff. And what about the swimming pool?' he asked.

Exactly.

'All the hotels now have to either pay for a lifeguard on duty all the time that the pool is open or they have to fit childproof railings all around it.' I nodded sympathetically although I realised that I would be quite safe – you have to find the pool first before you can drown in it. 'And no children drown in hotel pools,' he continued. 'All deaths that have happened in France have been to unattended children in garden pools but it is the hotels who have to spend the money.'

Before I left the hotel the *patron* and his wife kindly decided to ring Périgueux railway station to check whether I could take my bicycle on a train but all they got was a recorded message. When they tried the local station, they got no reply. Another shrug.

'*Bonne chance, monsieur.*' They waved me off up the road.

I was muffled up in my waterproof-that-isn't because it was raining. It had been raining all night and the deciduous trees were clean and heavy with water whilst the air was full of a fine rain that insinuated itself into my pyjamas.

I wound gently upwards with the road, puzzling at the discarded cigars that I saw glistening on the wet asphalt. One unsmoked cigar would have been unusual, but I was now going past my seventh. When I chose to ride over the eighth I discovered to my revulsion that they were not cigars but nine inch long slugs. If that is the size of the local slugs, how big are the hedgehogs?

By the time I squeak to a halt outside Périgueux railway station I am comprehensively damp. Where the rain has not managed to penetrate from the outside, the condensation has managed to permeate from the inside. It gets you one way or the other. The stupid thing is that we are bound by social mores to wear waterproofs that don't work and yet we humans have been fitted with a perfect weather-resistant covering called 'skin.' Rain runs off it very efficiently. If you went for a walk naked in a summer storm you would not come back with water sloshing around inside your kidneys or filling your legs from the ankles upwards. You would probably come back with a summons.

One July day, many years ago, I walked down the street from my bedsit to the small supermarket which served our neighbourhood of Paris. I wanted to buy some shampoo. Having made my purchase I regained the street at the very moment that the city was drenched by one of those sudden summer rainstorms. Others ran for cover but I could not be bothered. Within ten seconds I was soaked to the skin. The rain was not cold. The day was warm. I was wearing a tee shirt and shorts which, although they were soaked, would not degrade in any way so where was the problem? Then I realised that such a laid back philosophy not only gave me the fortitude to withstand the perfidy of the weather with equanimity but encouraged me to identify and exploit its advantages. Out came my purchase. *Glop, glop*, it went onto my scalp and I walked home, shampooing and rinsing my hair in the rain as I went. When it dried, it fluffed up like a dandelion seed head.

But here I am outside the railway station. I pull off my waterproofs and drape them over my bike because the sky down in the bottom left corner of the picture is bright blue and hopefully by the time that I have bought my ticket, my clothes will have dried. Yes, and I believe in fairies too.

The moment of truth has arrived. I have slid down the Pyrenees and braved raw tomato juice to bag four Golden Lions in a row. Will the SNCF be the upturned spoon under the tap in the kitchen sink of my life? If I cannot take my bicycle on a train to Limoges, my safari will stop right here.

Five minutes later I am back outside again, sitting in the sunshine and watching the rain steam from my bicycle. I don't condone this current fashion for criticising large organisations such as the SNCF. They are a very easy target and making them the butt of ill-informed complaint based on outrageous speculation is most unfair and I will not stand for it.

As I sit there, a young man swoops up on a red touring bicycle and installs himself at the terrace of the café next door. He orders breakfast and pulls out a map to study whilst he is waiting. I walk over.

'Where have you come from?' I ask in English. There is no point in embarrassing him with French.

'From a campsite just up the road.' He shows me his map. It covers all of France on one sheet. 'What about you? Where have you come from?'

'From a little place called Manzac. It's about there.' I make a vague stab at his map. 'But I am cheating. I am taking the train from here to Limoges. You are going south are you?'

'Yeah. I am going to a mate's wedding near Carcassone. Well, between Carcassone and Toulouse. I don't know exactly where it is. It's only a little village.'

'It won't be on a map of that scale. You'll need a 1:100,000 map at least.'

'Yeah, well I've got till Saturday. I'll go on the internet and find it. Or e-mail him. Trouble is, there are not many internet cafés in France are there?'

I shake my head with apparent authority. I have no idea what he is talking about. It strikes me that he has not made proper preparations for his trip at all. Unlike me.

My train will not be leaving for an hour and a half so I sit on a bench on the concourse and wait. I like watching people. Isn't it interesting that when French women grow old, their hair doesn't go grey or white, it goes red? Perhaps it's something in the water. Cycling down a boring *route nationale* encourages you to do silly things such as counting bicycles on the roofs of cars; sitting waiting for a train I find myself methodically picking the fluff out of my velcro. Well, it's got to be done at some time.

Eventually I thread my way out to platform C. Behind me at opposite ends of platform B two futuristic autorails are slumbering peacefully. They are all curves and shiny glass, as if sculpted from blue blancmange. I wonder whether they will trundle out into the station yard, couple together and come back on my platform to form my train.

My train is now due. Just as the recorded lady starts to make her announcement, the two railcars suddenly burst into life in a cacophony of diesels, drowning out the tinny voice like MPs at Question Time. We waiting passengers on platform C all look at each other, hoping that one of our cohort has been able to decipher the announcement. Vain hope! A man wearing an SNCF cap comes up the stairs and is besieged by people shooting questions at him as a portion of blue blancmange glides into the platform alongside us.

It is my train and the carriage with the section for bicycles pulls up right in front of me. Whilst I can see the advantage of designing a railcar with a slippy, curvy, smooth exterior that will slide through the air with the minimum of fuss, I do not quite see the advantage of continuing this style for the interior. I lean my bicycle up against the only unencumbered wall and it rolls away down the carriage because the wall is curved like a turret. I drag the machine back, speak to it sternly and reinstall it and it immediately attempts to shy backwards out of the open doors onto the platform.

But us cyclists have ways and means. Under the sardonic grins of the natives I start to unwind the bungee cord from my pannier rack. It is one of those short elastic ropes with a hook at each end which snags on everything except that which you want it to and then stretches, snaps back and hits you in the eye when you let go of it. But, properly tamed, they do have their uses.

Affecting a superior air, I unclip it, but then I am stumped. The locals are still grinning. There is nowhere, but nowhere to attach it: no hooks, no grab handles, no ridges, no useful little holes in the trim. Whilst I am casting around wildly for a purchase, the train starts and Dobbin decides to canter down the aisle. Now I am dancing back and forth from one foot to the other, waltzing with a loaded bike as the train lurches out of the station. I manage to manhandle the bicycle back and lean it against my curved wall. I duck down and wind the elastic cord several times through the front wheel and the frame, tying them together. This restricts the movement of the bicycle to a back and forth oscillation of about one foot. With a sigh of relief I sink onto the folding seat opposite.

And then things really start to happen. I think the driver must have been to Alton Towers. Or perhaps he was just trying to demonstrate how aerodynamically efficient the train was. He wound it up to eighty mph and then threw it into wheel-screeching turns and zigzags. My bike attempts a few cartwheels and handstands whilst I clutch at my seat. With a leg braced against the door, I thrust the other across the carriage and jam my foot into the back wheel. For an hour of swooping and swerving, swaying and sweeping I hang on grimly to whatever processes I can find and brace myself against greater forces than I ever remembered experiencing at Battersea Fun Fair.

And if that were not enough, I discover that the reason why this particular part of the train is curved is because it is the toilet and everybody wants to use it. For sixty minutes without pause the shell shaped door slides open and shut. I am treated to a symphony of water scouring down a pan complemented by a wafting of discreet fragrances. Is it more convenient for these country people to use the train for their ablutions than to undertake the time-honoured trudge down the garden?

Suddenly we are at Limoges and everybody wants to get off through the door at the side of which my bicycle is standing. They all have suitcases and they are all going to get off first. Every single one of them. Nobody is going to be second. They crash and crunch into me, wedging themselves into an immovable barricade that prevents any egress whatsoever. One lady makes it to the door and stands Messiah-like, a limb stretched to each corner, blocking the double doors like a giant letter X. She is going to be first. Nobody is going to get past her.

The brakes hiss, the doors open and mayhem starts as they surge into the barricade that they have built for themselves around my bicycle. I defend the spokes as best I can, kicking suitcases and ankles where necessary. There is no point in explaining to them that if, horror of horrors, they let me get off first with my bicycle, then everybody would be able to alight with the greatest of ease. Battered and not in the best of humour I at last manage to descend to the platform. I wheel my bicycle smartly over to an empty and unloved spot to get it out of everybody's way whilst they stampede out. I bend to reattach my bungee cord to my carrier and then I look up. I am penned in by a semicircle of fifteen travellers who are staring hard. Is there no place on this station that I can stand that somebody does not covet or own? Apparently I am blocking their view of the indicator board which, by the means of a line of miniature carriages, predicts the composition of the next train to arrive. But nobody gets past me and my bicycle as we ride up the escalator to the street. I make sure of that.

If you visit Limoges, you must not leave without seeing the Bénédictins railway station. All the tourist guide books and brochures recommend the picturesque old quarter and vaunt the porcelains and enamels for which the town is rightly famous but remain silent on this 1929 palace of modernism which, built in white stone with its tower straining skywards and situated near a flowering park, could almost be aspiring to the title of the 'Taj Mahal of the Limousin.'

The Hotel d'Orléans et du Lion d'Or is a few pedal turns from the station. The lady at reception searches for her ear ring on the floor behind the desk and answers my questions by bobbing up and down like a Titanic survivor, gasping out a syllable and then plunging below the counter again. The hotel used to be two hotels, side by side: the *Orléans* and the *Lion d'Or*. I can see the join inside and outside but she cannot tell me which half was which so I have to decide for the sake of the safari that I am sleeping in the Lion d'Or portion. She opens the garage for me so that I can store my bicycle. I dump my stuff in my room and hit the town.

It is still the early afternoon and although I have covered about seventy miles today, I have only cycled about ten of them. I should feel guilty or a bit of a cheat but I never said that it must be possible to *cycle* across France staying only at Lion d'Ors did I? And although I do not know it at the time, it transpires that those sixty miles endured in the train were to be the most gruelling of the entire tour.

The sun is seriously shining now and I sit at a streetside café and watch people getting on and off the buses. An African, as black as a lump of coal tries to sell me a carpet. I ask him if he does home delivery and the *patron* shoos him away and then scolds me for encouraging him. I walk around the town and sort out my exit route for the morning. Coming back to the hotel I note that there is a Basque restaurant across the street which guarantees authentic atmosphere and musical soirées and I decide that I will eat there tonight when it opens.

This Lion d'Or is a French hotel stuck in the 1960s. The stairs to the upper floors are all of different heights and the stairwell itself has been used as the main artery for every modernisation over the last hundred years. Fat sanitary conduits, twisted electrical cables, water pipes and central heating tubes twist organically up through the spiral funnel like liana vines in a tropical forest reaching to the sun.

My room is powder blue and smells like a traditional French hotel room. It must be a cocktail of the odour of clean but tired bedlinen, occasional wood polish and perennial toilet cleaner. But I have some homework to do before dinner. Tomorrow I go to Aubusson. The reservation will be no problem because I telephoned from the UK and then wrote a letter of confirmation as requested. But I do need to ring the new hotel that MyMateMargaret has found at Estivareilles, just north of Montluçon. If I can go there after Aubusson and avoid having to go into the centre of Montluçon that will be a good move. I succeed in booking not only that hotel but also the one at Nérondes for the following day.

Flushed with my success I decide to firm up my itinerary in the Loire. I was quietly pleased that my idea of not phoning the hotels until I got within spitting distance was proving to be the most practical procedure despite the criticism levelled at it from certain quarters. I would tell MyMateMargaret. Just for information, you understand, not for gloriation.

As things turned out I decided not to be churlish about my triumph.

'What's Limoges like?' she asked.

'Big, sunny, it's got trolley buses and some that run on natural gas.'

'Did the train work all right?'

'Oh, yes, no problem at all.'

'Thank you Margaret for doing the research.'

'Er, yes. Thank you. Whilst we are on the subject I have a little problem with the Loire.'

'I thought you had sorted all that out.'

'Yes, so did I but when I phoned the Lion d'Or at Amboise this afternoon they told me that they are only a restaurant now. They don't do hotel.'

'You could have found that out by telephoning from the UK before leaving.'

I think I have mentioned before this capacity that she has for reminding me of my underachievement. It is not a quality I find particularly endearing.

'The point is that I shall now need to cut straight across to Chinon.'

'So you save a day?'

'No.'

'Why not?'

'Because then I would get down the Loire to Ingrandes on Monday. They don't open till Tuesday. I shall now have to wait two days at Chinon.'

'Where do you stay the night before Chinon?'

'Oh that's no problem – I have a choice of three Lions: Romorantin, Mennetou or Selles. I'll choose one to suit.'

'So you don't actually know yet?'

'Look, I've got the hotels booked for three days ahead. That's pretty good isn't it?'

'Probably a record.'

Dinner. I crossed the street from the hotel to the lighted restaurant. I was looking forward to exercising my fluent Basque. *Ongi etorri* (welcome) would be easy. I was not so sure about *hurrengo geltokia* (the next station). I need not have worried. The waiter was about as Basque as a Bath bun and the musical soirée consisted of him singing odd snatches of songs along with the radio.

My first course was a *salade de ferme*: small bits of bacon, walnuts, toast and goat's cheese. Have you ever tried to pick up a well lubricated walnut with a knife and fork? The main course was *faux filet* and sauté potatoes. The latter were more '*plongé*' than '*sauté*' and the steak looked like the road map the English cyclist had shown me this morning. I left the portion of the meat where the blood was black. I prefer my *saignant* to be uncongealed.

All in all, it was an abysmal showing for Basque cuisine. On my grumbling stumble back to the hotel I walked past the Basque restaurant which was still in darkness. It did not open on Mondays. I had eaten at a Breton restaurant.

Well, all these ethnic minorities roll into one, don't they?

Hunting the Golden Lion

Limoges – Valençay

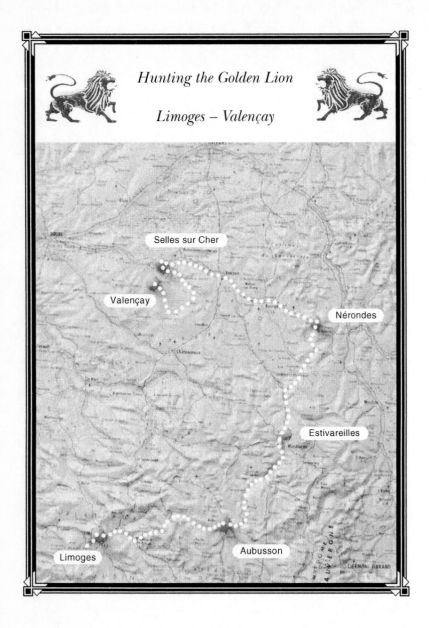

Selles sur Cher

Valençay

Nérondes

Estivareilles

Limoges

Aubusson

7 – Aubusson

I wake up with a smile on my face. I can feel it. I have bagged five Golden Lions and the difficult bit is now behind me. No more having to rely on outside agencies to get me to my destination; from now on the responsibility is mine and all the miles will be cycled.

And that is another thing. The cycling. Today is Tuesday. Since last Thursday I have cycled two hundred and forty one miles. I should, by rights, be crippled with cramp and straining with inflamed tendons but a funny thing has happened. When I had my bicycle built for me twelve years ago, my intention had been to exploit the 'many turns make light work' theory. No straining in high gears, no standing up on the pedals; this bicycle was to have a comfortable, many-springed saddle to sit upon and low gears to avoid my having to jump up and down. That was the theory but when I went out with MyMateJohn and the others I found I was always having to storm along in knee busting high gears just to be able to catch every third word of their conversations. My bicycle is built to last; theirs are built to go fast.

But now, as I spin the pedals to my own cadence and set out every day to a fixed destination at a known distance, I discover that I can pedal all day long in comfort. It has taken me twelve years of suffering to realise that I should have been selfish from the start. From now onwards, if they want to talk to me, then they will have to cycle as slowly as me, or suffer the consequences. So next time MyMateJohn lifts his bum out of the saddle I'll just threaten him, 'Chapter one, John, chapter one.' That should fix him. He is already terrified that I am going to put him in this book. As if I would!

Breakfast was a comprehensive buffet laid out at one end of the room. I was spreading a leisurely jam on my bread when I became aware of a feeling of agitation at the next table. There, a small, bald headed man in an ill fitting suit which suggested that he was a commercial traveller, if such a thing still exists, was scraping his spoon at the bottom of his cereal dish as he rose from his chair. He dumped the bowl and made for the buffet. He grabbed a plate and piled cheese slices and *saucisson* on it and then scurried back to his table. I was breaking open my little pot of honey when his fork clanged to the porcelain and he catapulted from his chair like a pilot ejecting from a fighter plane. The honey was twirling around my knife as he returned with a pot of yogurt and an apple. I had not, at that moment, noticed that he had placed three slices of bread in the automatic toaster but was appraised of this contingency when a few minutes later it clanged up and he was out of his chair in time to catch them on the rebound. His boiled egg was ready three minutes later. The croissants and *pain au chocolat* filled a corner for him whilst he contemplated whether he wanted a brown bread roll or a white. Without my telling you, you know how egalitarian his choice would eventually be don't you? And then, presumably, he spent the rest of the day sitting in a motor car.

Back in my room I take down my dry laundry and wind up my washing line and suddenly I have one of those brilliant flashes of inspiration for which I am known. In my kit has langoured, since the day I bought it twenty years earlier, a magic towel. This, the makers assured me, only weighed a few grams, folded up to the size of a final demand letter from British Telecom and would dry a human body to Kalahari dessication in less time than it would take me to write the cheque. So I did. When the towel arrived, thankfully not accompanied by any red letters, it revealed itself to be a patch of thin polyester cloth roughly hacked to the size and shape of a double page spread of a quality daily newspaper. The sheet that the instructions had been printed on was more absorbent than the towel itself but this was missing the point. Absorption was old hat; the current buzzwords were 'capillary wicking.' Apparently, all that was needed was to lay this cloth around one's wet bits and it drew the humidity from one's skin to the outer layer of the towel thus allowing it to evaporate.

Those readers who possess an elementary knowledge of Physics will have immediately seen the weak point. In order to transform itself into a gas and disappear off up into the greenhouse of our atmosphere, the water had to draw heat from somewhere and that somewhere was your body. So you stood there, partially wrapped in a ragged sheet of polyester, looking for all the world like a municipal statue half way through its unveiling... and you froze. You could not rub yourself because that would interrupt the capillary action. It might have restored your circulation but the fact that you were shivering had probably been included as a quotient in the calculation of the evaporation rate. The towel could not keep you warm because it was not large enough to wrap yourself up in.

So why do I pedal this utterly useless rag around Europe? Because I use it to wring out my wet clothes before hanging them up to dry. And as I collected my washing on that morning in Limoges I casually threw the towel around my neck to keep it out of the way and that was the master stroke of genius. Cycling through France in my pyjamas, from the point of view of style and chic, was already borderline.

The blue plastic clothes peg garnish had tipped it over into the mire of ridicule. What I needed was a scarf. Rather like the one that I had left on my bed in England. Now, if the French did not know that my shirt was my pyjamas, then they would not know that my scarf was my towel, would they?

The lady at the reception desk is not the lady of the ear ring. As I pay my bill I ask diffidently, 'Why is the hotel called the "Lion d'Or"?'

She neatly folds my bill over and scores it with her finger nail.

'It's a traditional name. Coaching inns were often called that. It came from the advertisement: *"Lit on dort"* that they used to hang outside. It sounds like "Golden Lion" you see.'

'Ah yes, I see.'

But I still don't believe it.

According to the map, the road to Aubusson will be undulating. It will take me to the east of the area of the Limousin, towards the Massif Central.

Did the Limousin really give its name to the 'limousine' style of motor car? Discuss. Time allowed, one hour.

Well, possibly. What do we understand by 'a limousine'? In Britain it has come to mean a large saloon car; 'saloon' from the French *'salon'* meaning a room in which one received visitors. This vehicle was something that the Americans would call a 'sedan' (cf Sedan: town in Eastern France) and the French, a *'berline'* (cf Berlin: former capital city of Prussia). The characteristic which distinguished this class of vehicles was that the roof was now extended to protect the driver as well as the passengers. Prior to this, the chauffeur was exposed to the weather in the *'landaulette'*, (cf Landau: town in Germany) rather as was the coachman of old. In the Limousin district of France, of which Limoges is the capital, shepherds and, more relevant to this disquisition, carriers, often wore a thick woollen cape to protect them from the weather. This cape was known as a *'limousine'*. In the nineteenth century if a felon declared that he was going to *'faire la limousine'* he meant that he would steal the lead from your roof. The fondness of the automobile industry for adopting the names of weather-proof clothes to describe their products was to spawn the memorable motor cars: the Austin Anorak, the Morris Macintosh and the Peugeot Pac-a-mac.

When I left the Pyrenees on the first day of this safari I could have cycled through the town of Condom. Are you glad that I did not?

I thought that the word 'undulating' meant that it went down as well as up. I have been cycling for three miles and it has only gone up. Limoges is way behind me on the river and I am plodding up its never ending valley side. It probably seems never ending because I am going so slowly. But not too slowly for a bit of excitement. Just past the taxidermist's, a motor cycle approaches from a minor road on a converging course. I have the priority. The old man is hunched up over his motor bike in a cloud of blue smoke and buzzing like a wasp. He is not going to stop. Neither am I. We play chicken, hurtling headlong towards mutual destruction and I win. At the very last moment he pretends that he has just noticed me and brakes fiercely, skidding on the loose road chippings. I nod graciously at him and he stalls. I feel vindicated. But the bloody road is still going up.

For the next fifty five miles the road comprehensively undulates. When it is not going up, it is going down. There are no flat bits between Limoges and Aubusson but the road surface is good, the carriageway is wide and the enormous lorries transporting the logs to the paper mills up the road at St Léonard de Noblat give me a wide berth as they sweep past. I keep spinning my pedals and am at peace with the world.

The sun is shining from a clear blue sky when I drift into the picnic spot formed as many of them are, from an old loop of the road. I had bought a small quiche on the way out of Limoges but had not found any fruit or tomatoes which was a shame since I am now starting my second bottle of water.

There is a map painted on a large board at the site so I use it to confirm my journey for tomorrow. The hills have all been glossed in three shades of green with trees on their slopes and the rivers are blue ribbons with red bridges. It is all very picturesque. I locate the valley by which I had intended to leave Aubusson tomorrow and it was a good thing that I did for it had a river but no road. This was a serious blow to my itinerary because the valley was pointing in just the right direction. I supposed that it was too much to hope that there would be a road. Life is like that. Full of disappointments. Hold on a minute. Do I really believe that in this hilly region, for generations the populace has preferred to clamber over the hills instead of slipping easily up the valley? I pull out my bundle of map extracts and choose the one for tomorrow. It shows a road where I need it and where you would expect it. I glance at the picturesque board. I can see that the artist has omitted the road because putting in a red line there would spoil the composition. From a patrician perspective I can empathise but I do feel that sometimes such considerations could be subjugated to the purpose of a map – that of representing faithfully the terrain. Or am I being churlish?

I move to double check my intended route with the man who has just got out of his car but he turns deliberately away from me and starts to pee into the hedge. I get on my bicycle and cycle away.

A short distance up the road I set up a flock of about one hundred small birds which had been busy doing something small-birdish on the verge. They rise as one body and fly straight through the hedge and out the other side, making a hissing noise like running water as their wings batter the foliage. Cyclists enjoy a strange relationship with other animals. The act of getting on a bicycle changes a person's threat profile in the eyes of various groups. If I meet a young lady alone in a deserted country lane I will say 'hello' to her. If I am on a bicycle she will smile and return the greeting; if I am walking she will bare her teeth and grab her CS gas spray. Wild animals react differently. All manner of rodents, herbivores, marsupials and reptiles will happily sunbathe or philosophise at the side of a thundering four lane motorway but should a bicycle try to sidle past them on the sly they will take to the air or whichever medium is theirs particular and scream murder to all within earshot.

And then a group of French racing cyclists passes in the opposite direction. They are red and blue, lean and leaning on slimline bicycles which glint and sparkle. I am upright and shaggy on a drab muddy bicycle with bags a-flapping. They try to ignore me so I further embarrass them by squeaking my bright yellow plastic squeezy duck which takes the place of a bell on my handlebars. Tail end Charlie lifts a vague hand in my direction. The others manage to talk over it.

Five minutes later as I steam steadily up another mile long hill a lorry toots its horn and the driver waves and gives me a thumbs up in recognition of the effort that I am expending. He probably rides a bicycle on his days off.

Aubusson lies at the bottom of a narrow valley. I have cycled fifty five miles and am content that the last mile should be a downhill run. Unfortunately, Aubusson has a one way system and to reach my hotel I have to clamber up a lung-busting street just to hurtle down the other side.

The Lion d'Or sits on the square. The front of the hotel is a terrace café surrounded by a low balustrade. I lean my bicycle against this and open the door. I find myself in the restaurant. A young lady in service black and white is walking through.

'Could you tell me where the entrance to the hotel is please?'

'Ah yes.' She waves her hand in the air. 'You go in the other door.'

'Which door? There is another door?'

'Yes, down to the left.'

'Down the side of the building?'

'Yes, you go out and turn left.'

'In the side street?'

'Yes you can go that way. It's along there. Up the steps.'

I exit, turn left, walk across the frontage of the hotel and enter the side street. There I find a door at the top of a couple of steps. I squeak it open and walk into what appears to be a sitting room. Nobody about. I cross this, go through the doorway and find myself back in the dining room. A little perplexed, I peer through the next doorway where I think I can see a small key rack. I walk through and there I find the reception counter and my waitress of earlier. She is standing talking to a rotund man in chef's uniform.

'I came the pretty route,' I explain to their enquiring faces and at the same time wonder where the breakdown in communication had occurred. 'I have a room booked for tonight.'.

'In what name, monsieur?' The chef pulls open a diary.

'Lloyd.'

He turns to today's page and studies it, shaking his head.

'And you have reserved it?'

'Yes. I did it by telephone.'

He looks vaguely at the key rack and hums to himself. The omens are not looking good.

'And you telephoned a reservation?' His gaze is still wandering up and down the page.

'Yes, about a week ago and then I wrote you a letter to confirm it.'

'You wrote a letter?'

'Yup.'

He flips to the back of the diary and pulls out an envelope. It is my letter. He slits it open and reads.

'Yes a single room, for one night. That's fine.' He hands me a key. 'First floor. Vanessa will show you.'

You see, a letter makes all the difference. I was sure MyMateMargaret would be proud of my prescience. I follow Vanessa onto the terrace.

'Where can I leave my bicycle?'

'At the bottom of the stairs.' She stands at the doorway and points along the facade.

'What, the steps around the corner, in the side street?'

'There are steps by the door. You can tuck it in there.'

I think of the dining room and the salon and cannot imagine where she proposes as a resting place.

'So, I go left there do I?'

'Yes, it's just there on the left. After the restaurant.' She waves her hand vaguely.

I walk back to the corner of the street. My bicycle is still leaning against the wall by the door which I know leads through the salon and dining room to the reception. I am going round in circles. I return to the terrace where Vanessa is clearing a table.

'Where do I go in for the hotel?' By now she must think that I am two sandwiches short of a picnic.

'Just there. It's after the restaurant.' She waves her hand again.

I am suddenly infused with a magnificent inspiration. 'Show me,' I say.

She threads her way around the tables and opens an insignificant door next to the restaurant entrance. She points at the staircase within.

'Up there,' she specifies, so that I would not think that the first floor was in the basement.

This little interlude, entertaining as it was, portended further amusements of similar confection for later in the tour but I was not privy to this morsel at the time.

I did my housework and then walked out for a quick look at the town in the evening sun. Some of the old buildings were lit by windows stretching across the entire length of the facade on the top floor. To me, this indicated an ancient workshop facility of some sort. Further investigation uncovered the mortifying fact that everybody except me seemed to know that Aubusson was famous for its tapestries. I had never heard of it, which just magnifies my stupendous ignorance and throws into question my qualifications for writing such a tome as this. My other discovery was that I had arrived a week too early to enjoy the washboard concert evening at the municipal hall. Damn!

When I returned to the hotel I met a cyclist drinking a beer on the terrace. His racing machine was propped up against the balustrade. When he learned that I was English he declared that he had English cousins and as a boy he had been regularly sent to stay with them in their boarding school for the holidays.

'*Mon Dieu*, how bored I was! You cannot imagine. I didn't understand a thing of what they were saying or what was going on. I am proud of one achievement – I learned to play cricket. Not many French people can do that.'

He was a biological researcher on his way from his home in Lyons to Royan for his holidays. His wife, he explained, was following in the car with the cat. As we sat there the lady herself arrived, clutching a travelling box.

'Oh, I had a terrible time getting here. The cat has been complaining. She is normally well behaved in the car. I don't know what was upsetting her. And of course the motorway exit is bizarre at Aubusson, you have to get off a funny way. I missed it and went on to the next.'

'I expect that was what the cat was complaining about,' I suggested. 'Cats have a sort of celestial navigation system haven't they? They always know where they are. She was probably shouting, "you've just missed the exit for Aubusson".'

They both looked at me and then at each other. Their unuttered riposte was deafening.

Dinner was a double treat. The food was out of this world. I started with *grosses crevettes et legumes marinés sur son sablé Cantal infusion de chèvre au lard.* It was magnificent and full of varied and complimentary tastes and textures. During its *dégustation* I discovered that my plate was plangent. Every time I knocked it, it rang like a bell. I expected at every instant for somebody to shout, 'seconds out, round two.'

The other treat was the ensemble. About eight tables were in use but only mine was in sole occupancy. This meant that I had nobody to talk to so I could listen to the conversations of the other diners. Of the four tables that I could hear, within a period of fifteen minutes they all mentioned either the English or England. If you were sitting in an English hotel dining room would you hear every table mention France or the French? I wonder.

My main course is served: it is *rosette d'agneau limousin* (presumably with a roof) *canneloni et courgette.* As the plate hits the table *(dong!)* I am aware of an unsettling effect. I suffer from occasional bouts of vertigo, which, by the by, can make cycling an interesting experience and at first I thought that I was due for a whirlygig but no, it was not quite the same feeling. The room is getting larger. No, not larger. The gap between me and the table to my right is increasing. The table is sliding away from me.

I bend lower to my plate and screw my eyes around in their sockets to try to ascertain what is happening. It's done it again. It's moved another six inches. The tenants of the table in question are a lady with a printed teeshirt that is too tight for her and a man wearing a suit that was the height of fashion twenty years earlier. Why is it that every Frenchman dining out with a woman behaves as if he is seducing somebody else's wife? I suppose the obvious answer to that question is probably the correct one. I tuck into my lamb and then notice that they are shuffling their chairs sideways on the tiles.

The problem was me. I was alone and thus not talking. They did not want me to hear their idiocies. When they had managed to open the gap to three feet by this underhand carpetbagging, they leaned across the boards and started to whisper at each other. Don't they know I am half deaf and foreign?

As I finish my cheese I remark to myself that the lady's tee shirt is an obvious forgery: the epithet embroidered onto it says, *'blaying cards'*.

Vanessa sweeps in.

'Coffee monsieur?'

I am confused for the menu has disappeared but I had recollection of a mention of *poire belle Hélène*.

'Don't I get dessert?'

'Do you want coffee?'

'I thought there was dessert.'

'Coffee?'

I give in. You have to know when you are beaten.

'Yes please.'

She comes back and serves me my dessert – *poire belle Hélène*.

What is going on?

8 – ESTIVAREILLES

Another sunny day. What a brilliant idea this safari is. I am not too sure about this road though. I thought it was supposed to follow a gentle valley. Perhaps the artist from yesterday was right.

I climb steadily upwards, winding left and right with the contours but either the gradient is not that severe or I am getting fitter. Eventually it levels out and I find myself in a pleasantly unspoiled pastoral countryside. It looks like the sunny rustic backdrops in the French B movies of the 1960s. Reinforcing this fantasy, a forty year-old, pale blue Citroen Ami-6 comes rattling towards me. It makes me smile. The car was never pretty and now it looks like a bug from Mars. How tastes have changed! In the garden of the next house a Simca 1100 is parked. I turn my head right and left, searching for the camera and clapperboard. When I see a blonde with sunglasses and a headscarf, driving a drophead Peugeot 203 I start to practise my interview technique. I must be on a film set. But I am not. The white cows (they show up better on black and white film), those fields of linseed (the pale blue just sets off the heroine's eyes a treat) and the *Touring Club de France* road signs are just what they do here. The cars probably go no further than a ten mile radius from their base and they are apparently untouched by any stringent MOT testing so they carry on forever.

But that lime green combine harvester the shape of a semi-detached house which is lumbering along the road towards me is definitely of the here and now. I edge my bicycle into a gateway to allow it to pass. It roars and belches a plug of black smoke into the cloudless sky and then stands looking at me as it bounces up and down on its enormous front tyres as if deciding whether to squash me into the mud or chop me up for chaff. When I deduce the reason for this behaviour I feel like a bucolic Humphrey Bogart. 'Of all the field gateways in all of France, I have to pull into that one.'

Have you ever tried to reverse a bicycle? If it has a 'fixed wheel' and you have the balance of a tightrope walker you can pedal it backwards. We have neither so I start to paddle my toes before me on the rutted earth in an attempt to push the bicycle rearwards. It begins to climb a mound behind me which means now that my feet no longer reach anything. I wobble like a dislocated ballerina whilst I try to choose between the two options: I can either try to recover my balance by giving a forward kick on my pedals which carries with it the risk that I will launch myself head first into the revolving blades or I can simply fall over. I go for the harvester option and succeed in cycling across the road in a beautifully executed arc. The lime green semi detached house roars and spews and then wriggles through the gateway into the field.

I set off down the lane again and forty yards further on I meet a big scarlet mechanical pitchfork. It is not touching the road. It rumbles towards me, its wheels flattening the grass on opposite verges and the prong of its blood red fork swaying from side to side in a clanging sweep. I can be pretty quick in assessing the main points of an argument. I turn around and I beat it to the field gateway by a short head.

Finished? Thank you. Now that they have the combine harvester and the mechanical handler, as I cycle down the lane for the third time I should be asking myself what are they going to put the bales on? It is this trailer the size of the Albert Hall which is coming towards me now. Back at the field gate, I wonder if they want any help with the harvest. It's a sunny day. I have no need to go any further. I could live here. I'm in no hurry.

Or I could try cycling down this stretch of lane for the fourth time.

I had fixed in my mind that I would stop for lunch at a little town called Chambon sur Vouelze and then cycle up to see the railway viaduct over the gorge of the river Tardes. When I reach the town I find that the river which it is *sur* is the Voueize not the Vouelze. This is the kind of minor inaccuracy which, had it occurred on a computer system, would have invalidated your car insurance or signed you up for a lifetime's subscription to the *Reader's Digest* but I demonstrate the remarkable superiority of the human brain over the electronic and decide to stop for lunch just the same. This town had twinkled briefly in the frantic firmament of my pre-tour preparations for, according to my *Guide Bleu*, it possessed a Hotel du Lion d'Or. When I had imparted this information to MyMateMargaret with the instruction to discover its address and tarif she had failed. I suppose I could have been a little lighter in my scorn of her internet prowess. She had busily flipped to the front of the book and then pointed out that the volume had been printed in 1923 and that the title *'Guide Bleu'* was a misnomer for, with the ageing of its pages, it should now be called a *'Guide Jaune'*. Until then, I had not known that she could speak French. It's marvellous what you can discover about people.

As I slide past the church, somewhere at the back of the town a factory siren sounds for midday. Down by the bridge I find a shaded picnic site alongside the river and spread out my lunch on the table. Three young ladies wander diffidently across the street and occupy the other table.

I am reminded of a time back in England when I arrived at a picnic spot which was furnished with only one table and so, perforce, I joined the party already installed.

I guessed it to be a father who had been entrusted with three children and instructed to get them out of the house for the morning. They had arrived on bicycles as I had and were well into their orange and green cellophane wrappers and pink squidgy plastic. Don't ask me what they were eating: children's diets nowadays are as quantum physics to me. I unfolded the twice-used-already aluminium foil and started to munch my sandwiches under the curious but polite glances of the children. I was fully aware that by not surrendering my aluminium foil I was holding up Spitfire production but if one has principles then one has to make a stand: I'll fight any man for the right to be a pacifist. Anyway, the foil was still intact.

When the father asks 'Wayne' what he has brought to eat, it occurs to me that probably not all the children are his. The two who answer to the labels of 'Rupert' and 'Alice' and are wearing earphones and designer lycra I readily assign as his progeniture but the dirty-sneakered crisp-eater I suspected was of another brood.

'Now, let's all play Interesting Facts, shall we?' Father suggests.

'Oh yes, Daddy.'

'Wot's that?' Wayne asks in a shower of cheese and onion.

'I'll go first, I'll go first.' Alice jumps up and down. 'Um... um... Did you know? ...Um... Where the Romans used to cross the River Thames in London it was not a bridge and they used to walk across at low tide? And they built a bridge and then when they were rebuilding it they found a load of old rotting piles in the mud from the old bridge.'

'Thank you Alice, that was very interesting.'

'Are your crisps salt and vinegar?' Rupert asks Wayne.

'Dunno.'

'What does it say on the packet?'

'Dunno.' He holds the bag out for Rupert to read. 'Make you thirsty.' He drops the bag to the table top and takes a hefty swig from an opaque plastic bottle.

'Your go now Rupert,' Alice reminds him.

'Yes, come along Rupert, let's hear your Interesting Fact.' Father endorses his daughter's reminder.

Rupert imitates Wayne and throws back his head to take a draught from his bottle. He regains his posture. 'Did you know that a woodpecker has a shock absorber in his head so that he can hit a tree a thousand times a minute without hurting himself?'

'No, I didn't know that. Well that was interesting wasn't it?' Father tries to draw Wayne into the enthusiasm for knowledge.

Wayne thinks for a second or two.

'Did you know,' he says, 'that if you swallow a burp it comes out later as a fart?'

'Thank you Wayne we don't really need to know that,' Father observes tartly.

I realise that my attempt to stifle any visible reaction is threatening to increase Spitfire production: I am gripping my tinfoil like in a vice and risk tearing it to shreds.

'Did you know,' says I, 'that the pond over there was dug out to supply the water for the stationary steam engine which used to pull the trains up from Whitstable?'

'Now that IS an interesting fact.' Father flashes me a grateful look. 'Did you know that Rupert?'

But Rupert is still cogitating.

'Does that mean that if you stop a fart it comes out later as a burp?'

'Rupert, I think we have finished with that subject now, thank you.'

Well that's definitely one more Spitfire.

I never went to see the viaduct. I started in that direction but did not like the weight of traffic. The lorries had squeezed the tarmac out and up into ridges at the edge of the road. Dobbin reacted by bucking like a bronco in a rodeo, so after a few hundred yards I turned back and took my proper road to Montluçon.

It is a long downhill run into Montluçon and I welcome it for the twenty miles before had somehow managed to have longer uphills than downhills although I had not climbed in total. This quirk of topographical improbability is well known to cyclists. I do not have a town plan, I shall have to find my way around Montluçon's western edge by following the railway line which is marked on the ragged portion of my cut-up map.

I find the iron road and hope that it is the correct one. Once upon a time navigating through a strange town was an easily practised skill. The settlement could be read like a book. The reason for the town's existence was evident on the ground. Perhaps two major trade routes crossed here or it was the only bridge on the river. You would aim for the church spire which you had espied from the outskirts. The church would sit just off the main square, opposite the town hall and at the point where the roads crossed. Here you would find all the road signs you needed and then you chose your way out of the town and the thing was done. Then they invented the bypass. When it was still new it was obvious and was signposted so that traffic which would formerly have travelled through the town would now be diverted from the centre. But then they built houses along the bypass and the road merged into the town. The give-away is where a formerly straight road which was aiming directly at the church spire suddenly veers to the left or right and what appears to be a minor street continues in the alignment ahead. The latter is your route. This is where you learn to now ignore the signs and use your instinct. But you can do nothing about housing estates. Here there is no history. All the roads have been built at the same time and their relative importance cannot be divined from their width nor their trace nor the traffic they carry. If you try to take a short cut off the main drag, the only landmarks highlighted will either be so parochial as to be invalid outside a range of fifty yards or so recondite as to be nonsense. What the hell is *'The Storks'* and why would I want to go there? And *'Zedyx'*? It could only have been invented to provide a bumper score in Scrabble.

The bus shelter has a route map so I cross the road to consult it. Not that I am lost, you understand. I just don't know where I am or where I should be going.

'Right then, Mr Map, I need the road to Vaux.'

'Who are you calling "Mr Map"? Can't you see that I am a schematic representation of the urban transport network of the municipality of Montluçon and its suburbs?'

'Right. Sorry if I offended you.'

'You come in here, insulting me. Calling me a map.'

'I said I was sorry.'

'I've got graphics you know. Not just wiggly lines.'

'Yes, I can see that. They are very nice. Colourful.'

'Well that's alright then. As long as you recognise it. Only people can be so ignorant.'

'How do I get to Vaux?'

'Number twenty-three.'

'What?'

'Number twenty-three. Goes via Auchan so you can do your shopping as well.'

'That's the mauve line is it?'

'I suppose you could call it mauve. I prefer 'purple'. It's more regal. Know what I mean?'

'But I don't want a bus, I'm on a bicycle.'

'You don't want a bus? What are you doing in my bus shelter then?'

'I thought you could show me how to get to Vaux.'

'I told you. Number twenty-three.'

'So if I follow the mauve–'

'–purple.'

'Sorry, the purple line it will show me the way to Vaux? Down here at the bottom left.'

'Oooh, I wouldn't go down there if I were you. Outside the urban ticket zone there you know. All kinds of funny stuff happens at the edge. Why do you want to go to Vaux anyway?'

'It's the road which will get me to Estivareilles.'

'Estivareilles? Never heard of it.'

'You wouldn't have done. It's off your map.'

'Wash your mouth out with soap and water. Nothing exists outside my map. I'll tell you what – why don't you go to the sewage farm, just down here?'

'I don't want the sewage farm, I want the road to Vaux.'

'Municipal rubbish dump? Very interesting place. See all kinds of stuff there.'

'The road to Vaux.'

'Look, I can see you're English. I'll do you do a special deal. What about this? – I'll give you a derelict Dunlop tyre factory complete with a chimbley with the letters all the way up it and a free company stadium thrown in. Now, I can't say fairer than that, can I?'

'I just want the road to Vaux.'

'I've told you already. Number twenty three.'

'OK. then. If I take the number twenty three, where do I catch it?'

'Here, of course. *Mon Dieu,* some people can be so thick!'

'Yes but the number twenty three goes in both directions doesn't it? Which side of the road should I be on?'

'It's no good asking me that. I don't know where I am do I? They don't tell me which side of the road they put me. Now was there anything else? Only I've got some curling up at the edges to do and I am a bit behind with me ultra violet fading.'

As I cycle past the derelict Dunlop factory, complete with chimney with all the letters on, company stadium and private railway siding (the map had kept quiet about the latter) one of those elusive facts that you had forgotten you knew, oozes into the foreground. During the Second World War we had sent the RAF over Montluçon on several occasions to bomb this tyre factory. Eventually, in July 1944, the French Resistance crept in with plastic explosives supplied by the SOE and destroyed the transformer, putting the factory out of action until the end of the war. But don't worry, we got another group to do the same to the Michelin factory in Clermont Ferrand, fair's fair.

The soil is red and the stream looks like tomato soup. Already in the seventeenth century Montluçon was an industrial centre for it had iron-ore. In nearby Commentry, coal was mined so the Canal du Berry was built to bring the fuel to the furnaces and foundries. The town did not have much luck though for by the time that the industrial revolution was getting into full swing in France, the coal was worked out and the foundries foundered.

To my surprise and satisfaction I debouch into the valley to the north of Montluçon without ever seeing a number twenty three bus. I cross the derelict canal and several branches of the tomato soup stream and then climb up to the main road. And there is the Lion d'Or sitting waiting for me. It is only mid afternoon and I can see no movement through any of the windows along the road frontage so I lean my bicycle against the gas meters and sit down at one of the tables on the terrace. I am in no hurry – the sun is still shining and although I have only covered forty seven miles today, I am ready for a halt.

Eventually a lady comes out.

'I am Monsieur Lloyd,' I tell her. 'I have reserved a room for tonight.'

'Ah yes.'

'Where shall I put my bicycle?'

'You can put it in the garage.'

I look at the garage door which is wide open to the world.

'Will it be locked?'

'Yes, yes, but we have to leave the door open a little for the swallows. They have just come back.' And as if to confirm it, three of the little blighters do a victory roll and then swoop into the blackness. 'They come back every year.'

They won't be back next year if they poo on my bicycle, I aver quietly to myself.

Given the proximity of several water courses and the affinity of mosquitos for such purlieus, I choose to dine indoors and not in the garden. This choice seems to puzzle the other diners but I stand fast. Once I am installed, the garçon starts me off with some *amuse-bouches:* a plate of fried garlic bread and dips. Every time he serves me he says 'hop' as if performing a conjuring trick.

'Hop,' and now I have two mini croissants and a prune wrapped in bacon, and, 'hop,' a melon dish doused in chablis. My starter is *effeuillé de moru en aioli aux asperges vertes* and it did not come out of a packet. This is followed by *boeuf charolais en pavé*. Then the chef-owner comes around to make sure that he has not poisoned anybody and we have 'hop,' a small plate of petits fours and then, 'hop,' a pineapple sorbet. I eat the cold fruit salad dessert but decide to skip the cheese. The food is excellent and I have just eaten far too much of it. Forty seven miles is not really exercise.

The hotel has three dining rooms plus a *salle de banquets* and a terrace. It is obviously known locally as a good eating place. I wander out to the reception and find the chef chatting to a regular customer who is casually undressing on the sofa.

'No, they're flying ants,' the customer insists as he pulls his lilac shirt out from his trousers. 'Look, thousands of them. I'm covered.'

I feel vindicated. The chef shows me his collection of red Michelin Guides displayed in a book rack. We discuss editions and printings. I divulge that I have a 1911 guide which is a year that he is missing. He says that he is always ready to buy the volumes he lacks. A 1911 would command about four hundred euros. I tell him I paid fifteen pence for it. Then I give him my promotion spiel.

'I started from the Pyrenees a week ago and this is the seventh Lion d'Or that I have stayed in.'

'Ah?' He can find nothing to say to that.

'I had intended to go to the one in Montluçon but decided to come to Estivareilles to avoid the town centre.'

'That was a good idea. The Lion d'Or in the town closed a few years ago. I think it's been pulled down.'

'This is an enormous hotel to be situated out of town. Why is it here?'

'There used to be a mill opposite. The farmers would bring their wheat to be milled and would have to wait several days for it to be done. At first the farmer's wife would put them up. Then in 1883 they built the hotel and it has been here ever since.'

'And why did they choose the name?'

'Some people say that it is an old inn sign. *"Lit, on dort"* – bed, one can sleep.' He rubbed his chin. 'But I don't know for sure.'

'Yes, I've heard that said.'

·LE LION D OR·

9 – Nérondes

The breakfast sun is pouring liquid gold through the large windows and onto the wood blocks and tiles of the foyer. This really is a Golden Lion, yet lying on the floor is not a feline but a canine. Old and white with black ears. He obviously lives here and moves for nobody.

I pay my bill. Madame has a dinner booking for the Rotary Club tonight – one hundred and twenty people with all the paraphernalia that goes with it. I come back to the subject of the collection of Michelin Guides. Where does her husband get them from?

'Oh he reads the small ads in the paper. Sometimes he finds one in an antique shop. He goes to *vide-greniers*'.

This expression literally means 'attic emptying' but translates into English as 'boot fairs'.'

'Are they popular in France? I know some people in England who make quite an income from boot fairs all the year around. They sometimes go to two or three a week.'

'Oh you can't do that in France – the antique dealers won't let you. You can only sell at a boot fair in your parish and you are not allowed to sell at more than four fairs per year.'

I had forgotten about France and its love of regulations.

'How do they know?'

'You have to get your card stamped to sell at a boot fair.

Four stamps and it's full.' She sucked on her teeth whilst I ruminated on the probable response that such a law would generate from the average Frenchman. She did not disappoint me. 'Of course, there are always ways around it. You get cards in other people's names, or you swap them about.' She shrugged. It was reassuring to know that France could still function despite its *'fonctionnaires'*.

I wrapped my towel cosily around my neck and tucked it into my pyjamas. Madame frowned as she studied the writing emblazoned across my chest. Why do they inscribe night attire with such pointless epithets? I can understand, without condoning, the decoration of a tee shirt; one could reasonably expect it to be seen in the street but, pyjamas? Who, under normal circumstances, is going to read your nightwear? What political statement can you usefully make to your pillow? Finally, unable to make any sense of it, she gave up and returned my bank card.

'Bonne route!' she said.

I dawdled out of Estivareilles because today was going to be another short day – less than fifty miles. The main road northwards was quiet. I soon entered the *Pays des Tronçais* – a region of oak forests and woodyards. The yard I was passing at the moment specialised in the wood for barrels. I stopped to inspect the branches of an oak tree which were hanging low over the verge. It was a peduncular oak and not a sessile. I mention this just to show how learned I am.

This forest is hundreds of years old and probably owes its survival to Louis XIV's multi-talented minister, Jean Baptiste Colbert. The State confiscated the *Foret des Tronçais* from its owner in the sixteenth century and then left it to go to waste. The neighbours cut the trees and made clearings for grazing and let their pigs forage in the undergrowth. Along comes Colbert in the seventeenth century and one of his responsibilities was Secretary of State for the Navy. He applied his energy to demonstrating the glory of France to the world by modernising and re-equipping the fleets and rebuilding the ports. Rochefort, Dunkirk, Toulon, Brest, Calais and Le Havre were all fortified and modernised under his direction. To sustain an effective navy he needed timber for ships. A seventy four-gun ship consumed in its construction about two thousand tons of timber and this would be the product of fifty five acres over the span of a century. Colbert managed to obtain for himself the position of Superintendant of the Waters and Forests and he planned for the future.

The forest of Tronçais was one of those which Colbert undertook to have re-seeded with oak trees whose felling would be forbidden before their reaching the age of two hundred years – forward planning indeed. His foresight was nearly rewarded but failed to predict the industrial revolution, and a century later many of the trees were coppiced to provide charcoal for the iron furnaces of the region. In the nineteenth century the forest was again taken in hand with re-seeding and thinning to allow full growth to the major stands whose felling is now forbidden until 2057 by which time I should imagine that there will be no oak used in shipbuilding at all. But we will still be able to enjoy the forest, global warming permitting.

What I had not remarked upon was that the day was becoming gloomy; perhaps I had been too engrossed under the canopy of foliage to notice the clouding of the sky or too preoccupied with my dendritic perorations. Ignoring the invitation of the signpost to visit a nearby hamlet called 'Hedgehog' I dropped into a shop in the village of Meaulnes to buy some vittels. There is only one other customer in the shop – an elderly lady – and she is where every elderly village lady ever is: in front of me at the till. This is a position which carries onerous responsibilities with regard to custom. She stabs and pokes into the depths of her handbag, like a heron fishing in a garden pond. She spears her fish and up from the depths she drags a wriggling cheque book – the mandatory method of settling her six euro fifty centimes bill.

My watch informs me that it is nearly time for my mid morning break. Incidentally, what a useful object a watch can be. I do not understand why MyMateMargaret made such a fuss about getting one. A watch will inform you of the time, night and day, without demur or insolence. I do not actually wear my watch on my wrist, I keep it rolled up in my waist bag. This removes from me the temptation to look at it when I am waiting for a train, or breakfast or a lady, or just when I want to know the time. To consult a timepiece in any one of these circumstances would be a gross impertinence.

Right on cue I come across a picnic site at a crossroads in the forest. The workman is just finishing cutting the grass with his ride-on motor mower. He sees me wheeling my bicycle towards the only table and bench and holds up his hand to stop me as he has not quite finished the cut. He swerves around the table like a destroyer hunting a submarine; his bow wave is a fan-shaped spray of grass cuttings. Having completed the circuit he acknowledges my restraint with a salute and charges past me to his lorry and trailer. I look down at my legs. They are green mohair. I try to brush off the clippings but they are wet and sticky. I shrug and wheel my bicycle to the table. It has grown a green furry coat. In sitting down, I amalgamate the bench and myself into the lawn. We become one unbroken expanse of green.

In my cycle bag not only do I find yesterday's *chausson aux pommes* which I had reserved for my elevenses but also an apricot. I scratch my head and try to recall when I last purchased apricots. I cannot remember but it is ripe so I eat it anyway. Behind me in the hedge are bouncing heavy knots of big shiny blackberries. That is what I should be doing – living off the country. I pull out a spare plastic bag and advance towards the harvest. There is no sign that anybody has ever tried to pick these fruit. I suppose that the reason is because all kinds of fruit are plentiful at this time of year and probably the French consider blackberries to be a bit mundane. I am in the act of stretching out my hand to grasp the first berry when an image flits into my mind. It is one of drivers alighting from cars in lay-bys and shuffling towards the hedge. I draw back my hand, empty. The blackberries giggle at me. 'Nearly caught you.'

By lunchtime I am sitting on a bench outside the church at Chalivoy Milon and watching the swallows catching flies. How much protein is contained in one fly? Look at the effort expended by these birds as they swoop and swirl. Surely they are burning up more energy in catching the food than will be provided by its ingestion? And do swallows come north in summer because they have eaten all the flies in the south?

The village is deserted except for one man. He is ruddy faced and slovenly dressed and making a beeline for my bench.

'*Monsieur,*' he says to me and proffers his hand. I ignore it and immediately feel mean for doing so. He sits next to me.

'Good weather today,' he says.

'Yes.'

'Do you smoke?'

'No.'

'I used to work, you know. I used to work for the boss. I don't now.'

'Oh.'

'If I did, I would be able to smoke. You don't smoke do you?'

'Still not.'

'Do you live here?'

'No, I'm just passing through.'

'Where have you come from?'

'Montluçon.'

'How far away is that? Two hundred kilometres?'

'No, about thirty.'

'Ah, thirty.' He peers intently at me and then floors me with his next enquiry. 'Are you Muslim?'

I stare at him. I am not anything, really. I am certainly not Muslim. At least, I don't think I am. One would think that it would be the sort of affiliation that one would be aware of.

'No, I'm not Muslim. Why did you ask that?' Perhaps it was because I do not smoke.

'That's what Muslims have. And Arabs and people like that.' He is pointing to the crescent moon decorating the front of my pyjamas.

'No, I'm not Muslim,' I decide not to point out that the oriental crescent moon rarely has a nightcap draped over it. Neither do I try to place the accompanying epithet, *'Sleepy Head'* in the worldwide context of transnational religious dogma.

'Do you smoke?'

'And I don't smoke either. I am a non-smoking, non-Muslim cyclist.'

That must have been the information he was seeking, for he got up and walked away.

Not being Muslim or anything else, I went into the church. When it was renovated in the nineteenth century, the builders discovered some frescoes dating from the tenth century. Gazing high up at the walls at the muted yellows and browns and blues I realised that these designs had probably been far more vivid when originally painted and time had faded their hues. I was wrong. These were the only pigments known to the artists of the time and those were their colours. I was amused by the artists' technique of picking out the tesselations of the stones and colouring them to resemble courses of brick and mortar. What was the point of that? Was such dissemblance the medieval equivalent to the modern day stone-cladding of a Victorian terraced house? I recalled a local perpetrator of such architectural dishonesty gazing disconsolately at the pile of rubble in his front garden one morning. His cladding had not lasted a thousand years, it had managed about four weeks.

The following wind was pushing me heartily towards my destination. No matter how much I seemed to backpedal, Nérondes was looming fast upon the horizon. I whooshed silently through villages, deserted except for the whiff of drains and whizzed along broad, empty main roads whilst wondering where all the cars were. I knew that I would have about seventy miles to do on the morrow, depending upon which hotel I managed to book, so when I arrived at Nérondes I cycled straight to the railway station to check out the possibility of shortening the following day's cycling.

The station was one of those help-yourself places. No human beings worked there, all provisions came via notice boards and electronic signals. I checked the timetable and discovered that there was a train which ran all the way from Nérondes to the Loire valley but that it would be of little use to me for the it ran only once a week, on a Sunday night and tomorrow was Friday. Otherwise, it would have been lovely. All the trains were the regional TER type upon which bicycles were accepted without problem.

I followed a lady in to the Lion d'Or and was a bit surprised when she passed behind the reception desk and then turned to face me.

'Monsieur?'

'I have booked a room for tonight.'

'Monsieur Lloyd,' she announced without looking at the book and confirms my suspicion that I am the only customer by giving me the key to the first room on the first floor.

'Is there somewhere I can leave my bicycle please?'

'Yes, you go through the gateway and you'll see *les offices* on the left. Just push it in there with the other bicycles.'

The alleyway under the gateway was surfaced with loose stones which were overgrown with weeds. *Les offices* is the generic word the French use for 'outbuildings'. Originally, *les offices* would have been the rooms in which the food was prepared before being brought into the kitchen. In my case I discovered that it meant the derelict outside toilet. I thought that Dobbin was going to recoil at the suggestion that it should sleep curled around the toilet bowl like a drunken rugby player but it took one look at the shapely French ladies' bike which was lounging racily against the wall and slipped into place alongside it with what I thought was a suspicious eagerness.

Up in my room I ran quickly through my housework and then turned to the telephone on the wall. MyMateMargaret had supplied me with three possible hotels: at Romorantin, Mennetou and Selles. The latter two both being on the river Cher which eventually flowed into the Loire. My preferred choice was Mennetou since it was the nearest. I grabbed the telephone handset and tapped out the number. The apparatus was only vaguely attached to the wall and it wobbled and wriggled everytime I touched it. Stabbing at the buttons was like trying to poke a tax collector in the eye, but less amusing.

I had no luck with Mennetou. The telephone just rang and rang. I could get no response at all. So much for MyMateMargaret's infallible internet research skills. I would have to speak to her about retraining or a refresher course. The Lion d'Or at Romorantin, on the other hand, came up trumps. They had a room, with a shower and I could have dinner there. Perfect. Is there anything else you wish to know sir? Oh yes, how much? I could feel the blood draining from my face as she told me. I replaced the receiver after having regretfully explained that one hundred pounds was too much for little old me in one bed for one night with breakfast extra. So that left Selles sur Cher, the furthest of the three. They seemed quite surprised that I had bothered to phone at all but reserved me a room anyway.

Flushed with success, and now knowing which route I would have to follow, I continued on through my list of hotels and managed to reserve all except Le Ribay and Neufchatel. I was doing well. The sun was shining, I had cycled three hundred and ninety miles in eight days and I had just bagged my eighth Golden Lion. I phoned in to Mission Control.

'Where are you?'

Why does she always want to know that? I am tempted to tell her 'Berlin' or 'Haywards Heath' or something equally facetious. It must be bloody obvious where I am.

'Nérondes,' I reply. What a wimp!

'And what about your handlebars? Have you had them fixed yet?'

'No but they are OK. They will last the trip.'

'I don't understand why they went wrong anyway. You always tell me how well you maintain your bicycle and that your machine is the best that was ever built.'

'Even Rolls Royces break down.'

'I've never seen one. Have you?' I try to give her a 'humph' just like she does to me. 'Have you got indigestion again? I put some magnesia tablets in your survival pack. You just chew them.' You do if you brought them with you, thinks I. 'Where are you going tomorrow? You should be turning towards the Loire, shouldn't you?'

My cue for a grumble.

'Yes, I'm booked in at Selles sur Cher. I wanted to go to Mennetou because it's nearer.'

'Well why didn't you then?'

'I could get no answer on the number you gave me.'

'I'm not surprised.'

'You're not surprised?' My voice rises an octave. 'What's the point of you giving me telephone numbers if you know they are duff? It's not the easiest job in the world, cycling across hostile territory all day long and then having to find a phone that works.'

'Your choice. My mum offered you her mobile phone. So did your mate John. Anyway, there is nothing wrong with the number I gave you.'

'Except that it gets no reply.'

'Well it won't will it?'

'What do you mean?'

'What day is it today?'

'Thursday. But what has that got to do with it?'

'Look on your hotel list. Next to Mennetou sur Cher. What have I written?'

I look. It says, *'closed on Thursdays'*.

Some people will go to quite extraordinary lengths to endeavour to be right. I feel that such obsession only demeans them.

I leave my key on the deserted reception desk and step outside for a breath of fresh air. Nérondes, I discover, is not much more than a street of houses and shops straggling along a main road. A car pulls up alongside me and a man gets out.

'*Pardon monsieur,* can you show me the way to the Place de l'Hotel de Ville?' he asks.

Always ready to accept a challenge and show off my learning I point down the road.

'It's where the road widens out a bit.'

'I'm looking for the drugstore.'

'There is a pharmacy up the street on the left,' I offer him. That shows just how ignorant I am. A drugstore, of course, is not a pharmacy. I would probably know exactly what a drugstore was if I watched television since everything on TV is American but I do not own a television so I commit the gaffe of exposing my unworldliness. His eyebrows shoot up onto his shaved scalp.

'Oh, is a pharmacy a drugstore then?' he asks.

His superciliousness riles me.

'Listen mate,' I lapse into my most familiar of back street

Parisian French, 'I had never been here before in my life until fifteen minutes ago and I'm English but I am still able to show you where the Place de l'Hotel de Ville is, which is more than you could do.'

His girl sitting in the passenger seat puts a hand to her face and snorts with laughter. I left him chewing the cud and wondering why an Englishman speaks French like a Parisian costermonger. I sometimes wonder that myself.

Back at the hotel, my key is still stranded on the counter like a beached whale. Nobody has put it in its pigeon hole. I scoop it up and return to my room. At eight o' clock I am sitting in the dining room. An ominous stillness pervades not only the room but the entire establishment. Ten minutes later I am still sitting there. I have seen nobody so I get up and leave. As I reach the doorway I stand aside to allow a couple to enter. I complete a short circuit of the hallway and then re-enter the dining room. They are now sitting at the table that I have just vacated. I choose another. Eventually a man wanders in and asks us if we want dinner. Astonishingly, we did.

I ate a tartare of *crudités* and smoked salmon with chopped salad followed by a brochette of roast pork on semolina. I finished with an apricot tart and ice cream. It was all very palatable.

Madame *la patronne* was sitting behind the desk as I made for the stairs.

'What time would you like breakfast?' she asks me.

'Half past seven,' I reply. Her enquiry reassures me that the hotel will still be running tomorrow.

10 – Selles sur Cher.

Friday morning dawned bright and sunny. Or at least I supposed it did. I was asleep at the time. I don't go in for this 'up with the lark' concept. But I had fixed breakfast for half past seven so I did apply a modicum of frenzy to my ablutions once I had realised that it was ten minutes past seven and I was still abed. Without that confounded watch that MyMateMargaret had made me buy I could have slumbered on in blissful oblivion.

I make it to the bottom of the stairs by seven twenty nine. Not a particularly spectacular achievement given that my room is at the top of the first flight. I greet the empty reception desk with an ironic 'good morning'. It was becoming a habit. The dining room is deserted and as silent as the grave. There is not even one of those loudly ticking clocks that grandparents customarily position on their mantelpieces to frown down and intimidate you when you come down too early on a Sunday morning. I retreat and cross the hall to the bar. The only occupant is yesterday's newspaper. I pick it up and sit at a table to wait. The paper informs me that somebody is going to cycle across the Algerian desert in fifteen days to follow in the famous Citroen 'raids' of the 1920s. Bah! Fifteen days to cross a desert. I bet he's not doing it in his pyjamas on a bicycle with broken handlebars. I cast the paper aside in disgust.

At that moment a young lady enters the hotel from the street and walks staight into the bar.

'Ah,' she says, 'are you waiting for breakfast?'

'Exactly that.'

'What time would you like it?'

'Half past seven was what I was told.'

She glances at her watch. It indicates that she has missed the deadline by ten minutes.

'We don't serve breakfast until eight o'clock,' she announces gaily. The grandeur of her insolence causes me to blink stupidly.

'In that case, I would like breakfast at eight o'clock please.'

You have to know how to negotiate in French hotels.

Three other guests appeared in the bar in time for breakfast. We all spooned the apple and plum confection onto our bread, bit into it and then exchanged discreet glances. It was not exactly jam, it was more stewed fruit. Unusual but quite edible. Needless to recount, by the time we are ready to check out of the hotel the reception desk is miraculously manned by a bill-totting *patron*.

'And don't forget the telephone,' I remind him, as I have had to remind nearly every hotel reception since I started this safari. Honesty, I propound, is always the best policy.

'Ah yes,' he says and raises his eyebrows in regretful sympathy. 'Twelve euros.'

I look at him, thinking he is making a joke. Two euros would have been expensive.

'Twelve euros?' I question politely, as if I had misheard.

He taps his pencil down an unseen sheet of paper on the lower level of the counter and his eyebrows rise again in a desolation of remorse.

'Twelve euros,' he confirms.

I decide not to tell him that my bicycle is lurking in his

derelict outside toilet, locked in a close embrace with a French lightweight, in case he fines me for indecency. Honesty, like all policies, must have its strict boundaries.

I am aiming to make my mid morning stop in the town of Bourges. Bourges is in the area known as *Le Champagne Berrichon,* which translates into English as 'Champagne Berry'. This makes is sound like either a yuppy name for the grape or a party-popping character in a Dornford Yates novel. It is neither. It is a region of rolling plains of wheat or whichever feculant happens to qualify for the biggest subsidy of the moment. I know not whether Champagne Berry figures prominently in the romantic poetry of the country, but if it does, the versifiers must have found rhymes for 'flat, dull, uninteresting, boring, monotonous, tedious, plain, soulless and dreary.' Unless of course they lied. The only monuments it boasts are water towers.

I stopped in the midst of this diorama of dreariness to take a mouthful of water from my bottle. As I stood there in the middle of nowhere, the water gurgling down my throat, I was convinced that I could hear somebody talking. I strained my ears. It was not so much talking as mumbling. I looked around me on a 360 degree scan. I was alone except for the occasional car which belted past me. There he goes again. I can hear him mumbling away in an uninteresting monotone. I shake my head, supposing this mumbling to be a product of my over-excited ears. I am accustomed to hearing random whistling and droning but this was the first time that the aural confections of my semi-circular canals had sounded like conversation – albeit a one-sided affair.

The sound would not go away so I had to accept it and ignore it if I could. I took a final swig and as my head returned to the horizontal I found myself looking straight into a pair of eyes. There was only one bush in the entire acreage on view. It was the size of a Punch and Judy tent and in it stood a gendarme with his radio clamped to his mouth.

As another car swished past me, lured inexorably into the speed trap by the straight road and apparently empty countryside it occurred to me that the gendarme had no cause to complain about my comportment. I had not given the game away and when one considers the use to which bushes alongside main roads in France are routinely subjected, he was very lucky that his shoes were only wet from the dew.

The sky was blue. The clouds were white and the planes were twin turbo-prop transports with sturdy tricycle undercarriages to enable them to alight on the rough landing strips in the Third World. There were two of them and they were performing 'circuits and bumps'– coming in to land, running along the runway and then opening up their engines to take straight off again and fly around the loop to repeat the manoeuvre. It was the Avord flying school for the French Air Force. If you discount the dangers inherent in attempting to open the foil-topped cream for your in-flight coffee, the landing and take-off are the two most perilous parts of a flight and the pilots were managing to perform one of each manoeuvre about every five minutes. Many years ago I knew a flight mechanic on one of these twin-engined planes who told me that they flew them across the Atlantic. Although, for safety reasons, civil airliners have to be four-engined to cross such an expanse of ocean, the regulations did not extend to military planes so they just got on and did it. He said it was a bit hairy though.

I did not wave to the aeroplane as it lumbered through the air above me. I had not forgotten the repercussions on the previous occasion when I had allowed exuberance to win over my natural reserve.

It happened like this. Frank and I were on a day's strenuous training ride inland from Calais. This meant that we cycled straight to the restaurant that we knew, ate an enormous meal, wobbled down to the supermarket to do our shopping and then took the most direct route back to the ferry. On the way to the restaurant, the minor road that I had chosen took us across the barren expanse of Calais-Marck aerodrome. This field had lived through several interesting moments during the British army's retreat through Dunkirk in 1940 but since then, one would not say that Calais-Marck aerodrome had played top of the bill on the world's aeronautical stage. A handful of brightly coloured monoplanes clustered around the gaping black void of a hangar indicated where the local flying club met; the orange radar scanner rotated like a mechanical ballerina and the wind sock, perhaps remembering the days of Dunkirk, pointed accusingly at Belgium.

But we were in for a surprise. High in the sky over the Pas de Calais, three tiny dots were flying in formation. We stopped to watch them.

'That's the French national aerobatics team,' Frank declared with authority. 'Or part of it. I expect they are practising.' And then he told me the type of aircraft they were flying. I cannot tell you because I was not really paying attention, I was watching the display. But Frank always knows these things. The planes broke into a fan and then dropped like bombs, flattening out over the aerodrome. 'Here they come,' he said.

Swooping along the ground at what seemed like head height, three red monoplanes made a low-level pass over the aerodrome and raced across the road before us. Then as one entity they stood on their tails and scorched upwards until they were the little black dots again.

'That was pretty impressive,' I said and I pushed off behind Frank whose stomach was obviously reminding him of the purpose of our day. About thirty seconds later, he suddenly stopped and pointed over to our right.

'There they are again.'

I put my hand to shield my eyes from the sun and once I had got my arm in that position, it seemed a shame to waste all the effort so I continued the movement and hoisted my arm to full stretch to wave at the aircraft as they hurtled towards us. It was the sort of harmless silliness which amused me. The fighters roared over our heads, leaving our ears ringing. In situations like this it often seems that the planes have almost skidded along your brylcreem although Frank assures me that in reality they are nearly always a couple of hundred feet up. They just feel close. These particular planes felt very close.

We set off again down the deserted straight road which would lead us to our lunch. We had travelled about fifty yards when suddenly we were shaken out of our skins as the three planes thundered directly over our heads. I could feel my chest resonating with the surge of their engines.

'Beware of the Hun in the sun!' I shouted to Frank, for the planes had jumped us from behind. But they had not finished. They wheeled around and, breaking formation, they swooped in from different directions.

'Bandits ten o'clock!' Frank warned and we both ducked involuntarily as the jet whisked across the road.

'Look out, there's another coming from the left,' I screamed.

'And one from behind,' Frank yelled.

The two planes crossed above us, doubling the noise and quadrupling our fright. Too late we saw the foolishness. In waving to the planes I had drawn the leader's attention upon us. I was wearing a fluorescent yellow jerkin; Frank was wearing bright orange. We wore startling colours to prevent motorists from pushing us from the road and pedestrians from diving into our spokes. Until now we had never considered aircraft as a factor to be contended with in our constant struggle for survival in today's traffic. Dressed as we were, the pilots could probably have seen us from the Alps. We were two unmissable tiddley-winks on the parlour carpet.

We pedalled on, glancing nervously from left to right.

Our pace was increasing as we aimed for the cover of the distant settlement. The planes would not be able to fly low over the houses.

'There they are,' Frank pointed at black dots, barely visible against the trees. We kept our eyes on them as we forced the pace up to eighteen mph; a bit too fast for me.

'I can only see two dots,' I shouted forwards. 'Where's the– Christ!' I bounced off the edge of the verge as the missing plane roared over our heads.

'Look out from the left!' Frank shouted.

'No, no. From the right!' I counterwarned.

We quailed as the aircraft centred on us as the focus of their display figure and then, once again, the world became ominously quiet and normal. By now we were whimpering as we sprinted the last five hundred yards towards cover. Four hundred yards. We are doing twenty mph now. Three hundred yards. Still nothing. By a superhuman effort I pounded up alongside Frank.

'I think we've lost them,' I gasped and then I dropped back because I could see traffic coming towards us. We could have done with some of that earlier. It would have kept the planes higher.

The oncoming traffic, as it quickly transpired, was the three planes. Head on down the road they charged in line astern, jigging right and left but coming straight towards us. Then with a cruel sense of humour, they began flashing the landing lights in their wings to make them look like machine guns.

We reached the built up area at such a speed that when we had to brake at the roundabout we skidded on the tarmac. Frank dismounted and turned to me to make his point more clearly.

'When you are with me, don't you ever, ever, ever wave at another aeroplane ever, ever again.'

I took a defiant stand.

'I think we did alright. Anyway, they are going to have

problems landing. They'll be skidding all over the show with the amount of brylcreem they must have on their tyres.' I don't think Frank understood my allusion. I trust you do.

Ten years later in the Far East, I was wriggling my route down Old Airport Road, Dhaka, in the turgid lethargy of the Bangladeshi rush hour – an oxymoron if ever there was one – jousting with motor-cycle rickshaws and wobbling tolly-garis when the Bangladeshi army realised that they had really wanted their helicopter to land on the other side of this road so they flew the machine across; about three feet above the road surface. It was not one of those bijou plastic bubbles with a dainty spinning arm on top; it was a gigantic green camouflaged monster scything through the traffic with two enormous four blade rotor arms. This thing could carry tanks.

On seeing the huge radar-encrusted nose butting its way into the traffic from the side road before me, my first reaction was to think, 'this cannot be happening'. I quickly remembered that I was in Bangladesh and so of course not only could it be happening, it was happening. I swerved directly to the side of the road and watched the Keystone Cops-style pile-up as rickshaws and motor bikes and hand pulled trolleys crashed into each other and tipped over. I bet if Frank had been there then he would have blamed me for that too.

I reached the town of Bourges in time for elevenses. As I sat on a bench, sipping water and pulling at croissants, I realised that there had been a constant traffic of walkers and cyclists passing behind me. I had managed to stop alongside a cycle track which I could not get onto because its boundary hedge and wire fence barred the way. I fared no better on my exit from the town. I started confidently out on a quiet road alongside the river until I reached an apparently minor junction but which was scarred by a crescent of worn tar and black rubber which scoured in from the right. I leaned my bicycle against the back of the direction sign and walked around to read the front. It informed the world that this road was now the quickest way to the *autoroute*. I abandoned it there and then.

The white fluffy clouds in and out of which the transport aeroplanes at Avord had been dodging were becoming rarer and rarer and the temperature was now in the low thirties centigrade. Twenty miles of pedalling under this sun and I reached the river Cher in the town of Vierzon. I found the layout of this town so confusing that I had to resort to my plastic compass to find my road out. Good job I had brought those trousers with me.

At a quarter past six I am sitting at the terrace of the Lion d'Or at Selles sur Cher. The street thermometer still indicates thirty four degrees and I am sipping a small black coffee with a Vittel-menthe. It is a strange combination but one I find admirably suited to my activities. The ice-cold peppermint water refreshes me and the scalding black coffee picks me up. My digestive system usually reflects a while before giving its opinion of this assault and the interregnum, as it were, is glorious.

The hotel bears a plaque on the wall which declares that Joan of Arc stayed there in June and September 1429. She must have liked it to have stayed twice, unless she was using her fidelity card. My room is up an outside, broken stone staircase to a first floor gallery above the former stables. The bedroom door opens directly onto the common verandah in the style of the planters' lodges in an Indian tea garden. The accommodation which I have been given is extensive. Even under ten foot ceilings the room appears large. The wardrobe is nine feet tall, its doors secured with massive double latches in brass; a chaise longue lounges, chaise-like, against the wall and the double bed sits in the middle of a football field. The television set perches precariously in the corner, bolted on a bracket at such a height that the viewer has to throw his head back like a star gazer. The electric flex winds three times around the bracket and dangles an adaptor at stomach height from which a jet of three plugs spurt a fountain of wires and flexes to the four corners of the room. I switch on the bedside light with no result. Two minutes later it self-illuminates for about five minutes then takes a sabbatical. Beside the door jamb, the base of a wall telephone is bolted but I cannot find the handset. This is the kind of electrical installation that characterised French hotels forty years ago. The management must have decided to preserve it for posterity.

I unpack my cycle bags and find the last apricot again. I thought that I had eaten it yesterday. To settle the argument I despatch it immediately and then wash my clothes. The bathroom is to the same scale as the bedroom, there is enough hanging space for me to peg out my entire wardrobe and still use all the facilities without the slightest inconvenience.

Down in the restaurant I demur at the suggestion that I would like to eat outside with the other guests; I remember cycling through some marshland immediately before entering the town and I have no wish to provide dinner for mosquitoes.

'Sit here, monsieur.' The waiter installs me at a table in the empty dining room. I order a gaspacho of melon with tarragon, lamb chops and white beans in sago, finishing with a peach parfait ice with a blackcurrant sauce.

At the side of me, through the open hatch, I can hear the pinging of the battery of microwave ovens as the two 'cooks' unload the instant meals onto plates. The waiter enters from the dining terrace and rushes past my table to the hatch.

'Deux pintades et un roti de porc,' he screeches and then scoops up the two plates on the hatch and passes up the other side of my table. Thirty seconds later the tall waiter thunders down the dining room with an armful of plates, bound for the scullery behind me. My table quakes with his passage. He bustles to the kitchen hatch.

'Faites marcher le quatorze,' he instructs and puts three ice cream concoctions onto a tray. As he whizzes up one side of my table, the other waiter sears down the other side. My shirt flaps in the breeze. He grabs a plate from the hatch and then pirouettes to me.

'Un gaspacho,' he announces and swerves the plate under my nose.

'I am in your way, sitting here,' I observe, not without reason. 'Let me move.'

'Oh not at all, monsieur, not at all,' he shrieks in my ear and then spins around to collect another order for the diners on the terrace.

The spoon is on its second voyage to my mouth when the other waiter charges by me.

'Le quinze,' he shouts, 'and don't forget the beans.' He grabs three plates which he slides up his arm and then he whooshes back to the doorway as the short waiter enters.

'Un beaujolais nouveau,' he shouts through the doorway to the bar. I had forgotten that one.

Thirty seconds later the barman hurries through from top left to top right, carrying a bottle of wine; the tall waiter enters top right to hastens bottom left to the scullery with more dirty crockery. He shouts across me to the hatch as he passes. The short waiter starts a shouting conversation outside. His voice is the most piercing and annoying screech possible. It rises an octave in interrogation at the end of every sentence, no matter what its sense. He minces through the doorway top right at ninety miles per hour, his elbow on his waist and his forearm swinging to and fro as if beckoning traffic to overtake him. His screeching rises in volume and pitch as the distance from his interlocutor increases. The tall waiter whisks past my chair from bottom left to top right; the barman hurries back from top right to top left.

I am the only guest eating in this dining room and they have put me in the table which is the roundabout of their manic activities. There are nine, empty, tranquil tables and I am crammed onto this one. I am in the middle of a pin ball game. My clothes swing in the breeze of their passage; I am getting dizzy, my ears are ringing.

On my way out, I accost the barman who doubles as the receptionist.

'I cannot find the rest of the telephone in my room. I wish to make a call.'

He looks at me, bewildered.

'Where have you seen a telephone in your room?'

'Well, that is the point. I am in room twelve. There is half a telephone by the door but it has no handset.'

All seems clear to him.

'Ah I see now. Yes, that would be right. Yes. There aren't any telephones in the rooms.'

Behind him, the poster on the wall informs the world that the band of the medecine school of Tours is called 'La Vaginale'.

I have cycled for just over seven hours today. I have covered seventy miles and reached my ninth Golden Lion in a row. I decide to be satisfied with my lot.

I go to bed.

11 – VALENÇAY

I am not a narcissist, which is just as well given the paucity of my finer attributes, but as I lie on my back in the middle of that enormous carpet, running through the physical exercises which I employ daily to remind my body who is boss, I observe that bits of me are indubitably toning up. Four hundred and seventy miles of pedalling is having an effect. The muscles on my legs are tauter and, dare I believe it, the rolls of fat around my waist are perhaps a little firmer?

The morning sun casts the shadow of my neighbour onto my curtains as she passes along the verandah on her way to breakfast. When she reaches my bedroom door she, naturally, glances in. Had I forgotten to tell you that my bedroom door was furnished with three-quarter length windows which one is supposed to obscure by drawing curtains when one desires privacy? No? Sorry, it slipped my mind. I freeze rigid like an Agatha Christie corpse and catch a snapshot of her startled face as she occults in the gap of my curtains. Not very clever. She will probably now go straight down and ring for an ambulance.

I walk into the bar to take my breakfast. The customers are arranged at individual tables stretching along one wall leading to the door; they form an appetising perspective of steaming coffee cups and golden croissants.

'Breakfast?' the barman asks me.

I nod as I sweep my eyes down the line to identify and defuse the potential ambulance summoner. It must have been this distraction which prompted me to comply with his suggestion that I should, 'Sit there, monsieur.' I do, and he immediately rushes past me to serve a customer. The other unoccupied table in this perspective of busy break-fasters is opposite me and it beckons me but before I can respond, an elderly couple appear at the bottom of the staircase and are drawn to it in the same way that the last piece of jigsaw is to the nozzle on the vacuum cleaner. I am stuck where I am. On my left the coffee machine is wheezing and hissing like a mainline steam locomotive crawling up Shap; on my right a baby is crying and its elder sibling is enquiring in a piping voice if it has 'done a poo'. If that were not enough, the darling child then demands the right to inspect the final product of its younger sibling's digestion. And naturally, the barman bumps into my chair every time he passes. Why is everybody else allowed to choose their table? Why does this establishment doggedly believe that my purpose in life is to serve them as a traffic roundabout? Then I think of one of the hotel's previous guests. Could it be that the personnel are punishing me as the representative of the nation who burned their Joan of Arc? When I later propounded this theory to MyMateJohn he pointed out that it was not the English who had burned Joan of Arc it was the French. The whole concoction was a political myth. The two countries had been at war for a hundred years, all the reigning families had intermarried and the conflict was really a civil war. Joan was condemned by a jury of French bishops and burned by Burgundians. They were about as English as King Henry VI was French. I accepted the validity of his disquisition with alacrity. You have to. If you let MyMateJohn talk for more than three minutes he always steers the subject around to Christopher Marlowe and then you do have to lay down your trowel.

From the point of view of my itinerary I am more than half way up France now but this is where an important technical factor is forcing me to veer westwards across the country. The gaps between Golden Lions on the direct northerly route are too great for my little legs to close in one day's cycling. Having decided to go west I am obliged to disrupt my itinerary further to allow for the differing opening and closing days of my projected staging posts.

As a result, today will be a frustrating dawdle. I need to go to Chinon but today is Saturday and the Lion d'Or at Chinon will not open until Sunday night. So I have decided to creep slightly nearer by cycling to Valençay and bagging their Golden Lion on the way. Unfortunately the town is only about eleven miles away and so I arrange my route to visit a dolmen to inflate my mileage to thirty three. Dolmens and menhirs are far more widepread in Brittany so an example south of the Loire, to my mind, is worth a visit. A dolmen is an ancient stone monument in the form of a table, usually standing on three rocks. A menhir is a stone standing upright. I expect that you had already come to that conclusion from your knowledge of ancient Breton. *Dol* = table; *hir* = pillar and *men* = stone.

However, before I leave Selles I need to provision myself for the day. Yesterday's quiche was like bacon in custard. I would like something a little more serious for today. As I criss cross the compact town, looking for a patisserie, I remark that the street is named after a former mayor: Docteur Massacré. I wonder if he was a medical doctor? *'Doctor Massacred'* would be a forbidding nameplate to screw alongside one's front door.

I ignore the first patisserie because of the length of the queue. Daft really: I shall be twiddling my thumbs all day long and yet I am reluctant to waste some of that time in a queue. Ten minutes later I am back at the shop for the simple reason that it is the only one in the town. So I've wasted ten minutes already. I squeeze myself onto the tail's end and we shuffle forwards very slowly towards the two serving ladies. They are chatting far more than they are serving. At shoulder height on our right is a glass counter on the top of which is displayed a selection of the patissier's larger and more expensive creations. Suddenly a man, three customers ahead of me, throws back his head and gasps. Is it a heart attack? Has he seen a vampire bat on the ceiling? No, he is going to sneeze. Ah... ah... ah... *plam*! and that's one for the meringue and ah... ah... *plam!* one for the apricot tart and *plam! plam!* two for the chocolate gateau.

When I finally make it to the front, I purchase vittels whose provenance from the depths of the glass cabinet assure me that I would not be engorging any extra vitamins.

The sun was already high and hot as I wriggled a route out of Selles and it retained those qualities for the duration of the day but it was a day which was strangely empty. Until now I had been struggling to achieve frightening mileages and this had given me a purpose but now I felt that I was killing time.

I stopped for an early lunch on a deserted village square somewhere. It seemed to have been carved out of the back gardens of a block of houses who had turned their backs on the square, shunning it to enjoy a different prospect. The sun beat down on the white stone and concrete. As I munched a *pain au chocolat,* a day cyclist in bib shorts and cycling shirt rolled into the top of the square. He rode around the four sides of the *place,* passing before me and ignoring my greeting and then he rode back out along the way he had entered. It's a funny old world, ain't it?

One highlight of the day was that of passing by several fallow corners of fields along the way which had been sown with a wild flower mixture entitled, according to the notice, *'the blossoming fallows'*. No doubt the farmer had received a substantial encouragement to undertake this patrician act but the effect of those bobbing heads of lilac, mauve, pink, purple, red, orange, yellow and white was quite delightful.

And they were thrown into higher contrast by the mundane monotony of the hectares of sun baked stubble which seemed to stretch in all directions.

I arrived at Valençay in the early afternoon. I never did find the dolmen. I had looked for it but the heat and my inability to form a working partnership with the portion of tattered map that was my day's ration united to beat me.

I neatly avoided visiting the chateau by slipping instead into the nearby motor museum. There I spent a jolly hour wandering amongst a cool arrangement of burnished brass and wooden wheels, of flapping hoods and yellowing side screens, of creased leather seats and black metal steering wheels. One of the more modern exhibits took me back a few years. It was a Citroen 2CV (that's the car that looks and drives like a chicken hutch). This particular specimen had completed the Citroen 2CV Raid of 1973 where a convoy of these vehicles had crossed the Sahara Desert.

One of the men in my office had undertaken, and paid, to embark upon this madcap adventure. Whilst preparing for the journey he had entertained us by cataloguing the hardships and trials that the convoy was sure to endure. He had even shown to anybody who had sat still long enough, the small handgun which he had procured to protect himself from the marauding riffs. Upon his return he had appeared somewhat subdued. When pressed, he admitted that the most frightening part of the expedition had been the drive down the autoroute A6 from Paris to Marseille.

And here was a photograph of a Tilbury – a two wheeled horse-drawn cart named after the English coachbuilder who had popularised the design in the early 1800s. And did you know that in 1941, whilst France was reeling under the heels of the Nazi jackboot – I think that is the standard expression – the government passed a law prohibiting the use of any vehicle that had been registered before 1st September 1925? Concern was raised by the decrepit state of such vehicles and this measure of control was introduced not for safety reasons but to conserve fuel since the older engines were far less efficient than the modern versions

The Lion d'Or lurks in one corner of the town square. It blazons its name across the facade in attractive golden letters which are enclosed by a green neon frame. It did not look tawdry but at first sight I did mistake it for a pharmacy.

The *patron* is small with an undefinable sadness rubbed softly into his face like thumb-smeared clay. He undertakes to show me the rooms before I make my choice. This used to be the custom in many hotels but it has fallen into desuetude due, no doubt, to the increasing infirmity of aged hotel proprietors and the number of stairs needed to be climbed in one day.

'I will show you a room at the front and one at the back.'

So, thinks I, they have at least two empty rooms. My powers of deduction have often been favourably remarked upon. I follow him. Climbing stairs at the end of a day's cycling is a jolly good exercise. It uses muscles differently and gives some interesting variety to the cramp that will later wake you up screaming at three in the morning.

'This is the room at the back.' He throws open a door. I go in. It is a hotel room. What do you expect? There is a bed, a wardrobe, a small table and a chair. Had the door been flung back to reveal an atomic reactor or a troupe of dancing girls I would perhaps found something intelligent to say. I nod. He closes the door. 'And this is the room at the front.' He follows me in. 'It overlooks the square. You can have whichever room you like.' He looks at me sadly. 'Although it will probably be quieter at the back.'

I go to the window and look out. It provides a charming view of the square. Hot, white, tranquil and completely deserted. There was no reason to believe that the noise that could emanate from such a mausoleum would disturb anybody. For a reason which I do not understand, I choose the room at the back which has a view of a flat roof. He sighs and hands me the key.

I manage a complete clothes wash, including my cycling shorts and as I am hanging them out to dry on my line I notice something catastrophic. I quickly haul down the line and crush my laundry into a bag to hide it. I hurry down to the reception and collar the *patron*.

'Sorry to be a nuisance but I will have to change to the other room. My room has no curtains. I will not be able to sleep if I cannot make the room dark.' This is an important factor when the sun starts climbing out of bed just after four in the morning.

He scrutinises me, his soft features hardening slightly as he decides whether I am taking the mickey or just plain stupid. He eventually decides on the latter.

'Well, close the shutters then.'

'Ah yes, the shutters. Silly me. Ha. The shutters.' I start to back away. 'We don't have them where I come from,' I explain lamely.

To his initial assessment of 'idiot' he silently adds the qualification, 'from Mars'.

Having completed my domestic chores and checked that I could operate the shutters, I walked around the town to identify my exit route for Sunday morning and to find a patisserie which would be open. Somebody nearby was playing their radio loudly with the window open. The booming bass was clutching at my stomach and as I filtered back through the side streets towards the hotel an electric guitar suddenly clanged out with a crescendo of notes that rattled the roof tiles. This was no radio, it was a real live rock band. I turned into the square. The band was setting up outside the front door of the hotel. Right under the window of the room that he had offered me with the observation that 'it probably will be quieter at the back'. The technician checked the microphones with an ear splitting '*un, deux, un, deux,*' which I took to be a candid revelation of his limited numeracy and then a gorilla in a red shirt smacked his fist onto his guitar and split another five ear drums.

And this was just the calibration of the equipment; the 'concert' itself would not start until later.

We all ate in the courtyard. A mixture of hotel residents and passers-by. I was going to choose the *'paté berrichonne'* which I suspected would be a French version of ham and egg pie but I noticed that the other table had been given a slice of this local delicacy as its *amuse bouche* so I ordered melon and *canard à l'orange* to follow. I need not have worried – my menu did not include *amuse bouches* so I never did eat any *paté berrichonne*.

As I eavesdropped on the other diners I realised that a fair proportion of them were passing motorists who were taking a break from the 200km of traffic jams which were clogging up France on this change-over weekend. Near the top end of the shaded courtyard, a family of Parisians were established. Forty years ago the contrast in dress and manners between Parisians and countryfolk was striking; the two classes could have been distinguished along the length of a street. Today the difference is much less obvious but exists nevertheless. This family were talking rather more loudly than was strictly necessary, laughing often to demonstrate how much at ease they could be in such bucolic surroundings, and chopping and changing their choice from the menu and commenting upon the reasons for such vacillation to show the waitress how worldly-wise they were. The latter was a venerable lady of ancient years who could easily have been the *patron's* mother. She impatiently tapped her pencil on her pad whilst they deliberated. Having eventually taken the order, she turned from the table and strode back to the kitchens exclaiming loudly for the benefit of any person who might have been curious that, 'people like that make me shit.'

I cut my Charentais melon and raised a few eyebrows by sprinkling it with salt and pepper, as I had been taught by the natives of the Charente, and eating it with bread and butter. I had been aware of a vaguely familiar odour for some time and, at the very moment that I identified it as the disinfectant used in the metro toilets in Paris, I traced its provenance: the large lady friend of the effusive gentleman sitting on the next table. I do not know how much she had paid for her perfume but whatever the price, had I been in her place I think I would have changed my patronage.

There was a sudden flash and the lady grumbled.

'Oh really! You could have warned me. I do hate my photograph being taken.'

Her companion soothed her ruffled feathers with what I thought was a rather ambiguous assurance. 'Don't worry my dear, it was not a close-up.' She huffed and puffed some more so he swivelled the camera around to show her the screen and added, 'See, I had to use a wide angle.'

I do not know to this day how he got away with it. I am damn certain that I could never have done.

By the time that I telephoned MyMateMargaret, the rock band was in full eruption; a thudding bass to take your breath away, a clanging guitar to set your teeth on edge and a raucous yelling and shouting that encouraged you to hurriedly barricade your door to avoid being dragged off to the guillotine.

'Where are you?' she asked.

Boom, boom, boom.

'In the Lion d'Or at Valençay.'

Chang! Cheeeeaaang! Wawawa!

'No but where?'

Yeah, yeah, yeah.

'In the hotel, like I said.'

Thud, thud, yeerrrrr, thud, chang.

'Have you got a disco going?'

'No, it's a–' *bang, boom, cheeeang* '–band in the square.'

'Are you sure you are not in a disco? This is not supposed to be a holiday, you know. You've got a job to do.'

I envied the impregnability of the man with the wide angle lens and wisely said nothing.

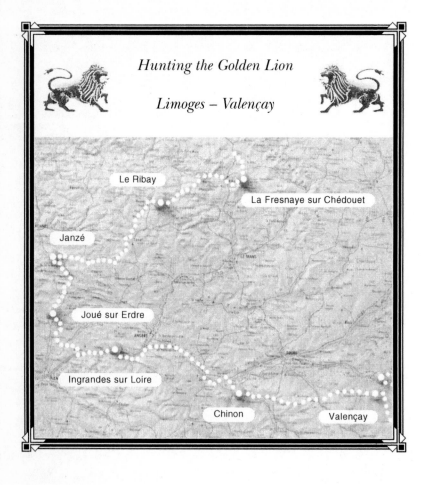

Hunting the Golden Lion

Limoges – Valençay

Le Ribay

La Fresnaye sur Chédouet

Janzé

Joué sur Erdre

Ingrandes sur Loire

Chinon

Valençay

12 – Chinon

Islept like a log. This is an expression whose origin has often intrigued me. Why a log? Why not a brick, or a plum pudding or some other utterly moribund object such as a car on the M25 for instance? Does it perhaps hearken back to the French fairy tale of Perrault, *The Sleeping Beauty* whose French title, *La Belle au Bois Dormant,* translates as, 'The Beauty in the Sleeping Wood'? There, one would presume, all the trees would have slept like logs.

We stood in the cool, tiled vestibule which promised eventual access to the bar and we tried not to look at each other. Seven of us, waiting for breakfast. I had been there only since a quarter to eight having taken with a pinch of salt the *garçon's* insistence on the night before that breakfast would be served at half past seven. He had said it with the ecstatic confidence of one who knew that he did not work on Sundays. We sat on disparate chairs arranged around the walls and whispered to each other like patients in a doctor's waiting room. I did not have anybody to whisper to so I occasionally squeaked my sneakers on the floor as my contribution. It's eight o'clock and we are straining our communal ear to detect any sound of the hotel owners getting out of bed, preparing coffee and making breakfast.

At ten past eight the door bursts open and a head appears. It belongs to the crabby grandmother who had railed at the laxative properties of Parisians.

'Tiens! Are you waiting for breakfast?'

Now how did she know that?

We file in and she crashes crockery onto table tops with the violence of a tropical storm. Somewhere around the corner I can hear the rasping of a serrated knife sawing through bread crust. The French breakfast is a great leveller. There is no macho 'full house' with extra beans and a double side order of fried bread to be shovelled down with a few swings of the elbow. In France, everybody has to fiddle about with pats of butter and pots of jam or they don't eat.

The poster on the wall behind me informs me that next week in the neighbouring village they are holding a 'Mr Wet Swimming Shorts Competition' and from another notice I learn that the band on the previous evening had been playing 'punk garage'. I am sure that the following disclosure reveals a dreadful lacuna in my education or even a seismic fissure in my worldliness but, believe it or not, neither of these snippets of information makes any sense to me at all.

The sun is beating seriously through the patisserie window as I stand in line to buy my lunch. I look over the shoulder of the lady in front of me and read her newspaper. The projected temperature for today is 34 degrees. Now that is seriously hot. There has been an outbreak of foot and mouth disease in Guildford but more worrying to me is the headline warning that Chinon has been invaded by ten thousand *'gueux'*. What the hell is a *'gueux'*? Does it sting? Does it bite? I make a mental inventory of the contents of the emergency pack that MyMateMargaret had tried to press upon me. Totting up all the discarded components, I realise that the only item that I had actually brought with me from the original pack was a small tube of Savlon antiseptic cream. That is expedition planning of a high calibre: Savlon is just the thing for insect bites.

I am in high spirits as I leave Valençay. The sun is bright,

I have bagged my eleventh Golden Lion in a row and I am wearing clean pyjamas. It is the simple things in life that matter.

The road which passes by the monumental entrance gate to the chateau has been relaid in ancient granite setts. Very pretty, I am sure, but have you ever tried riding a bicycle over them? It is like sitting on a pneumatic drill. When I drew up the specification for my bicycle, I chose from the depths of the Brooks catalogue an obsolete saddle which had been designed for use on butchers' delivery boys' bicycles. It has enormous coil springs front and rear but even with this cushioning I can feel my eyeballs rattling in their sockets like the ball on a roulette wheel. And the noise of the loose handlebar bolt clanging in the steering tube sounds like a stick drawn along the park railings.

As I bounce over a particularly prominent lump of dressed igneous rock I hear a *twang* and something stings down the inside of my thigh and then falls behind me with a metallic rattle. Panic! I immediately think of the nut from the end of my handlebar bolt. It must have finally shaken loose and dropped out. If I don't find it I will never be able to tighten the bolt. I stop in the middle of the street and begin to search the road. Several Sunday motorists show surprise at rounding the corner and finding an Englishman wheeling a big green bicycle around in circles in the middle of the road. After the third close encounter I abandon my prospection for I suddenly realise that it was based on a faulty deduction. The nut could not have dropped out of the tube because there is no hole for it to drop through. It must have been something else. I test the brakes and the gears – they work perfectly. The pannier racks are still firmly attached, the mudguards do not rattle any more than they did before and the squeaky plastic duck which I strapped to my handlebars to serve as a bell is still firmly seated. There is obviously nothing wrong with my bicycle at all.

I was making for the town of Loches for lunchtime, it being approximately mid way to Chinon. It promised an interesting old town and a magnificent formerly-royal castle. The road was quiet and undulating. The sun was hot. When I wanted my elevenses I could not find a picnic site on my side of the road. It seemed that in straightening this particular *nationale*, the engineers had left all the dead corners on the other side of the carriageway. I ended up in a bus shelter where I uncharacteristically crawled into the shade like a beetle under a stone.

The *pain au chocolat* I was munching was particularly scrumptious. As I rinsed the cloying chocolate down my throat I glanced at my saddle. It seemed somehow different from normal. Perhaps my angle of view was distorted by my leaning the bicycle against the hut. I was not convinced. I gingerly lifted the nose of the saddle. It reared onto its hind springs like the stallion at the opening credits of each television episode of *Champion the Wonder Horse*. It should not do that, I thought. This was not what Mr Brooks had intended when he built it.

Further investigation revealed that the bracket holding the nose of the saddle onto the stretcher bolt underneath had sheared off. Not content with simple fracture, it had decamped entirely and it had been this sliver of sharp metal which had stung down my thigh on its successful bid for freedom. What was I to do? Even if I found a cycle shop open on a Sunday it would not stock an obscure accessory for an obsolete English saddle. I decided to employ the same rationale as I had for the handlebars: yes, the saddle was broken but did this stop it from functioning? With slight provocation the saddle could point skywards like the graph on the cost of living index but as it seemed to share the same destiny in life as me, viz: to be sat upon, it would have little opportunity for such flamboyant behaviour.

At this point you might be forgiven for encouraging me to abandon the trip utterly because it was obviously heading for disaster: I had forgotten my clothes, my handlebars were loose and my saddle unhinged but I would respond to such a suggestion with the upbeat contradiction that you knew not the meaning of the word 'disaster'. Let me tell you about Lloyd's Kiss of Death Tour of Northern France.

It unfurled some years ago. My cycling companion was Hairy who had figured in *The Trouble with France*. (At this point, publishers traditionally insert a footnote informing the reader of the price, binding and availability of the title which the author has alluded to. Sometimes they expand this to mention that it is available in talking book form and that it was followed by an equally successful sequel, *The Trouble with Spain*. You will be pleased to learn that I have dissuaded them from any such opportunist indelicacy.)

We rode in early June. This meant that I could leave my cycle lights at home for with the long days and short mileages, we would be tucked up snugly in bed before dark. This was fortuitous for, on its way through London, Hairy's rear lamp had jumped from its bracket and committed suicide under a passing truck. No portion larger than a conker surviving.

The first day was spent cycling in pouring rain to the town of Fruges. The hotel there was recommended in the current year's local tourist guide. Recommended it might have been; open, it was not. When I state that it was closed I would not like you to labour under the belief that the *patronne* had just nipped down to the corner for a baguette. This hotel was closed with a capital F – no curtains, no furniture and a pile of uncollected mail rotting behind the door. Fruges had been a one-hotel town; now it was a no-hotel town.

The rain was thickening as we staggered off to cover the extra twenty kilometres to the next town. Five kilometres up the road I ignored the diversion sign, as cyclists always do, because roads are never closed to cyclists — if you can walk it you can ride it, and in any case it would have involved us in an extra ten kilometres. A little further on, the road dissolved into a quagmire of orange clay. We slithered and slipped, staggered and dragged. The clay clogged up our pedals and cloyed in our wheels, making them into solid discs. We could not walk it. This road was only practicable by tank. We were forced to retreat and do the extra ten kilometres.

The following morning our sodden leather shoes were not only cold and damp but had managed to contort themselves into objects that you would expect to see in the Tate Modern. We hobbled out to our bikes and set off towards the wide blue horizon. The moment it started to rain, Hairy got his puncture. Knowing that it would be me who would mend it for him, and intent upon making my task as comfortable as possible, he wheeled the bicycle through a farmyard to the shelter of a barn: a farmyard spread with glutinous bright yellow cow poo which lovingly adhered to the flat tyre.

I was the proud possessor of one of the early electronic trip computers of the day. Compared with modern versions they were fairly clunky and when, later that morning, mine registered our speed as 124 mph I drew this to Hairy's attention. 'Funny,' he said, 'I didn't think we were doing much above seventy.'

At the lunch stop, Hairy's saddle swivelled sideways as if it had just seen a big-busted blonde on the pavement. We spent our lunch hour removing the seat pillar in order to pour shampoo down the inside of the tube in an attempt to dipserse the grease that the cycle shop had smeared in there. That afternoon we stopped on the road to Bapaume to take a photograph: the shutter on my camera jammed open and ruined the shot. But at least we could look forward to a familiar welcome at the Hotel de la Gare. We had been there before and liked the food and the beds. It was closed: no curtains, no furniture, a pile of mail rotting behind the door.

It was not until early the next afternoon that Hairy collected his next puncture. I suppose I was in some way responsible because I was leading and I had a penchant for diverting down bumpy tracks as short cuts, which, paradoxically, usually turned out to be longer. I mended the puncture and we then discovered that the track evolved into a ploughed field. On the way back up the track he got another puncture. I mended it just before the rain broke. I need not have hurried. Fifty yards further on, he got his third puncture. I did make the neutral observation that perhaps thin city tyres were not the ideal equipment for a loaded touring trip to France. That evening we made a triumphant entry to the town St Quentin to the musical accompaniement of Hairy's cycle bell as it rolled down the gutter alongside us.

The following morning I experienced difficulty finding the correct road out of the town but, as it turned out, it allowed me to stop under a shelter, get out my adjustable wrench and tighten the headset on Hairy's bicycle. The weather cleared in the afternoon and we enjoyed a pleasant time alongside the upper reaches of the river Somme. Hairy enjoyed this interlude more than I because I was bent double with greasy hands, removing the ruptured links on his chain before rejoining it. It had worn so thin that a link had actually snapped. I was very good. I did not say a word.

The advantage of the hotel in Ham was that it was near a cycle shop. I marched Hairy straight around to their front door the moment they opened and got them to fit a new chain and make a permanent adjustment to his headset which they did willingly and by breaking only one of the two wires vital to the functioning of his computer. A deserted bus shelter in the drizzle was the next stop while we mended a puncture in his rear tyre and then again, a few miles further on but out in the open rain this time.

I was remarkably self restrained. There was Hairy with this liability of a bicycle, shedding ironmongery like a cluster bomb and picking up thorns quicker than Androcles' lion and did I make a snide comment? I did not. Did I make any remark about poor maintenance? Not a word. Which was just as well, for the following morning my handlebars snapped in half.

So when you talk to me of disaster, I assert even more strongly, that you do not know the meaning of the word.

Having taken the decision to continue, I left my bus shelter, straddled my bicycle and set off up the road. Around the corner I found a picnic site on my side of the road. I made a note of it for next time.

A gentle breeze was blowing into my face which served to disguise the real temperature. Every time I stopped I could feel the crisping heat frying me. By the time that I reached Loches at about midday I had drunk a litre of my water and was still thirsty. The combination of the heat and the drying wind was dessicating me. I probably needed those rehydration sachets that MyMateMargaret had tried to convince me to carry. Instead I decided upon an ice cream.

I was not convinced that the shop was open because it had adopted the abandoned look that French commerces do at lunchtime – the door is unlocked, the lights are on, the goods are on display but there is nobody in attendance. Eventually, however, a young lady appeared and I ordered a pineapple and vanilla cornet.

'Just the weather for an ice cream,' she said.

'Yes, I am suprised that the shop is not full.'

'I'm not. We are closed for lunch.'

'The door was open.'

'Yes, we leave it unlocked but everybody knows that we are closed.'

'Sorry, I'm not from Loches. I didn't know.'

'Don't worry yourself, monsieur. Now, can I get you anything else?'

I unscrewed the cap from my water bottle.

'Do you have a tap please? Could I have some water?'

'Just tap water?'

'Yes, that will be fine.'

She handed me the ice cream and I passed the bottle over the counter. She filled it at the sink behind her and then offered it back to me.

Do you remember those nauseating problems that smug people who already knew the answers would challenge you with at parties? You've got a fox, a rabbit and a lettuce to carry across the river in a boat but the boat is only big enough to take two at a time. If you take the the fox and the rabbit the former will eat the latter. Likewise with the rabbit and the lettuce. I was always tempted to suggest obtaining a bigger boat or arguing that if the boat was large enough to carry a fox and a rabbit together then there would surely be room enough for a lettuce? Or finally, why not let the rabbit eat the lettuce and the fox eat the rabbit and then carry the whole lot over in one journey?

The counter in this shop was a glass dome. It had no flat surface. She could not put the bottle down. I could not take it because I held an ice cream in one hand and the money and the screw cap in the other. We looked at each other.

'If I give you back the ice cream to hold for a moment then I can separate the cap and the money,' I suggested. She took the ice cream. I picked the money out of my other hand and offered it to her. She looked at me, an ice cream in one hand and a brimming unlidded water bottle in the other. 'Oh no that won't work.'

'Look, why don't I hold the bottle whilst you screw on the cap?' she suggested and held out the bottle whilst I gingerly screwed on the cap, keeping a wary eye on my ice cream which was wobbling in her other hand.

'Right, now you give me the bottle in my left hand and I'll give you the money with my right.'

The exchange was effected without spillage. That left her with the money and the ice cream.

'You'd better take your ice cream before it melts,' she smiled.

I took it and turned to the door.

'Ah,' I said apologetically, 'could you open the door for me please?'

'Just let me put this money in the till.' She opened the door. 'I would suggest that you eat you ice cream before you start cycling again monsieur.'

'Thank you for the advice, mademoiselle. *Bon appétit.*'

Of course, the trouble with an ice cream is that it leaves you thirsty.

I rolled down to the modern square at the bottom of the town. Here there were dozens of empty benches scattered under the trees. The place was deserted. The locals were all cowering in the shade of their houses. Occasional holiday cars wandered around looking for a cool place to park and failing. The sun beat mercilessly up from the white stone. I chose a bench at random and unpacked my lunch. There was only one other person in the entire square. He wandered over to my bench, sat next to me and lit up a foul-smelling cigar.

Loches has a royal palace and a castle and a pretty old town. I cannot tell you anything about them, it was too bloody hot, I just wanted to get cycling again to feel the cooling breeze.

That afternoon, I cycled to Chinon. The wind searing across miles of sun-scorched stubble came at me like the buffet of air from the oven door, carrying with it the dry, dusty perfume of après-harvest. I stopped for a drink and a refill of my bottles in a bar in the old part of St Maure de Touraine. Seven men were standing smoking cigars and watching the horse racing on television. In the square, wedding guests in shorts and tee shirts were milling around the town hall. The bar counter was wet, my forearm lay in the puddle. I could not be bothered to move it and in any case, it would have made no difference for the water was coming from me. When I had been cycling, my body had been pumping out sweat to evaporate in the passing breeze and cool me down. I had drunk litres of water. Now I had stopped moving but my body had not stopped pumping. I sat and watched the perspiration ooze from my skin as if squeezed from a sponge.

The last ten miles were along the river Vienne which flows into the Loire a few miles downstream from Chinon. They seemed to take ages – my sense of time had been set awry by the heat. At seventy one miles, I found the Hotel du Lion d'Or on the square in Chinon. I was very glad to see it. I dumped my bicycle in the hotel cycle park, washed and changed and wandered into the town centre to a café. I find it useful to walk for a while after a long ride to stretch different muscles in my legs.

The sun was harsh and golden on the waters of the Vienne but suffused under the cream arches of the bridge. I found a pavement café and sat with a *diabolo-menthe* and an espresso coffee and settled down to watch the residents of Chinon go about their business. Demonstrating the unquenchable and insolent humour of the *commerçant*, the garçon immediately stacked up all the other chairs and tables against the wall, leaving me isolated and stranded on the pavement, thirty yards from anywhere. The crowds of pedestrians re-occupied the liberated space and expressed surprise and annoyance when they discovered in the middle of their trajectory, a man sitting at a table and drinking coffee.

I had been made into another roundabout.

13 – Chinon again

Rest and recuperation – that is what it is all about. Athletes and other dedicated sportsmen always allocate a day to rest and recuperation. So, does this make me an athlete? Hardly. And in any case, it is not me who has chosen to stop; the hiatus has been imposed by the awkward opening times of the various Golden Lions which I am hoping to bag. My next, at Ingrandes sur Loire is seventy miles down the river and is closed on Mondays, so here I am in Chinon.

I had forgotten just how disgusting some breakfast cereals are but at least now I have drunk some milk. I must try to keep up my calcium and vitamin D intake, says MyMateMargaret. But then, she says a lot of things.

Breakfast in this place is a silent affair. How I long for the screaming kids and noisy traffic of yesterday. Here, nobody is speaking; all communication is achieved in hoarse whispers. After a few minutes of failing to intercept anything worth a drop from the eaves I notice that not only is everybody talking in whispers but they are also coughing. How did they pick up their sore throats and coughs? Perhaps they don't cycle with a towel around their necks, or in their pyjamas. Or is it the attack of the *gueux,* ten thousand of which, the newspaper had informed me, had invaded Chinon? Either way, I decided to give this sickly lot of inmates a wide berth. The last thing that I wanted was to catch some foreign bug. Not because of the inconvenience, or the discomfort, or the debilitating sickness of it all. No, I knew with an unshakeable certainty that whatever sickness, malady, ague, canker, pox or lurgy I might contract, MyMateMargaret would insist that she had provided the prevention, antidote, cure and relief in her emergency pack. This was the pack, the contents of which were still sitting on my kitchen table. Apart from the miniature tube of Savlon which, still in its virgin state, was snoozing contentedly in some obscure fold of my pannier bag.

This group in the breakfast room must all be Spanish because they have tied their sweaters around their waists to dangle behind them. Oh, that's a clever idea, where did they get their trays from? That would have saved me commuting to the buffet every five minutes.

I fiddle with the menu card and other paper ephemera which garnishes the empty spaces on my table. The hotel proudly proclaims that it is run by *'les hoteliers avec l'accent'* – 'the hoteliers with an accent.' I puzzle over this expression. Does it mean that they are foreign and you won't be able to understand their French or perhaps have they a strong regional dialect? I give up trying to work it out and return to my room to change into my sandals.

I sit on the bed to think. I have a day to spend in Chinon. The prospect is unattractive to me. I realise that I do not like holidays. Until now, this Golden Lion Safari has been work, but today I shall not be on my bicycle. How can I write about that? What am I going to do? I shall be bored to tears. Could I not excuse myself this chapter on the grounds that nothing is going to happen and at the end of it, I shall still be in the same place as when I started it? Whatever I decide, I cannot sit here all day. I must go out.

I switch on the television. This is quite a treat for me because I do not have such apparatus at home. It does not require many minutes of viewing for me to be reminded of the reason why I decided ten years earlier to eschew this audiovisual medium. Words like 'vaccuous' and 'tedious' figure weightily in the argument.

The programme is being broadcast by a company called CNN. A few weeks after I returned home, I was telephoned by a charming young production assistant at the London office of the same company.

'Mr Lloyd, we are compiling our next month's *Business Traveller* programme and would like you to come on to speak about the history of the passport.'

Rather than jump from the sofa and punch the air, shouting 'Yesssss!' I would entreat you to read further and learn the realities of life. An old media campaigner like me has seen all this before. The first precaution is to avoid telling them that a) you have never heard of them and, b) you do not possess a television.

'I see. And what is the format of the programme?'

'It's a monthly half hour slot that goes out worldwide on CNN. We present subjects which will be of interest to our business traveller viewers.'

'And is it 'live' or a pre-record?'

'It's pre-recorded in our London studios.'

'A pre-record 'as live' or edited?'

The former is a technique whereby although the programme is recorded for later transmission, no cuts are made in it. This is to create an impression of freshness and intimacy. With such an interview you have to remember not to mention days of the week or times of day because the television company will want to dupe the viewers into believing that you are in the studio at the very time that the recording is broadcast.

'No it will be edited. There are two other guests.'

Three guests, thirty minutes.

'So I get ten minutes do I?' I am pretty good at mental arithmatic.

'The time allocated will depend upon the editor.'

'What are the other guests talking about?'

'One will talk about biometrics and the other about the European visa regime.'

'Fine. You realise that my subject is the history of the passport? Don't expect me to talk about current frontier controls because I know little about them, in fact, your viewers will certainly know far more about them than me because they are passing through them every day.'

'Yes we understand that.'

'Although of course the other two topics do impinge upon mine. Biometrics for instance, I have traced back three and a half thousand years. The Ancient Egyptians had a–' I interrupt myself brutally. I have just heard that *chock, chock, chock,* that I always get when talking to MyMateJohn. She is typing on her computer. This is where alarm bells begin to ring with any writer who has a specialist knowledge which is in demand. Media companies love to ring up specialists, tempt them with visions of instant fame and fortune, pick their brains for ten minutes and then go off and make the programme without them. She is creating programme content from my words. 'Do you have a copy of my book, *The Passport, the History of Man's Most Travelled Document?'* I ask pleasantly.

'Er... no, we haven't.'

'Would you like me to send you one?'

'Oh yes please,' she gushes, 'that would be so kind.'

I take her name and address and then hit her between the eyes.

'Now, let's talk money. How much are you going to pay me for this?'

There is a gasp and the sound of an insensible body falling to the carpet. Well not quite, but it took her by surprise.

'Oh, we are a news channel. We do not pay our guests.'

Writers have to be versatile. Whilst talking to her I have managed, one-handed, to extract from the bookcase my current edition of *The Writer's Handbook* and open it at the relevant entry.

'You are the leading 24-hour global news network and you are owned by Time Warner. You have twenty six cable television channels and a worldwide viewing audience of one billion.' I remind her. 'And you want me to give you ten minutes of free television?'

Well, she had rather hoped that I would. I hung up. Everybody in that studio would have been paid: the anchor man, the production assistant, the cameraman, the sound engineer, the producer, the lad who makes the tea and the person who sweeps the floor. Everybody, except me. And without me, they could not have the ten minutes of programme content to earn the revenue to pay everybody. And they were going to try to do it without even spending £9.99 on a copy of my book.

When I told MyMateMargaret of my success in turning down the opportunity to go global for free, she was a bit short with me. She is a bit short anyway but I am too kind to mention that. Spurred on by her tight-lipped silence I decided to investigate. I telephoned Michael, a friend who is the CEO of a vibrant company in the City. I outlined the scenario.

'Well, Martin, we would have gone on CNN for free. We would see it as raising the profile of the company.' I was flabbergasted. If he raised his company's profile any higher he would need oxygen. 'In fact,' he continued, 'we did go on. Last year they had us on that very programme. We had just published our latest management book and we took the opportunity to promote it.'

This all made me look rather silly. And yet... Michael, of all people, was the kind of chap who would investigate the return earned.

'And what was the result?' I asked, fearfully.

'Zilch. Not one enquiry, worldwide, did we receive as a result of our having appeared on CNN.'

'Thank you Michael, keep making your millions.'

When I told MyMateMargaret she just sniffed. She had been looking forward to qualifying for a new London outfit and hat, dinner and a show and probably a bouquet and box of chocolates. And just after I had typed this bit, I went downstairs to turn off the radio and heard Michael talking on the BBC World Service. I wonder how much he was paid for that? I must ask him.

But here I am in Chinon. I switch off the television, put my stuff into my green plastic string bag and go downstairs. In the hotel's bicycle rack twelve identical bicycles are leaning into each other's ears to discuss their previous day's ride. The Loire valley is a region favoured by companies who organise gentle cycling holidays for otherwise reluctant cyclists. Apparently this Lion d'Or is a staging post for one of them.

Outside it is raining. Oh goody! I do not mind cycling in the rain, you get wet, but at least you are going somewhere. If you wander around a town for the day, you just get wet.

I got wet. My belongings got wet because a string bag is not waterproof. It is nothing-proof. My feet got wet because I wore my sandals to keep my shoes dry for tomorrow. My lunch got wet.

I hate being a tourist. I visited the tourist office because it had a roof. At the counter a German couple were lodging a complaint about their holiday let because the underwater light in the swimming pool did not function. A light in a swimming pool? What for? Does the water need to see where it is going? Is anybody likely to steal it? A ten year old boy was swinging around his father's arm and treading on his mother's feet whilst the parents valiantly tried to read a map. The exasperated father sends him outside to play in the rain. Silly move – they will now have to deal with a sodden, bored child. Was it incidents such as this that gave rise to the phrase which, in my infancy, I remember my father often expectorating – 'sodden kids'?

I get the feeling that people are coming here to be arty and draw and paint and be English, so I visit the museum. The still lifes belong to the 'sterling effort but could do better' school of painting.

For the sake of something to do I buy some pastries for tomorrow's lunch. The serving lady is a West African with a mat of thick black hair. She does not understand what I am asking for so I point out my desires one by one. I wonder whether I have got the names wrong – they can change from region to region or perhaps it is her first day. It possibly is but the problem reveals itself to be a little more fundamental than that – she cannot understand French. Nor can she add up. And she does not recognise French money. It's a wonderful thing the European Union.

Chinon is on the river Vienne. The river ambles by whilst the town pulls back its toes and retreats backwards up the hill. The river contributed to Chinon's development. Most traffic came by water and in the nineteenth century the prosperity of the town was aggravated by the town walls which hindered the unloading of vessels and the movement of cargoes into the town so, after a deal of procrastination, the good burghers of Chinon decided, in 1840, to demolish the town walls. They now had unembrangled access to the river. A few years later, along came the railway and the river trade died overnight.

But the town itself has narrow street upon narrow street of ancient buildings. Interestingly, in the same year that the Chinonais were hastily pulling down their fortifications, an archaeologist and writer called Prosper Merimée was suggesting the administrative concept of the 'historical monument' although laws supporting his idea were not passed until seventy years later. His idea was important for the survival of medieval Chinon because in 1962 the laws were further refined to recognise the idea of an entire area being classified as an historical monument and Chinon quickly got this definition applied to its town centre.

But the town was stagnating, its economy was crumbling. Along comes a saviour called Vitry. He sees that the future of Chinon lies in tourism and he proposes in 1971 a radical rethink of the purpose of the *monument historique*. The town was dying because the narrow streets prevented vehicular access. What the town needed was a wide thoroughfare and car parks, so in order to exploit the wonders of the old town he suggested that they widen the streets which would involve demolishing hundreds of ancient buildings but would open up the settlement to motor cars. Had his plan been implemented it would have allowed the tourists to drive in to the centre, park easily in the car park and then look around them and wonder why they were there.

I return to the hotel for an afternoon tea. The style of the bar is imitation English pub. I remark upon this to the serving girl.

'It is very 'English' here.'

She looks around and shrugs.

'I don't know, I've never been there but all these pictures on the wall make it look different.'

I look at the pictures. They are large black and white photographs of men; six of them, and they are all smoking cigars. That suggests to my suspicious mind that they might be prints provided for publicity purposes. But, I am a bit behind on the local news and I really need to know about these *gueux*.

'Mademoiselle, do you have a local newspaper that I could read?'

She glances over to the bar.

'We do, but it is in use at the moment.'

'Thank you.'

I spend the next fifteen minutes with my unblinking gaze fixed on the man reading the newspaper at the bar. I am poised on the edge of my seat, ready to dive in and grab the discarded broadsheet before it hits the counter. We enjoy a few false starts. My muscles are tingling with tension. Eventually, he calls a farewell to the barman, tucks the paper under his arm, and walks out. My jaw drops at such cheek. Whilst I am deciding whether to challenge him on the pavement like a store detective outside Woolworth's, another customer comes in, orders a coffee, picks up the newspaper which had been lying ignored on the counter for the last fifteen minutes and begins to read every word, starting methodically at the top left corner of the front page.

I ring MyMateMargaret after dinner.

'I'm bored,' I complain.

'Nobody is forcing you to do this trip. What did you have for dinner?'

'I was very good. I took to heart what you had said about needing fresh vegetables and vitamin D. I ate a *salade paysanne.*'

'Good.'

Well, not quite. When it arrived it was a plate full of hot bacon and steaming potatoes. The only piece of greenery was one floppy lettuce leaf adhering to the plate in the guise of garnish.

But I shall be on my bicycle tomorrow. Yipeee!

14 – Ingrandes sur Loire

'And tell me, madame, how did the hotel get its name?'

Madame looked up from the calculation of my bill. She was squeezed into a cubby hole, the dimensions of which made an average shower cubicle appear like a Victorian assembly room.

'It's a very old name. It's always been the Lion d'Or.'

It might be an old name but the hotel was not old. It had only started appearing in the guide books ten years earlier, however, I sensed that she would not be interested in my fascinating adventure so I left it at that. At least she had not trotted out that absurd story about 'a bed, one sleeps'.

'Don't forget to charge for the telephone.'

'Ah yes.' She ducked below the counter in order to read the meter.

Throughout my tour I have been surprised by my having to persistently remind hoteliers to add charges to my bill. This is a delicious contrast to the egregious arrogance of the luxury chain hotels who believe they have a hereditary right to take a deposit from your credit card at check-in just in case you baulk at the outrageous charges they hope to ensnare you with. And when you leave, their computerised billing system will unfailingly insist that you have consumed a bottle of champagne and a bag of nuts from the fridge. Is this programmed into the software or is there a corps of spectre-like beings who occupy your room in your absence and conduct wild orgies of pop and peanuts?

Anyhow, I paid my bill and pushed my bicycle out into the sunshine. I was leaving Chinon, unlike King Henry II who died here in 1189 to be succeeded by his eldest son, Richard the Lion Heart. But I expect you know that.

The tall white plumes of water vapour streaming skywards from the nuclear power station over the hill in the Loire valley indicated that I would probably be cycling into a headwind all day long. This was unwelcome news. I had seventy miles to achieve; I needed every little bit of help that I could get. Against my better judgment I decided to get out of town straight away and then worry about buying my food later.

Getting out of town was easy. It was a simple case of cycling down the right bank of the river Vienne towards its confluence with the Loire. Finding my route to the bridge was more difficult. I will not lay the usual blame on the deceiving road signs and inaccurate maps I will just admit that I cocked it up. Never mind. I got across the bridge but did so accompanied by some heavy lorries who would rather I had found the minor road that I had been seeking.

I was now following the left bank of the Loire as far as Saumur where I would cross and pick up the cycle route that I had been told ran down this side of the river towards the sea at Nantes. To my left I could see caves carved high up into the chalk valley side, many of them apparently used as wine cellars for the viticulteurs of the region. Between the houses and trees on my right I caught glimpses of strands of the Loire – sand, slack water and here and there, a rotting skeleton of a boat, half swallowed by the mud. I even passed a creperie called the *'Creperie du Lion d'Or'*. Had it been a patisserie, and open, I might have provisioned myself in style.

As it is, I see the first beggar of my journey at Saumur. He is sitting cross-legged outside the patisserie where I do purchase my lunch.

I have been through the Saumur before and I recall that part of it was built on an island and so I have to remember to cross two bridges. My first visit, many years earlier, had been as a staging post on a marathon journey to Spain on my, as then, brand new bicycle. In this very town I had purchased a small tin of a leather dressing, a smidgin of which, I lovingly rubbed into the leather of my Brooks saddle. It is essential to mould a new leather saddle into the contours of one's bottom. It is hard work but the ultimate rewards last forever. That is what the pundits claim. From the discomfort that I experience occasionally I deduce that once the saddle has been forced into the mould, you alter the profiles of the matrix at your peril. And inevitably, the shape of one's bottom changes.

I crossed the second bridge and turned left towards the sea. I noticed a cycle track wending through some trees and although it would certainly be slower than cycling along the road, it tempted me. But not for long. The tarmac was rutted and rucked by tree roots – it scored seven on my clinkometer and the jarring on the handlebars was bruising my hands. 'What about that pipe lagging that you fixed on the bars in the guise of padding?' I hear you say. Oh that! It split and dropped off days ago just as MyMateJohn had predicted it would. And my smug assurance that such an eventuality would be of little consequence to me was based upon the knowledge that I had an abundant store of the lagging in my shed. I have not brought my shed with me.

With the wide expanse of the Loire on my left reflecting the intense blue of the sky, and Angers somewhere before me, I tucked down my head and pounded the pedals up to twelve miles per hour. The wind was against my right shoulder but I ignored it and pushed on as if it were not there. The miles began to clock up. This was what I needed.

Do you ever puzzle over the heiroglyphs that interested parties paint onto the road surface? Whenever the cutting of a trench is projected, somebody comes along with cans of spray paint and draws onto the asphalt the routes of the existing conduits so that when the workmen make their excavation they do not deprive the locality of essential services or, indeed, provide them with entertainment such as impromptu firework displays or decorous fifty foot high fountains. Rather as artists adore a clean sheet of paper, so these highway daubers prefer to desecrate absolutely pristine tarmac, preferably within two or three weeks of it having been laid. My observations have suggested that everything is colour-coded. The pipes and conduits are coloured according to function and the paint marks reflect this: red for electricity, blue for water, yellow for gas, white for telephone and green for others like cable television.

With my head bowed before the wind I begin to log strange symbols as they appear on the road beneath my wheels. A number fifty in a circle, now what could that mean? A square with three dots in it? In England, dots usually signify the number of conduits in one trench. Now a triangle with three dots. Then the word *'feux'*. That is fairly obvious – it means 'traffic lights', so this is where they are going to install lights in order to dig up the road. And that number fifty in a circle probably means 'put the 50km limit sign here.' My bicycle lurches alarmingly as I perform a double take to check the next instruction. It says 'TNT' I find, unaccountably, that my speed has suddenly reached sixteen mph.

For some time now a railway line has been keeping me company. It is the textbook 'lines of communication' situation: river, road and railway running parallel down the valley. Along this track towards me now trundles a diminutive diesel locomotive. It looks as if it has been taken from a child's train set. It has a long nose and a dumpy cab sitting squatly on four wheels. I can see a man in a red shirt at the controls. It looks so toy-like that I find myself smiling. He toots his horn at me and waves. I squeak my plastic duck and wave back. It is an incongruous exchange of greetings rendered more charming by its spontaneity. When did you last get a wave from an engine driver?

I am approaching Angers and need to find somewhere to stop beforehand to eat some lunch. With my speed I am overhauling another English family on bicycles. I have seen several groups all enjoying the Loire cycleway, although this particular bit of it was not that pretty. The mother is riding a trailer bike – one with a third wheel and saddle attached to the back so that a small child can ride and share the pedalling. A virtuous idea, in my opinon. The contraption is the cycling equivalent of an articulated lorry and as I approach it I give a series of squeaks on my duck as a warning. Every time I do so, the little girl on the back looks right and left, up and down, and all around the bicycle, lifting her bag and looking in her pocket to try to find where the noise is coming from. When I eventually pass her, she ignores me completely. The story of my life, really.

In the village of La Daguenière I find a bus shelter opposite the town hall. I install myself and partake of a little lunch. The weather is glorious – blue sky, bright sun and that little headwind is sufficient to cool me as I cycle. It is half past eleven and I have already covered thirty miles. I cannot understand where my strength is coming from.

As I sit there, pensively sucking on a tomato, I discover that I have company. Into the car park behind me rattles a strange cortège. First comes a boy of about twelve, swooping in on a knobbly-tyred bicycle. A young lady behind him solemnly steers a bicycle and trailer around a similar curve and parks alongside him. In the trailer sits two rucksacks, a child's bicycle and the child.

'Where are you going?' I ask.

'We are going to stay with family at Bourganeuf,' she replies as they began to unpack their lunch.

'Oh that's near Chinon isn't it? I've just come from near there.'

'Yes. Where are you going?'

'Ingrandes sur Loire.'

She laughs and flicks her fingers through her hair. 'We come from Montjean. It's just across the river from Ingrandes.'

'We are swapping places.'

We chatted as we ate and my respect for this diminutive French mother grew enormously. She had started out early this morning to undertake a sixty mile journey on bicycles with a twelve year old and a seven year old. She was towing a two-wheeled trailer of robust construction such as would be used by a gardener tending his allotment. It was not designed to be lightweight. In this trailer she had loaded their clothes for the holiday and a day's provisions. When, after ten miles, the seven year old had announced that he could cycle no further, she had calmly hoisted him and his bicycle into the trailer and carried on. That was an awful lot of dead weight to be towing behind you for sixty miles. With the discretion that comes with age, I made a disinterested assessment of her body. She was no amazon. She was petite with a very trim figure, healthy skin and bright eyes. A superb advertisement for cycling, and what a woman!

Before we separated, she showed me on my day's portion of map where the cycle track ran to avoid Angers. She handed it back to me, turning it over curiously as she did so.

'I didn't know they made such small maps. It's quite handy.'

'Oh they don't,' I explained proudly. 'I cut out the bits I need and leave the rest at home. It saves weight.'

She looked into her trailer and nodded thoughtfully. I was worried about a few extra square centimetres of paper? I felt very foolish. She kindly said nothing. It made me feel worse. What a woman!

I made my way around Angers as directed. At Pont de Cé I paused to gaze at the stumps of a now-disappeared railway bridge which jutted through the water in the middle of the river. Today was the 7th August. Almost one hundred years earlier to the day in 1907, a wagon and a third class carriage of the Angers–Poitiers express had plunged from this bridge into the river, drowning thirty people. Somewhere I had seen photographs of steam traction engines with cable drums, hauling the carriages up onto the beach. Now even the bridge had gone.

On the west side of Angers the river Maine flows into the Loire. I was now cycling on an enormously wide stretch of fine, compounded gravel which ran level with the water. From this altitude it is difficult to establish how wide the river is – it is peppered with sandbanks and knots of trees. I knew that the thick belt of dark green foliage which was separated from me by three hundred yards of sand and meandering water channels was not the left bank of the river. It was probably only a sandbank and the main course of water would be flowing on the far side of it. The river banks hereabouts were over a mile apart and the Loire wandered randomly across this mile. I learned from a plaque on the wall of a nearby ancient property that the trees were on an island called the *Ile aux Chevaux* – the Isle of Horses. It was nothing like London's Isle of Dogs. It was about two miles long and boasted a human population of two. A hundred years earlier the population had been in the low fifties. I suppose, over the decades, some had managed to swim ashore. Had they known it, they could have stayed put and saved themselves the trouble because the island is inexorably creeping across the river towards the right bank. In a couple of centuries they will be able to jump the gap.

The breeze from Nantes is now blowing steadily into my face so I cheat and cross the river to Montjean where the French family had started from this morning. This takes me out of the wind and avoids my using a main road. A few miles further down the valley I cross the next bridge straight into Ingrandes sur Loire. The main street climbs gently up from the old river port by the bridge. At the top I find the

Lion d'Or, tastefully nestled alongside the railway line. As I postulate on the status, vis-à-vis railway traffic, of this ferrovial axis and wonder about the implications of the happy juxtaposition of line and hotel, a TGV thunders through at a million decibels and my unformed question is answered.

But the hotel has a designated bicycle parking. It is in an outbuilding with a sliding door at the back of the garage which I get to via the yard. The receptionist is a cheery young lady, rotund of humour and of physique.

'Just for one night, monsieur?'

'Yes just one night.'

'A business visit?'

'Well, sort of. My publishers have challenged me to cycle through France from bottom to top and to stay only in hotels called the Lion d'Or.'

'Wow! That's an adventure. And are you writing a book about it?'

'As soon as I get home.'

'Where did you start from?'

'I left Cauterets, in the Pyrenees, on 27th July and you are the twelvth Lion d'Or in a row.' She made a 'suitably impressed' face. 'The trouble is, the hotels are not always where I want them. I have had to zigzag about France to get this far. I wanted to get here last night but you are closed on Mondays.' I faltered as I watched her mobile face pucker into a frown. 'Don't tell me that you were open last night?'

'Well, yes we were, but I won't tell you if you don't want me to.' An impish smile wriggled into the corner of her mouth.

'But I had to stay two nights in Chinon to waste time.'

'There are worse places to stay than Chinon.' She looked at my face and then shrugged. 'Well, perhaps not.'

'I was stuck there for an extra day. I wanted to be writing. I should have brought my computer with me but it would have been too heavy.'

'Yes you travel with the bare minimum on a bicycle.'

I become sordidly confidential. 'Actually, I left with just below the bare minimum. I am cycling in my pyjamas because I forgot my clothes, but don't tell anyone.'

She dissolved into giggles which I found quite satisfying.

The staircase was an uninterrupted run of narrow stairs of an unusally severe gradient. One false step at the top and you would tumble all the way to the bottom. Waiting in my bedroom was a hospitality tray; now that was an innovation for France. I kicked off my shoes and lay on the bed with a cup of coffee. I felt happy with the world. You can't beat a smiling welcome and a cup of jolly old instant coffee to buck you up.

The dining room had originally been three rooms. This was indicated by its three different ceiling heights and the not quite square doorways. Some sort of unifying harmony had been attempted by running wood panelling around the walls at waist height but this had at some later time been painted white which rather spoiled the effect.

I ordered a *crudités* followed by a fish called *colin*. This could be a hake or it could be a cod. I cannot tell the difference either in French or on the plate. Don't expect great eulogies of cordon bleu cuisine from me. Funnily enough, I had a schoolfriend called Colin but he was not a fish. The hake or cod was served with sliced sauté potatoes and a mini ratatouille. For afters, I chose *le crumble* which happened to be pear and morello cherry crumble and it was served with Chantilly cream and ice cream.

Each time the lady served or removed a dish from my table she peered over to try to read what I was writing in my notebook. On one occasion I was actually writing that sentence. Perhaps the receptionist had told her that I was a famous author. On the table in front of me, two men spent the entire mealtime reading their mobile phones and exhanging single words with each other. I wondered whether they were playing a game of telephone Scrabble.

Time to phone MyMateMargaret.

'I thought you said that Ingrandes was closed on Monday nights?' I waded in. I was still annoyed about my wasted day.

'How are you Margaret? Oh quite well thank you Martin. Would you like me to look at my notes about Ingrandes?'

I think she was trying to make a point. It's always safer to play her game.

'Yes please.' I thought that was quite conciliatory.

'Do I assume that you are in Ingrandes?'

'Correct.'

'Have you eaten?'

'Yes thank you.'

'Well, you would not have been able to dine yesterday because the restaurant is closed on Monday evenings.'

'The restaurant? Ah. Not the hotel? Anyway, I had a good ride today. Plenty of sunshine, I really cracked on. At lunchtime I met a fantastic French woman.'

'Oh yes?'

'You know the type – cycles all day and still looks like a million francs, not a hair out of place.'

'Ah ha.'

'She was towing this trailer with one of her kids in.'

'So she was married then?'

'And she was really slim and wiry. What a tremendous woman to be able to envisage such a journey.'

'I see.'

'Lovely complexion.'

'Mmm.'

I got the impression that she was not paying attention. Or was she trying to say something in that obscure manner that women do when they know you cannot see them?

15 – Joué sur Erdre

Never a train did I hear, once I had rolled into bed. Nary a clang, nary a whistle. That's what a clear conscience and seventy miles pedalled can do for you.

I was offered the chance to enjoy breakfast out in the courtyard but declined it because I knew that the glaring bright sun reflecting on the white walls of the hotel would cause me eye problems. The guests passing by my table on their way to their al fresco nourishment cast pitying glances upon this unadventurous foreigner who chose to eat in the gloom, but they soon revised their patronising sympathy when a breeze sprang up and brought to their tables and their noses the sharp odour of silage which the energetic farmers had spread on the fields around the town.

I sat indoors and annexed the local paper. Casually turning the pages, my random journalistic peregrination suddenly stalled on a picture of a crowd of persons wearing strange old fashioned clothes and painted faces. They were parading down a street in Chinon. These were the *gueux*. Chinon has an annual fair whose origins date back to mediaeval times and the people who attend this fair traditionally dress in whatever they consider to be nearest to mediaeval attire. Ten thousand of them had invaded Chinon. Of that possibility I had already been alerted and my immediate reaction, you may recall, had been to reach for the antiseptic cream. How silly of me! Had one of these pests bitten me I would have needed a surgeon not Savlon, but I had seen none of the *gueux*, of course, having missed the fair by one day.

'Where is your next Lion d'Or?' the smiling receptionist enquired as I paid my bill.

'Not very far. It's just up the road at Joué sur Erdre.'

'How far is that?'

'About fifty six kilometres, assuming I don't get lost.'

She handed me the bill, cocked a humorous head at my chest and pouted. 'I preferred your yesterday's pyjamas.'

The man waiting to pay at the side of me stared, his gaze shifting in growing wonder from her to me. The girl exploded in spluttering giggles and sank majestically below the counter on an urgent but obscure quest.

'Thank you for making my stay so pleasant,' I called to the abandoned counter as I picked up my cycle bags. I selected the expression for its scandalous ambiguity and I was pleased to see that its effect on the man was not wasted.

The hotel buildings had been a priory two centuries earlier, with vines and the remains of a chateau in the grounds. When the cattle market in Ingrandes began to assume importance, the three houses had been knocked into one to lodge the dealers, and the garden and courtyard were used to accommodate their animals awaiting market. I could see the proof of this activity in the layout of the outbuilding from which I retrieved my bicycle. It had obviously been stabling in a previous time.

I only had thirty five miles to cover today. If I pedalled hard I could do that before lunch which would leave me stranded at my destination with nothing to do so I decided to kill time by taking a look around Ingrandes before leaving. First stop was the town hall. Like many such offices in settlements of this importance it hides behind a facade fashioned in the 'administration style' of architecture and gazes pompously down a square populated with benches and parked cars. It can do this because it is always closed. But every town hall has a notice board.

The first notice was an official communiqué forbidding the importation of any meat from the UK because of the outbreak of foot and mouth disease there. You see how the country goes to rack and ruin the moment my back is turned? The next notice was an apology from the mayor that the annual swimming pool could not be erected this year because the level of the Loire was too high. Fifty years ago, Ingrandes was well frequented for its beach along the Loire. The present day seasonal swimming pool was presumably the natural development from that. The third poster informed me that the nearby town of Beaune would be holding its annual *rillettes* and *paté aux prunes* fair on the first of July. Quite why pork and plums should share a celebration, I could not imagine. I supposed them to be the fruits of the region's agriculture.

Just across the road, the tourist information centre housed a collection of ancient clocks which had been presented to the museum by a local clockmaker. They came mostly from the towers of local churches whose priests had recognised at an early stage the autonomy provided by electricity. No more clumping up endless spirals of uneven steps in a poorly lit tower in order to hand wind the clock with an enormous windlass. With electricity you could install a remotely controlled motor to rewind the clock or replace the entire timepiece with an electrically powered unit. As the tentacles of the electricity grid extended to the outlying villages, the clockmaker was called upon to dismantle more and more church clocks and replace them with newfangled sparky ones. Being a man of vision, or perhaps he just did not like to throw things away, he amassed a collection of some of the more interesting examples. As I marvelled at the size of these machines I could not but feel sympathy for his wife. Many of them looked as if they had been built by a blacksmith which, as it turned out, was true. They sported an entanglement of huge, viciously toothed iron cogs, clacking in three planes as they ground out the time through a system of forged tines and crudely hacked levers. Some were powered by a weight or pendulum which had been fashioned from a rock, roughly smoothed and then bound in iron hoops. With their serrations and sawteeth and riveted constraints these clocks looked more like mediaeval torture engines than reliable timepieces.

Anthony, the young man in charge, rattled some chains and hefted a rock and then stood back proudly as one of these monsters took up the cadence of unstoppable time with a ponderous *tack, donk, tack, donk*. I encouraged him further and at the end of ten minutes the museum sounded like a drunken centipede walking downstairs.

Out in the street again and the sun is still shining and the pong is still ponging. I make my way down to the river. At Ingrandes the river Loire takes a swerve to the left. This is caused by an outcrop of very hard stone upon which the village is built. Even after thousands of years, the river has not managed to erode it. A failure for which the inhabitants of the said village have been grateful for generations. The influence of this right-angled bend upon Ingrandes has been beneficial because it took vessels out of the wind and they then had to lie up to await a favourable breeze and whilst they waited, the sailors would go ashore and frequent the taverns. A journey from Orléans downstream to the sea at Nantes, would take about fifteen days. The upstream journey took at least a month even with sails.

And here on the old river front I find an impressive town house built by a Monsieur Walsh de Serant who was a prosperous boat builder of the town and who had settled here from his native Ireland. But Ingrandes has not finished showing me its treasures. It is dribbling them out bit by bit. I am intrigued by this talk of the town being 'at the frontier'. At the frontier of what, I ask? This plaque marks the spot of the frontier stone. When France became an indivisible one with the Revolution in 1792, the stone was sold to a local quarryman. What benefit would he earn from buying a stone in the middle of the town? I suppose it saved him the effort of transport.

In the district where I used to live in Paris there is a street called the *rue du gros caillou* – the 'street of the big pebble'. This stone marked the limit of the pasture lands rented to the commoners by the Abbeys of St Dominique and Les Clercs. When it was decided to remove the stone in 1738, it was demolished with explosives but the name lived on in the street and, incidentally, in a well-frequented brothel of the neighbourhood. And even to this day there is a church of St Peter of the Big Pebble which is a bit of ecclesiastical tautology which rather amuses me.

This stone in Ingrandes marked the frontier between independent Brittany to the north west and the province of Anjou. The importance of distinguishing between the two areas was bound up in a tax on salt which had existed since the middle ages, called *'la gabelle'*. In Brittany and Calais, salt was not taxed at all; in Anjou, it was taxed heavily; south of the Loire, the rate was lighter. It is not difficult to predict the outcome of such a state of affairs – everybody tried to smuggle untaxed salt into Anjou. The administrative border between this province and Brittany ran through the western end of the town and still does. Most of Ingrandes is in the *département* of the Maine et Loire whilst the former Brittany part is in the Loire Atlantique.

Here, in this former customs house, *douaniers* would check on the boats crossing the Loire from the lowly taxed south or coming upstream from untaxed Brittany and further up the street stands an ancient salt warehouse.

I was now really on my road out of town. I was leaving Ingrandes. I had crossed the frontier into the *département* of the Loire Atlantique but even then the town had one more surprise for me. It came plunging down on my right; a road as straight as an arrow flying from the country and targeted on the river. It was an old *chemin noir* – a black road. Why was it called 'black?' Because of coal. It was a road which had been straightened in the eighteenth century to make it easier for the hauliers to get their waggons of coal down to the boats for loading on the river. In 1746 the local coal concessionaire brought in Belgian miners to help develop the reserves of the district. They suggested importing from England a Newcomen steam engine which they did in 1760 – one of the first steam engines in France. It was used to pump water out of the mine and would have been an enormous stationary apparatus requiring a substantial building to house it. Not an investment to be undertaken lightly and yet, twenty years later it was obsolete and replaced by a Watt engine, also from England. When we complain today that our desktop computer we purchased five years earlier is now obsolete we are more voicing a conservative disgust at the speed at which technology has advanced than complaining at the expense involved. Compared to purchasing and installing a stationary steam engine the outlay of capital and effort is piffling.

Under this countryside, men were toiling to dig up coal, peat and iron-ore to feed the growing industrial demands of the port of Nantes with its iron foundries and shipyards By 1864, the district contained 287 steam engines which produced a total power of 2544 horsepower. But by then, three quarters of the coal they used was imported from England. Only 354 men worked in coal mines; ten times more than that were employed in the sea salt pans of Nantes.

Ingrandes – what an interesting little settlement! As I left on the road for Anetz, I was met by a golden retriever silently padding homewards with a rabbit in its jaws. The road turned down towards the Loire and under every railway bridge, fiteen foot high steel flood gates had been fitted so that they could be swung across the road to convert the railway embankment into an extra flood defence. I turned left at the road sign depicting a car falling into a dock and discovered that they were not joking. Two hundred yards later, with no further reminder, the road – tarmac, white line and all – dived straight into the river.

Ancenis is the town where I will strike away from the Loire and enter the fringes of Brittany to resume my route northwards to the Channel. The town is on the right bank of the river and linked to the other bank by the inevitable suspension bridge. As I pedal towards the old centre of the town I become aware of a pervasive odour; it is organic but thankfully not of the genus that we had endured at breakfast. I rack my olefactory memory to place it but all that springs to mind is Christmas. And for a reason. The smell is indubitably that of sage and onion stuffing. Why, I could not tell you. The area is known for raising cattle, growing maize to feed the aforesaid and making the fine rosé wines of Anjou to refresh those who looked after the cows.

I sit on a bench in the little square to eat my sausage roll that I purchased in Saumur yesterday. It has travelled eighty miles since and I am sure that the savoury odour supplied by Ancenis only adds to its palatability. The sun is shining hard now. The day is heating up. Thank goodness I am only wearing pyjamas. Suddenly I flinch as I feel a small claw-like grip on my shoulder. It is similar to a sort of nerve twitch. I turn my head and look straight into the small beady eye of a sparrow. He abruptly changes his mind about the availability of the sausage roll in my hand and flies away, flacking my cheek with his wing as he does so. I feel shivers of Alfred Hitchcock run through me as I glance uneasily at the numbers of birds assembling on the rooftops.

As I cleared up after my meal I noticed an empty key ring lying on the ground. It was a simple split ring so I picked it up and passed it through the loop on the back of my saddle. You never know when you might need something like that. Ask any cyclist and they will amaze you with tales of what they can pick up from the highway. Some of my best tools have come from the tarmac. I gleaned a sturdy screwdriver in Teddington High Street and found its crosshead twin in Boulogne; I have a gas fitter's huge iron spanner and an interesting fifteen inch long bolt. The former would be of use should I ever need to dismantle my gas meter whilst the latter's utility is best described as a conversation starter along the lines of, 'a fifteen inch bolt must be holding together something fairly massive and important, would you not think that somebody would have noticed that it had dropped off?'

Just for interest, for one whole year I made a list of every object that I picked up whilst cycling the eighteen miles to work and back. It reads thus: three screwdrivers, nine assorted spanners, two paint scrapers, one pair of insulated wire cutters, one pair of pliers, one protective hard hat from the channel tunnel site, ten yards of blue plastic rope, one French number plate, one metal cycle pump, one pair of brown woollen gloves, one pair of bright green socks, two raw onions, one mudguard reflector, one roll of self adhesive labels, one hardback children's novel, one fluorescent green reflective tabard, one fake Rolex watch, one cycle lamp complete with batteries, one squash racket, three strong rubber gloves, one German number plate, three rubber cat's eyes each with a complete set of reflectors and two pounds twenty in small change.

Leaving aside the great service that I am performing for the community in clearing the roads of debris, this harvest is not entirely without benefit for me. I still wear the socks; the rubber gloves I use for gardening; the sticky labels lasted five years; the tools all loll in my tool box; the rope went into the tree house; anything for a bicycle goes into the shed; the book I gave away as I did the squash racket, having no pretensions in that direction. The one article which I see most commonly on the road and in the hedgerow but which does not appear on the list is the escapee plastic hub cap. These are of no use to anybody and so I do not take them home; I use them as a frisbee into the nearest field. The small discs from the Mini Metro used to fly the furthest.

I dawdled out of Ancenis so that I did not arrive too early at my next Golden Lion. Since I had turned into Brittany, clouds had begun to appear in the blue sky. Their presence did not worry me but it was a useful reminder to me that it always rains in Brittany. For the next three days I would be navigating through that part of France of which I had school trip memories of short steep hills and strong winds. If the district really wanted to delay me, it had the facilities – rain, wind and inclines. I must try not to upset it.

The Auberge du Lion d'Or welcomed me at Joué sur Erdre. It crouched opposite the *place aux foires* and stared straight up the road to Petit Mars and Nantes. I sat in the bar with a coffee whilst I awaited the man who would show me where I could put my bicycle. Three men in working clothes were smoking and drinking at the counter and discussing gloomily the agricultural crisis which had just hit this locality. Twenty miles up the road was the town of Chateaubriant whose weekly cattle market sold seventy two thousand head of cattle per annum. This week's market had been cancelled. Restrictions on the movement of cattle had been imposed because of the outbreak of foot and mouth disease in England. I buried my face in the local newspaper as they maligned the perfidious British Government, the greedy English farmers, the shortsighted cattlebreeders, inexperienced transporters, and incompetent laboratory administrators.

'Don't understand why they have to keep the disease in a laboratory at all. What good is that?' the red haired man said.

'They didn't keep it, did they? That's the point.'

'Bloody obvious,' said the third, 'that it would get out eventually. They've got no proper controls. Look at the way that the English sell their milk.'

I puzzled over this last observation and even to this day, I cannot see its relevance.

'They need sorting out properly these *rosbif.*' His red bushy moustache bristled as he bridled. 'It's not the first time they've pulled a trick like this.'

At this juncture, the barman leaned over the bar and said something in a low voice. As one man, they all three turned from the bar to look at me. I like country folk; there is no subterfuge; no hypocritical persiflage.

'Monsieur is English?' the red haired man enquired.

'Proud to be so,' I replied brightly.

'Well what do you think of this crisis?'

One of his two companions pulled at his sleeve and tried to nod him back to the bar. They were beginning to feel embarrassed, bless 'em.

'Well,' I began cagily, 'it's a tragic situation but you don't want to believe everything that you read in the newspapers.'

'They're not wrong on this. That's a French newspaper and it's of the region. Obviously they'll say it differently in the English papers.' He tugged at his moustache.

My heart gave a leap as my eye slid down the column of text on the table before me.

'Do you mean to say that you believe what is written in this paper?' This was challenging and confrontational and his two mates were now squirming and looking miserable. He, of course, could not now back down.

'Of course I do.'

'So what they write down here is true then?' I tapped the newspaper.

'Naturally.' He was now beginning to wonder.

'Good. Then you'll permit me to read it to you. *"It is thought that the virus escaped from a laboratory south of London. The negligent enterprise is owned and managed by a Franco-*

American company." I looked up at him and grinned. 'So it's half your fault and nothing to do with me. I'm English.'

His two companions clapped him on the back and guffawed at him. The barman smiled in relief and the red moustache twitched and then he laughed louder than the others.

'Permit me to pay you a glass, monsieur.' His offer was genuine and presented in all good nature.

'I will gladly drink another coffee, thank you.'

'Another coffee for *Monsieur l'Anglais*,' he said to the smiling barman. '*Ah les sacrés Anglais.* They always wriggle out of it.'

The dining room sat thirty. It was the front room of the house with a marble fire surround in the corner and a central electric chandelier. The walls were unpainted half panelling topped by Regency stripe wallpaper and finished with decorative plaster cornices and ceiling rose. In the bar a girl is laughing and somebody is playing an automatic game with a motorbike sound track. Travellers are stopping from the road and dropping in for dinner.

There is one item on the menu that I must have – the *salade du lion d'or*. The waiter regrets that there is none left.

'Oh, have you run out of golden lions?' I ask innocently.

'Ha, ha. Run out of lions. I like that. That's really funny.'

The other diners laugh. He takes my order out to the kitchen and I hear him recounting my riposte to the cook. He laughs as well. Good hearted, uncomplicated laughter is one of the most uplifting sounds that I know.

Two of the other diners must be staying at the inn for some shooting or fishing because they are wearing solid country clothes and talking about the land, rivers and lakes with that knowledge and familiarity that hunters develop.

The auberge has five rooms, arranged in a line at the top of the stairs. I am first in line. On the other side of me, bright daylight pours down the stairwell from the attic.

I fit the long shanked brass key into a bedroom door that unlatches only if you flex it. My room is rustic. The shower and toilet corner is constructed from baulks of timber nailed together like a cow shed. A curtain provides privacy for the WC. There are two bedside lamps but only one electrical socket: you choose which side of the bed you wish to illuminate. It is simple, straighforward and honest; just like the people, the auberge and the cuisine. And I like things like that.

The hunters move in to the room next door. The partition wall must be single-ply hardboard. I can hear everything that I don't want to. I ring MyMateMargaret to report progress.

'One of my sandals broke at dinner time,' I tell her. 'The strap holding the buckle just came off the cloth.'

'Get it mended. They have shoe repairers in France.'

'Cobblers.'

'I beg your pardon.'

'Shoe repairers,' I explain. I like to label these things correctly when I can. 'Anyway, that won't work. The strap is only stapled on and the cloth supporting the fixing has just frayed away. There is nothing that a cobbler could do.'

'That is what happens when you buy cheap stuff.'

'Yes but they are very lightweight.'

'And broken. Who is that talking?'

'It's the chaps next door.'

'They are in your room,' she accuses.

'No, they are not. It's just that the walls are very thin.'

'What? Speak up.'

'If I speak up,' I whisper, 'they will hear me. I said that the walls are very thin.'

'Strikes me that all your excuses are pretty thin.'

Now what did she think I was doing in my room? Running a poker school or something? I don't know the first thing about stoking fires.

16 – Janzé

Something niggled at me during the night. A sense of unease or of something left undone. When I awoke I checked all my functions, as one does, but nothing seemed amiss. I found it hard to believe that a broken buckle on my sandal would give me disturbed sleep. I failed to dispel the feeling at breakfast, try as I might so I shrugged like a Frenchman and said *'bof.'*

Whilst the man unlocked the barn across the road to free my bicycle I watched the *boulanger* load bread into his van. I had thought at first that he was unloading it into the shop. Many of the villages now no longer support a bread baker so they have what is called a *'depot de pain'* – a shop where a baker deposits bread for sale daily. But this village has its own fully functioning *boulangerie* and it is their baker who supplies the surrounding villages.

The tyres on my bicycle had picked up straw from the damp earth floor of the barn and as I wheel it across the road to my bags which I have dumped outside the hotel, the stalks flack and tick and swish through my mudguards.

Today I have about forty miles to do to reach my next Lion at Janzé. I shall be penetrating further into the fringes of Brittany and as if to remind me, the sun has decided to have a day in bed and has just left me its duvet. And it is a bit grey around the edges.

I look up the main road in the direction of north. Chateaubriant is the town I must make for – the town whose cattle market has been suspended. Get out the appropriate map segment for this stage, Martin. That unease surges to the forefront again. I don't remember actually seeing a map showing this part of the route and this, I discover, is for the simple reason that I don't have one, but this time it is not my fault. Not really. The two maps that I had cut up and which should have overlapped, were from different editions and did not. Today had fallen down the gap. Students take a gap year; I shall have a gap day.

The Erdre here is only a stream but it was used well into the nineteenth century to transport coal and iron around. The pretty wooded lakes which the lower reaches link together, supply water for the Nantes-Brest canal by means of a feeder canal. The country is hedged and undulating. It is a region of pigs and *charcuterie*, organic wheat and loose *bocage* lightly scattered with the remains of ancient iron forges. I cycled through a village on a main road which was crossed by no fewer than ten pedestrian crossings and a few kilometres further along, the highway was daubed with giant letters declaring somebody's rejection of genetically modified crops and demanding that José Bové be liberated. This latter personage I assumed had carried his objections to the aforementioned cultivation to the point where it had clashed with the desires of Authority and he had been incarcerated for his trouble.

I turned from the main road and went into the village of Moisdon la Rivière to buy myself some lunch. Here they had a *rue des vignes* and a *rue du pressoir*, suggesting that at some time in the past, here they had grown grapes and pressed them but there are no vinyards in sight today.

The customer in front of me was buying fruit. She asked for *'un livre d'abricots'* – a pound of apricots. But I thought that France went metric with the Revolution two centuries ago. In fact, they invented the blight. This is true but habits die hard and out in the country, the older generation still uses the word 'pound' to denote the weight of half a kilo which we in Britain have to call 500 grams.

I have on occasion been teased by the French about several aspects of British life and have learned to give as good as I get. E.g: why are you the only country in the world to drive on the left? We are not. So do the billion people in India, also Pakistan, and Japan and anyway, how long do the French think they have been driving on the right? I have an ancient copy of the French Highway Code which states quite clearly that you should drive in the middle of the road and only pull over to the right in the face of oncoming traffic. I know some people who still drive like that. We British have allowed ourselves to be stigmatised by our desire to drive sinister-wise as if it were some unique defect or perversion. But let me tell you, in 1923 the following countries all drove on the left: South Africa, Rhodesia, Argentina, Australia, Austria, Ceylon, China, CzechoSlovakia, Malaya, Hungary, India, New Zealand, Portugal and Sweden. Oh and if you went to Italy you drove on the right in the country and on the left in the town. How's that for a practical arrangement?

And then there is always that silly problem over our twelves and their tens. Why don't we go metric? Well you just tell them that we will go metric when they do. Go into a French restaurant and order oysters or snails – they serve them by the dozen not by the ten. We don't eat snails, so it is not Britain forcing them into a duodecimal straitjacket. Try buying a five-pack of beer at a French supermarket – you can't, it does not exist. And make them count on their fingers. How high do they get? Ten? Watch the thirteen year old lad who operates the ferry across the Meghna in Bangladesh as he counts up to a gross on his fingers. I did. He uses his thumbs as the markers and ticks off the three segments of four fingers to make twelve. The right hand does the units up to twelve, the left hand does the dozens up to twelve. And when you match that with the twelve pennies we had in a shilling, it all falls into place.

Well that did me good. I'll get off my high horse now. Oh, look what I've trodden in. Did I say all that?

The ostrich farm on the road at the entrance to Chateaubriant has gone kaput but it has been closed for months so they can't pin that upon the foot and mouth outbreak in England. Rather like my map with the bit missing, Chateaubriant looks like a town with a bit missing but I cannot think what. It seems somehow, not quite finished. I wheel my steed into the square by the church and sit down to eat my lunch. I have to sit on the wall since there are no benches anywhere. Perhaps that was the missing item on the council's shopping list.

Sitting on the wall opposite me is a middle-aged man. He is wearing blue trousers and a white shirt, open at the neck and a thin jacket. His hair glints with threads of silver as he turns occasionally to glance around him. He looks down at his trousers and brushes his knees with the palms of his hands. Then he scratches his head and folds his arms in his lap. Soon he gets up and paces in regular, steady steps towards the church entrance then he turns with his hands clasped in front of him and his thumbs tapping together. He returns to his wall and sits then suddenly rises again and brushes the seat of his trousers. He walks to and fro a couple of times, stopping to look at the flowers in the raised beds. It is obvious to me that he has no particular interest in them. He just looks at them because they are there.

Somebody waves to him. His face is suddenly aglow as he turns. Walking towards him is a lady wearing a light green raincoat over a plum coloured skirt. Her grey hair is elegantly coiffed and she holds a magazine in her hand. They meet. He puts both hands up before him as he greets her as if he needs to touch her to reassure himself that she really is there and she realises that she cannot shake hands anyway with the magazine in her grasp. They exchange stilted greetings whilst she fumbles to free up her right hand. She drops the magazine and they bang heads as they both make a lunge at it. The paper flops to the ground and they apologise to each other as they rub their own heads and exchange polite laughs. He picks up her magazine and says something to her. She nods agreement and they turn to walk down a side road. It leads towards the restaurants. They walk and talk, still maintaining the gap between them. The scene was like an excerpt from a French version of *Brief Encounter*. I was longing to know what happened next.

What did acually happen next was that the church clock struck for midday. First it sounded all the quarters: *ding, dong, dang,* four times. Thence followed a pause, broken by a tinnier bell which struck twelve times. A minute later, a much louder bell rang nine times then somebody started to rattle a bucket at the top of the tower and that was the signal for all the bells, tin cans, spades, cymbals and dustbin lids in the town to express themselves freely. It was a random percussive free-for-all which lasted for about five minutes.

Time to go. But which road should I take? I knew my next Golden Lion was at Janzé and it was to the north. Two roads left the town in this direction, one went to Vitré and the other to Rennes. I recalled the surreptitious research that I had undertaken at the map shelves in Otterstones and plumped squarely for the road to Rennes.

The road became the first of several *'routes de la liberation'* along which I would travel in the next few days through Brittany and Normandy. Every village had renamed the road along which the allied troops had arrived after D-Day in June 1944. This particular artery was staked out with huge commemorative marker stones at each kilometre. They were all leaning backwards. The reason being that they were not stone at all but moulded in glass fibre and the dominant wind here is northerly so they all lean to the south. Today, the wind had started at about a quarter to eleven and was quite insistant in its desire to push me back to the Mediterranean.

In the village of Rougé I pause to inspect the cross that the people had erected to celebrate the return of Monsieur Durnae de la Minière who, during the seventh crusade, had deflected an arrow from the body of the king Saint Louis with his gauntlet. The king had bestowed the highest honours upon Durnae de la Minière who had returned to his village in triumph. That had been in 1250; the cross was not erected until 1994. I suppose they were waiting for an EC heritage grant.

I know that I only have thirty nine miles to cover today. I look at my counter. I have already done thirty two and a half. I start to pay great attention to the direction signs because Janzé should soon be signposted off to my right. The wind has now blown away the duvet and the sun is dancing around the bedroom, clutching little scraps of white cumulus to its nether regions to preserve its decency. Another side road crawls by and it is not Janzé. The statue of the Virgin Mary gazes hollow eyed at me. Once I had evaded her gaze I enjoyed a good snigger. When I had first come to Brittany on a school trip, the guide on the coach had announced, 'Now we are in Brittany so you will find a virgin on the corner of every road.' She could little have imagined the effect that this would have on a coach load of teenaged boys.

But I am not looking for a virgin. Well, not at this very minute, I am hoping to find a road sign. I begin to have doubts. Did I choose the correct road out of Chateaubriant? Perhaps I should be cycling towards Vitré? I decide that I will try one more junction and if that does not serve, then, heaven forfend, I would ask somebody. As soon as one takes this decision, the indigenous population of the country immediately burrows under the nearest stone and puts out on the shelf the village idiot and an assortment of nomads who happen to be passing through on their way to Siberia.

'Sorry mate, I'm a stranger here myself.' You know exactly what I mean.

Today, the natives have simply hidden and left the shelf empty. I glance at the road sign. There is a *'road closed'* barrier pulled across the tarmac and somebody has taped over the names on the sign. All that I can read is the road number, D92. It means nothing to me. They obviously do not want anybody to go down there. But I am a cyclist. I lean my bicycle against the post and peel back the tape. Underneath it says, *'Janzé'.*

The road was not really closed. Some workmen with a tipper lorry were building up the verges with ballast and earth and did not want to be disturbed by passing traffic. I did not trouble them at all.

The afternoon was turning out quite pleasantly. I cycled to the railway station and sat on a bench in the sun. An elderly lady came out of a nearby house and settled next to me to read her paper. It was a bit early to turn up at the hotel so how could I employ my time? I thought of my sandals. They were a really handy part of my equipment. I could use them as slippers in the bedroom and I could walk around the town in them and wear them in the dining room. It was relaxing to slide one's feet into footwear of a different shape after many hours pounding the pedals. Perhaps I should try to repair them.

I pulled the deficient sandal from my bag and studied it. The buckle and strap were intact; it was merely that they had been ripped from the cloth of the shoe. If I had a fixing I could make a hole there in the cloth and reattach it. But I did not have one and I would need an apparatus for making holes. The ideal tool would have been the scissors that I had derisively jettisoned from MyMateMargaret's survival kit. Funny how that kept cropping up. I could hear the sound of my chickens shuffling along the roosting perch to make room for latecomers. Here I was sitting on a bench, wearing my pyjamas and towel. My handlebars were disconnected, my handlebar padding had long since fallen off, the bracket on my saddle had snapped and now my sandals had failed. Did I worry that I would not succeed in this safari? Not for one moment. Not whilst I still possessed my remarkable resourcefulness and stamina. Oh and my modesty, I nearly forgot that.

I frowned at my saddle. Dangling from the back was the key ring that I had picked up yesterday; a split ring that could be attached to the buckle and then passed through a hole yet to be made in the cloth. I searched in the bag containing my toothbrush and dug out my nail clippers. They were not scissors but a pair of vicious little spring loaded steel jaws. When squeezed, they gaily amputated whatever you placed between their teeth without question or compunction. The old lady at the side of me took an intense interest in my operations as I wrestled with the sandal, twisting the ring through the buckle, chipping away at the flesh of the fabric with the corner of the clippers until I could insert the key ring. This must be what it is like to have to pierce a navel, I thought.

I took off one shoe and slipped on the sandal. I walked in a gentle circle around the station yard and then returned to my bench.

'*Ça marche?*' the old lady asked.

'*Ça marche.*' I confirmed.

'*Eh bien, bravo mon gars.*' She rattled her newspaper in a businesslike manner. I could feel my sandal swell with pride at such an unsolicited endorsement.

I check into the hotel, do my housework and then go out to sit in the sunshine outside the café. At one table sits a man with two young boys. An East European woman in long skirt and headscarf comes and begs a cigarette from him. At another table sits a mixed race couple; she, European, he, North African. He has thick spectacles and an even thicker book. His wife looks around at the children playing across the street whilst he reads and drinks from his enormous glass of beer. A mechanic with *'Peugeot'* embroidered across the back of his overalls walks past me to go to the bar. A lady with a child perched on the back of her bicycle calls out to ask if 'Henri' has arrived yet. The *patronne* wanders out and reels in the sunblind a little to protect it from the tugging wind; cars go by, tooting greetings which are returned by various of the customers. The *patronne's* son runs out of the bar. He is wearing white trousers and has long hair. He hops into his mate's car which has pulled up in the street. The lady with the bicycle returns, props up her bike, still with child strapped on the back and goes into the bar to ask for a light for her cigarette.

I become aware of a man behind me who is talking in a desultory manner, as if nobody was listening to him. I don't think they are but I am too feeble to turn around to check and I cannot see a mirror in which to find a reflection. Suddenly the voice becomes louder and more intrusive. It is apparent that the man has imbibed considerably.

'Look at him, Monsieur Perniche, in his white suit. Dressed up like an angel but he's not an angel. He's the devil is Monsieur Perniche.'

A man in a light suit was picking his way across the square before the church.

'Well I never knew that,' the *patronne* replies.

'In his white suit, standing in front of the church like the Angel Gabriel himself. But he's not an angel, he's the devil.'

'What has Monsieur Perniche done to you then?'

'What has he done to me? What has he done to me? I'll tell you what Monsieur Perniche has done to me.'

'Go on then. I'm listening.'

'I'll tell you what he did.' The *patronne* waits. I wait. I can imagine the man drawing himself up in indignation. 'He refused my Jesus Christ, that's what he did.'

I almost turn around in surprise. Luckily the *patronne* is as suprised as I am.

'He did what?'

'I did him a lovely Jesus Christ. The boss had saved me a lump of cherry wood, beautiful it was, I did it out of that. But Monsieur Perniche said he did not want it. He refused my Jesus Christ.'

'Why didn't he want it?'

'He said... he said... "He's got no beard. Jesus Christ had a beard". I told him, "when I do Jesus Christ he is always shaven. My Jesus Christ never has a beard." But he wouldn't have it. He refused to pay for it. The boss was livid with me.'

'Well it wasn't your fault. He should have specified a Jesus Christ with a beard.'

'That's what I said but Monsieur Perniche said that Jesus Christs always have a beard. When he ordered a Jesus Christ he expected to get one with a beard. The boss asked him to take the carving anyway and he said "no, it doesn't look a bit like him." "Doesn't look a bit like him!" I said, "how do you know what Jesus Christ looked like? Have you met him? Have you got a photograph of him? Have you seen his passport?"'

The voice drops to a sodden mumble and I can hear the *patronne* collecting empty glasses from the bar top.

'I didn't know you did carving,' she says.

'I don't now. I used to.'

'Who for?'

'Benoit. He had a workshop over there.'

'Where?'

'It's gone now. They knocked it down to build the super-market.'

'But, the supermarket has been there all the time that I've been here and that is at least six years. When did this happen?'

'About twenty years ago. Look at him, devil in his white suit.'

Across the busy square, the much-maligned Monsieur Perniche, in his white suit, is making for the newsagents, utterly oblivious of the calumny that is being shovelled at him, or of the English cyclist furiously scribbling in a notebook.

Dinner was *fond d'artichauts aux langoustines* as starters – a better class than the weary prawn cocktail of yore. After that I ate a local farm chicken cooked in cider accompanied by roast potatoes and apple. It was delicious. Apples will figure more frequently on the menus now because I am getting close to Normandy. Also, butter is automatically served with the bread, another indicator of the proximity of this prosperous dairy region of France.

At a neighbouring table sit a couple and their adult son.

'And how do you want your steak?' the *patronne* asks him.

'Well cooked.'

'We don't do it well cooked. The furthest we go is medium.'

'But–' his father starts.

'We will bring it medium cooked.'

'But–'

'If he wants it cooked more then we can pass it across the flame again. It's quite simple to work out. You can always cook a bit more but you can't uncook something.' She shrugs this dictum off in the direction of his mother and adds, nodding at the blustering father, 'he's only like this because I was always above him in class.'

Behind me tocks an enormous grandfather clock. It has a date hand on the face and the inscription of the maker, *Neret-Anger, Chateaubriant*. Below, gently swings a pendulum, ornately decorated with wheat sheaves and grapes. At eight o'clock grandfather strikes eight times and then two minutes later it does it again. At half past eight it strikes five times. I discreetly untangle my electric wristwatch from my handkerchief and check the time.

I must go to my room to do some serious telephoning. I have not yet managed to book tomorrow's Golden Lion.

I climb the ten stairs to the two split stairs; I take the eight to the left leaving the seven to climb away at a tangent. Another eight stairs and another split: eight to the right, six to the left. I take the six to my bedroom. But even then I am apparently not high enough: the floor of my room climbs towards the window.

I dial the number of the Lion d'Or at Le Ribay. I had tried to make enquiries of this hotel when in England and the man had told me not to worry, there would be room, just telephone the day before.

'*Allo?*' a woman's voice rings out.

'Is that the Lion d'Or at Le Ribay?'

'I'm his mother.'

Well, I suppose even Golden Lions have to have mothers.

'Have you a single room for tomorrow night?'

'Yes. When will you arrive?'

'I am not sure, it might be after seven o' clock.'

'That's alright, the hotel is closed but we have room.'

I did not like the sound of that. Of course they have got room. If the hotel is closed all the rooms will be empty.

'So, you have a room for me for tomorrow night?'

'Yes. The hotel is closed at the front but I am in the kitchen. I'm his mother. Come into the courtyard and you'll find me there. I'm in the kitchen.'

I had to leave the arrangement there. It was not the status of confirmed booking that I would have liked but one must not be fussy. After all, she was his mother.

17 – Le Ribay

The breakfast room was unlit but madame bade me take a seat so I made for a table by the window so that I could look at my maps whilst waiting. I calculated that by about eleven o'clock in the morning I would appear on the edge of my next map. I was on my way home, I realised. I was now actually making for the Channel. Four more Golden Lions and I would be there. But I still had some serious cycling to do. Today's journey would be over eighty miles but if I found my way correctly, about half of that mileage would be on old railway tracks which would make it easy and fast. The tricky bit was navigating across the gap from the hotel to get me onto the next map. All I knew was that I had to leave Janzé in an easterly direction.

But here comes breakfast so I'll eat first and worry later. I shuffle away my papers whilst madame throws down a paper place mat and lays out plate, cup, croissant, bread jam and butter.

'Tea? Coffee?' she asks.

'Coffee please.'

She retires to her top table and I stick my knife into the bread roll. It explodes like a grenade, showering splinters of bread crust into my pyjamas and across the table top. I glance guiltily across at madame but she does not look up. She is eating her breakfast at a table on a dais by the till, lording it over me like the chief teller in a Dickensian bank. There is no radio and no talking. The only noises are the occasional swish of the newspaper as she turns a page and the varied explosions and eruptions from my battleground as I fight my way through the bread and croissants.

It is not yet eight o'clock. I want to set off early today to give me a good start. I expect it to be a long and tiring day. I have nearly finished my breakfast; the field has been cleared of corpses and unspent ordinance and I can now see the earth beneath. And what stares up at me is a map of the region around the hotel. It is printed on the paper place mat and is rendered in a pictorial style intended to appeal to tourists but it does have the villages and other landmarks clearly identified. I scrape a blob of jam from the local chateau and fold the paper into my pocket.

Half and hour later I am roughly on the blob of jam. The fields are still heavy with dew. It is an autumn morning yet we are in August. A convoy of four stock lorries trundles past me and for the next mile I waft along in a pungent pig pong. At a crossroads a small white van pulls up alongside me. It is absolutely full of asparagus. The fronds are flattened to the glass of the windscreen. Somewhere in there sits a driver but I cannot see him and he certainly cannot see to his right. This must be a disappointment to him since he needs to turn onto the main road. I wait, immobile and invisible whilst he edges blindly out of the junction waiting for the sound of a horn or of crunching metal to warn him of approaching traffic.

This is no longer a region of houses built in white dressed stone; everything is ragstone and brick topped by grey slate roofs; chimney stacks are tiled on all four sides to keep out the wind-driven rain and north facing walls often carry slate cladding which slides to ground level like a huge black waterfall.

By eleven o' clock I have been into three patisseries and still found no savoury pastries. It would seem that north of the Loire the *patissiers* only make sweet tarts; no quiche lorraine or *tarte à l'oignon* or meat pasties. I wonder why? In desperation I buy a pack of ready made sandwiches, just like the examples one sees rotting on the shelves in the local supermarket. The filling is ham and emmenthal and the producer informs me that this offering is part of the *'Grand Jury Sandwich Club'*. What on earth the French make of such a nonsensical use of English I cannot imagine. Neither can I picture them ingesting these sandwiches. I have eaten more appetising dishcloths. Oh yes I have.

The sun breaks through the mist at midday and I am now on my map. The paper place mat I have discarded with the uneaten remains of the disgusting sandwiches. I reach the first of my cycle tracks. It is largely straight and remarkably deserted and it leads me sixteen miles to the town of Laval. Where the track crosses roads on former level crossings the authorities have erected warning signs for cyclists; they are cartoon representations of a cyclist smashing into a car. No other warning necessary, really. Under the shade of an avenue of trees, I disturb enormous green lizards which zig-zag away, and a four foot long grass snake. At least, I tell myself it was only a grass snake.

I want to avoid mixing with the town of Laval. It is large and busy and in my way. The only fact that I can recall about it is that it was known for its manufactory of duck cloth. Whether this is still the case I could not say and I did not wish to find out. Thankfully, the old railway line curves around towards the north of Laval and just when it feels like making a feint for the town centre, it stops, dumping me in a sprawling partially finished development of dispersed industries and housing estates linked by flyovers and fast dual carriageways. This is not such a disaster as it sounds since the highway engineers have provided broad cycle tracks alongside the motor carriageways. A road graded for cars, with its long straight descents and swooping bridges is less enjoyable for a cyclist and the new embankments of bare earth provide no cover from the wind, when one encounters it, but all I have to do is follow the blue cycle signs to La Mayenne. I debate with myself for a while upon the meaning of this information since I need to go to the town of La Mayenne by cycling up the bank of the river La Mayenne, so is the sign directing me to the town or the river? As it transpires, I am a little previous in my anxiety because here I am back at this roundabout again, having followed the signs and cycled in a three mile circle.

I must have missed a turning somewhere. I start off again, checking at each underpass and crossing that I am following La Mayenne. At some crossings there is no sign and so I have to guess. When I see a park full of brand new minibuses I recognise the style of coachwork as being that of the company Gruau. This is bad news because on my previous attempt to follow the signs I distinctly remember passing along the front of the works. I cannot deduce what the inconsistency is in the signing. Is it deficient or is there some element that I am misunderstanding? I turn back towards the original roundabout and start to pick up the signs again. And then I notice what the quirk is: the signs are all right-pointing boards. Not one of them points to the left. I did not know whether they had forgotten to order the left-pointing signs or whether they were still waiting for them to arrive, but it meant that only the right hand turns would be signposted; the left turns you guess at. I realise that wherever I come to a possible left turn I need to take that road, even if I have to cross through an underpass, until I come to the first right turn. If there is no sign pointing to La Mayenne I need to turn back and pick up my original route. By this process, forty five minutes later than I should have done, I reach the river La Mayenne.

When planning my route I had dithered over choosing this track. It was not an old railway track; it was a path along the river. My experience of such paths had been that they could vary between two extremes of quality: one might be a four metre wide strip of billiard smooth tarmacadam whilst its sister might offer a rugged donkey spine of brickbats, broken glass and potholes. This was a risk that I had to take. I needed the path to give me the mileage to reach today's Golden Lion but it could only do so if it were navigable. It was beautiful. The surface varied from loose gravel, with the occasional puddle to good tarmac. I sat under the shade of trees at a picnic bench and ate some lunch. Out on the broad Mayenne, the occasional pleasure craft would drift by, usually with a broad-bellied captain standing at the wheel whilst an hour glass female in a bikini selflessly did her best to protect the superstructure from the deleterious effects of the rays of the sun.

The Mayenne seems to be a broad river in a narrow valley. In the nineteenth century it was rendered navigable by a system of weirs to maintain the depth and reduce the speed of the current. At each weir there is a lock and lock-keeper's cottage... and a power station. Set into the weirs are water turbines. I can hear them whining as I cycle upstream. They are called 'micro power stations' and supply the French electricity grid.

It is now a sunny Friday afternoon in August and as I pass each lock cottage I often say '*bonjour*' to a keeper sitting outside on the step or a deck chair. At the next lock I watch as the lady keeper operates the lock to pass a cabin cruiser downstream. The captain ignores her completely and does not even thank her. She waves and shrugs and then climbs into her car and drives down to the next lock to operate that one as well.

When I espy the café on the river bank, I stop. I have already covered over sixty miles and consider that I am entitled to a drink. This is obviously a popular spot for the tourists as well as the locals. The terrace spreads its silver chairs and tables across the towpath and the four waitresses are dancing a constant ballet of bottles, glasses and cups. These aluminium tables are all very nice and do not rot in the winter but they are most inhospitable in bright sunlight. Whichever way I sit there seems to be five or six bright reflections of the sun flashing kaleidoscope designs into my sun specs.

A confused shuffling starts at the far end of the terrace and then customers begin to stand up and drag their chairs and tables aside. A huge camper van is on its way to the campsite and has to drive through us to get there. Some of the customers are reluctant to make any effort at all, rather as if the wife were vacuum cleaning the front room and they hope that if they just pick up their feet the van will be able to squeeze under.

At the town of La Mayenne I call in at the tourist office and try to charm the young lady there into telling me how to get onto the last of my cycle tracks of the day. She is very interested in my safari and precociously attempts to order a copy of the book before it is written. I refrain from hurting her feelings by pointing out that by her inability to direct me to the cycle track she might be putting the whole enterprise into jeopardy; instead I wheedle out of her the probable location of the railway station.

No trains run now into La Mayenne. The station lies abandoned in an enormous yard – acres of derelict ground scattered with crumbs of railway engineering. I find the track and cycle past the station and onto smooth tarmac. This path is very popular; people are walking their dogs or teaching their children to ride. After about ten minutes of slaloming around tricycles and outrunning dogs I began to feel that something is wrong. Why is the sun over there? If I am cycling eastwards, it should be more over *there*. I turn around and return to the station. Crossing the road I find the trace of the lines departing northwards. I plunge into a copse of dark green and when I am presented with a choice of three tracks I take the extreme right, working on the theory that it must turn to the east. It does and soon I am out of the town and alone, running alongside a gentle stream, the track bordered by low hedges.

What is this up ahead? It looks like somebody pushing a bicycle. It is a lady wearing orange trousers.

'Have you got a problem?' I ask.

'Puncture.'

'Shall I mend it for you?' I look at her great knobbly tyres and then ask the clinching question. 'Do you have a pump? Mine won't fit your valves.'

I know what the answer will be.

'No, I don't have a pump.'

'There is not a lot of sense in my repairing the puncture then if we can't inflate the tyre.'

She looks down at her tyre and pulls a face.

'I'm trying to get to Grazay. Does this go to Grazay?'

'The last sign I saw was for Marcillé la Ville.'

'That's not far then. I think I'll walk.'

The stream was too shallow to swim in. Unless she could fly, I could see no other choice for her.

A few miles further on I left the track to complete the final five miles to Le Ribay. By now I had cycled seventy nine miles and I felt it. It was not really necessary for France to provide me with a one and a half mile gradient at 1 in 9 to warm me up. I slogged up it in my bottom gear. I slowly crept by a house standing on a bank at the edge of the wood. A family were sitting at a dining table in the garden, silently eating their evening meal.

'Good evening,' I called in English. They could only be English if they were eating in silence. The UK-registered car parked in the drive merely confirmed my deduction.

Le Ribay eventually loomed into sight. It was a small settlement spread along the main road. I could see the Lion d'Or from a distance. It was a rectangular building on the road frontage. As I got nearer I could see the white paper stuck over all the windows and when I dismounted outside I was able to read the note on the door, *'closed for the month of August'*.

Was this anything to worry about? Had his mother not said that the hotel was closed? I freewheeled down into the yard. One car was parked there. It had Brittany registration plates so it was not a local for we were now in Normandy. What had the Golden Lion's mother said? 'Come around to the back I shall be in the kitchen.' She was sitting waiting for me. She opened the door and gave me a key.

'It's up the stairs. The room has three beds, choose whichever one you want. The shower is along the corridor. Come down when you want dinner.'

I had a choice of three shampoos and four body gels in the shower. Whether they belonged to the hotel or the other guests, if there were any, was unclear but I helped myself. When I came down to the dining room, a couple were just leaving the table. I say 'table' because there was only one table.

'Ah monsieur,' said the lady, 'you will be cosseted by this lady. You will be cosseted.'

Well, they seemed pleased with their stay.

The Lion's mother sat me at the table and came in with a blackboard upon which she had written the menu. I started with *melon au jambon*, followed by a venison steak served with chips and green beans. The chips had been peeled from proper potatoes, not moulded in a press from reconstituted potato flour, and every one of them was crisp.

The Lion's mother came to sit with me.

'I was a bit worried when I saw the sign saying that the hotel was closed,' I admitted ingenuously. Actually, I had been devastated but I hid it well, didn't I?

'It is closed. My son runs the hotel but he has gone to Guadaloupe to play golf so somebody has to look after the hotel in case of leaks or fire. And in any case, the gendarme cadet from up the road comes in for his lunch and dinner and if we closed he would have nowhere to eat so I am cooking twice a day. And if anybody phones up for a room then I tell them to come. It gives me somebody to talk to.

I'm seventy four and I have a friend I used to walk with but I walk too fast for her and now I have nobody to talk to. I can't talk on my own. It's depressing here especially in the winter; always in the dark. This way I get the chance to talk and chat.' She waved her arm around the room. 'The hotel is being painted at the moment. Normally we would eat in the dining room through there, with proper napkins and that.' I could see tables and chairs stacked against the wall and covered with dust sheets. 'The beans and potatoes are from our garden just across the road. We eat vegetables from the garden for eight months of the year.'

'Do you get many people in?'

'When we are open?'

This conversation was veering towards the surreal.

'Yes.'

'We sometimes have about sixty for lunch. Lunch is always nine euros eighty. We get lots of lorry drivers in. And for dinner we get about thirty five, because we've got the President just up the road.'

'And having the President up the road brings in trade?'

'Oh yes. The men come to do a job for perhaps a week at a time and they stay here. They don't mind sharing rooms.'

'Has Monsieur Sarkozy ever eaten here?'

'Monsieur Sarkozy? No. Why should he come in here?'

'You only get the workers then?'

'Sometimes we have eight or nine at a time. I think the company pays them a lodging allowance and by coming here and sharing rooms they can save a bit. Yes they are often here. I suppose with a factory of that size there are always machines that need repairing.'

And it was at this point that I remembered that in France there is a company which makes butter under the brand name, *'Le President.'* Good job I remembered that or it might have led to misunderstandings.

18 – La Fresnaye sur Chédouet

The sun was shining from a suspiciously pale sky when I strapped my bags back onto my bicycle after breakfast.

'Do you carry everything you need in those bags?' the Golden Lion's mother enquired in wonder.

'Yes, but when you cycle you learn to do without a lot of non-essential things.' Like clothes, for instance.

'Well I guarantee you a fine day today.' She aimed a fragile hand at the sky. 'It will stay fine like this all day.'

Perhaps the sun always shines on the Golden Lion's mother but for me, three kilometres down the road it went into cloud and I did not see it again for the rest of the day. This main road was part of the route of the traditional Paris-Brest cycle race as was confirmed by occasional ancient cast iron plaques which I could see bolted high up on walls and which announced the distance in kilometres from Paris in one direction and Brest in the other.

The motor traffic was busy in a bustling sort of way. It was not dithering, it had places to go. It was Saturday morning and I was astride another one of those frenetic 'all change' weekends that the French build into their holiday periods to provide the tension necessary to poison any enjoyment they may have harvested on vacation. I decided to conduct a traffic census and I compared the registration districts of the first one hundred vehicles which I saw at nine thirty, ten thirty and eleven thirty. The first result was fifty strangers to fifty local; that was a ratio already heavily distorted by the number of out-of-district cars setting out or returning from their holidays. By ten thirty the ratio had diverged further to sixty versus forty locals. At eleven thirty, the locals must have all arrived where they were going for the ratio was a staggering eighty five to fifteen. This data collection and analysis proved absolutely nothing but it did fill in the time.

I had been looking for a decent patisserie since I had set off but such an establishment had so far eluded me. The last village had offered me only half a bread shop but two thriving veterinary surgeries. That was a settlement ripe for a searching sociological study, I would opine.

The first picnic site of the day loomed up and I stopped for elevenses. At first view I thought it was a cemetery. It was a neat garden surrounded by a six foot hedge. I wheeled my bicycle into the enclave like a sheep entering a fold. Outside was a road full of noisy wolves. What had I got that I could eat? I unearthed a soggy pizza from the strata of my luggage. This was real archaeology. I remembered buying this morsel at least two days earlier. It had travelled one hundred and twenty five miles since then. I was impressed by its resilience in the face of such an ordeal but reasoned that structural integrity should not be an overriding factor when assessing the suitability of a pizza as appetising nourishment. If it could stand up that well to nearly three days' pounding on the roads of Normandy would it succumb quiescently to my molars? I chose to halt my investigation at that challenge and threw the disc into the rubbish bin. In the same bag I found two soft nectarines. In the same bag! I ask you, who would be so stupid as to put two nectarines into a bag with a pizza?

As punishment, I ate them both and detected a slight cheesy tang in them. Whilst I was sitting there, I heard the sound of a car slowing to a halt on the verge outside. A door slammed and then a woman in a red shirt and blue slacks came through the gap in the hedge. She looked around, stepped forward and then espied me grinning a welcome with nectarine juice running down my jowls. She hesitated and then retreated. Ten seconds later she reappeared, grasping a pink toilet roll before her like a ceremonial sword. With eyes afront she marched straight up the garden and through the hedge into the field beyond.

By consuming the fruit and discarding the pizza I had committed the inexcusable crime of leaving myself without any provisions at all. Long ago I had made it a rule to never discard the old food until the new food was in the bag. Yes it was soggy. Yes it was unappetising but who is to say that I would find anywhere to reprovision myself today? When you face the prospect of cycling all day on an empty stomach even the most compliant of tepid pizzas can be lovingly unfolded and wolfed down. But I had bunged it into the bin. It was a reckless move.

But man cannot live on predetermined action alone; he must take risks to gain reward and at the entrance to the next village I was rewarded by the sight of a mountain of patisserie squatting on the counter in a small shop. I went in. The shop was the front room of the old house. The only piece of furniture in it was a large counter with a marble top. In the middle of this had been dumped a pile of bread and croissants and other patisseries. And I mean 'dumped'. It looked as if somebody had just emptied a sack out onto the table. As I stood looking at it, a man came in from the back of the room. He was thickset and ruddy faced. His sleeves were rolled up in a businesslike manner and he was wearing blue overalls.

'Help yourself.' He designated the chaos of croissants with a wave of his hand; a hand whose every crevice and finger nail was ingrained with white. I had thought from the outside that this was merely a *depot de pain* but from the state of his hands it was obvious that he was the master baker. I rummaged through the pile as if I were at a jumble sale, discarding loaves and burrowing under baguettes to pull out a *pain au chocolat*. 'Bags are on the string. Just pull one off,' he suggested. I ripped off a bag. 'Have you got the right money?' I nodded. 'Just leave it on the counter.' He disappeared back through the door.

I piled up the coins and twisted together the corners of the paper bag. I had obviously interrupted him in the middle of some culinary operation and that had been the reason why he had not wanted to touch anything with his hands. Having satisfied myself with this deduction I cycled away, only wavering slightly to acknowledge his *'au revoir'*. He delivered it to me from the top of a ladder which he had propped up against the side wall of the house. There he stood in his overalls, a paint roller in one hand and a paint pot in the other, methodically resuming the whitewashing of his house from the point where I had interrupted him.

I pressed on along the road, tucking my towel closer into my pyjamas because I was beginning to feel a little chilly. The sky was elephant grey, the traffic was a monotonous stream of cars in both directions. The next picnic stop was a large crescent of the old road which lunged out over a valley side. I sat at a wooden table and ate a snack. On the far side of the curve a small hatchback was parked with its tailgate raised. A man and a woman stood at the back, using the small area of load platform which was not stacked with holiday goods as a kitchen table on which they tartined and saucissed and drinking red wine from clear plastic toothmugs, no doubt rescued from their last night's stay.

It was all rather civilised. So far, nobody had appeared cuddling a toilet roll. The door of the car nearest to me opened and a lady's many-ringed hand dropped a dog to the tarmac. The dog wandered off, attached to his mistress by one of those infuriating dog leads that unreel like a surveyor's measure to about a hundred yards, sweeping innocent walkers from their feet like felled timber and, more importantly, physically distancing the owner from any pangs of guilt or compassion they might have felt at the ruction caused by their errant canine. The dog in question suddenly made up its mind. It waddled straight over to my table and cocked up his leg against the strut nearest my foot. Thank you madam.

A black spot was dangling before my eyes. For a dreaded moment I took it to be another floater, heralding an acceleration in the break up of my retina, but it wriggled and then began to climb back up to the rim of my cap. It was a spider. What nourishment did a spider think it was going to catch by spinning a web on the peak of a cap as it whisked through the air at twelve mph?

Before setting out again I pulled my anorak on over my pyjamas because I was definitely feeling the chill now. Back on the road the traffic was ceaseless, cars cruising slowly by, nose to tail, all looking for a peeable hedge.

I reached Alençon, the *préfecture* of the *département* of the Orne, and made a few purchases at the food shops before they closed for lunch. Then I sat in a small garden and, under the gaze of a Mauritian lady seated on the opposite bench, I pushed tablets of cream cheese into croissants and ate them with an enormous tomato. When my lunch was finished I wrote my latest postcard to my daughter. I had sent several cards so far. I always chose a card which featured a cow since she was more interested in animals than churches. And I usually inscribed it with a witty, some might say, inane, epithet to amuse her. In all I mailed her nine postcards from my safari. What a pity I put the wrong house number on every single one of them. She never received them. Somewhere in her street there is a kitchen whose fridge still wonders why it has nine assorted foreign cows stuck on its door.

Alençon had a brief period of fame in 1944 during the allied invasion of Normandy for it was through Alençon that the American troups had charged on their hurried way to trap the German Army. The XVth corps of the US 12th.

Army had been fighting its way southwards through Normandy to the Loire. When they reached Le Mans, way to the south of me, on the 8th August, General Bradley, aware of the rapidly developing strategic situation, had asked permission to reverse his advance. He turned his corps northwards from Le Mans and in three days passed through Alençon on his way back towards the beachhead and the town of Falaise. It was this force which provided the southern jaw of the pincers which were intended to close on the enemy at the Falaise gap.

In the nineteenth century Alençon was known for its linen products and lace. The *département* temporarily exported workers to neighbouring regions, most went to help with the harvest but some worked as specialist mole destroyers, roaming Northern France and Belgium in search of employment

Now Alençon is just a county town. But only just, for the county boundary runs along the river Sarthe and thus the southern part of the town is annexed to the neighbouring *département*. I blame it all on the river. I have remarked before upon this imperial attitude that French rivers display. The Sarthe is a land-grabbing opportunist usurper. It rises in a *département* named after another river, the Orne. Taking umbrage at this slight it then tries to drag the head town, Alençon, into its own *département*, the Sarthe. As if this were not enough, having flowed through one *préfecture*, it runs through its own, Le Mans, and then sets its sights on another by joining the Loire at Angers, which is the county town of the next *département*.

The old red brick offices of the *préfecture* hide behind an imposing grill. The road outside it is ruptured tarmac laid on rucked up pavé. One minute I was bouncing along the crenellations of an enormous pie crust, the next I was wobbling along the top of a split baguette. It was a patisserie of potholes. Around the corner, the sterile five storey office blocks of the *cité administrative* housed today's civil servants.

I realised belatedly that I had made too much progress for the day. I was not far from my next Lion at La Fresnaye and it was still the early afternoon. Sitting in a public park under a distempered sky, flinching at the strident scream of the town's allocation of underpowered motorcycles as their helmetted pilots, looking for all the world like coloured map pins, spurred them on to decibels unbelievable, was not my idea of a relaxing afternoon. In an unexpected but welcome lull, the church bells rang out a shaky version of the first line of *Ride a Cock Horse to Banbury Cross*. I looked at Dobbin, Dobbin looked at me and we decided to concur with its suggestion and finish our day's journey.

I knew by which direction I needed to leave the town, I just didn't know how to get there so I popped into the tourist office and posed my problem to the lady there.

'Where are you going?'

'I'm cycling to La Fresnaye sur Chédouet.'

'Why? There is nothing there.'

'I rather hope there will be a hotel called the Lion d'Or, since I reserved a room in it several days ago.'

'Oh really?' She did not sound convinced. 'And you are cycling there?'

I nodded. 'So I don't want to go on a main road. According to my map–'

'What happened to your map? This is only a piece of it. Where is the rest?'

I thought I would introduce too many complications into her life if I replied, 'on my kitchen floor' so I told her that it was on my bike. She pulled a photocopied street plan onto the counter and inked in a street.

'That is what you need – the Avenue de la Republique. You're lucky, it crosses just up the road.'

She was right in a manner of speaking. It crossed on a bridge, access to which was by eighteen very steep steps up which I had to carry my bicycle. My route out to the village of La Fresnaye was by a series of quiet back roads. I could

understand the tourist office lady's bafflement as to why a
cyclist should want to rusticate himself thus but then,
perhaps like me, she had not known about the Bicycle
Museum at La Fresnaye. It was huge and modern and well
stocked and I managed to spend an interesting hour
amongst the frames and wheels and posters and film clips.

As I left the museum I could hear music booming out in
the village. Was it a local fete day? Was it a carnival? The
village itself was deserted. The only animation came from
the inane rock music which was bellowing from the open
door of a hovel on the crossroads. It was some kind of bar
but of the meanest order; a ramshackle single storey shed
which joined the ends of two streets on the right angle like
a rusty bracket on a rotten sash window. It was dowdy, it was
a flea pit, it was the Hotel du Lion d'Or.

I stared at it in utter dismay. I did not want to cross its
threshold. In parts of the Far East where I had worked, such
an establishment would have represented the latest luxury
and I would have patronised it gladly but in rural France
the norms are different.

Where is your fibre? Where is your resilience? Here you
are at your sixteenth Lion. Only two more to go and you are
baulking at a little squalor? I heaved a majestic sigh of
resignation, looked for and failed to find a sympathetic
audience, and went in. Madame *la patronne* was a child of
the French Commonwealth; whether from Polynesia or the
Indian Ocean I could not say.

'I phoned some days ago to book a room.'

'Ah yes, Monsieur Lloyd, isn't it?'

'That's correct. Where can I store my bicycle?'

'I'll open the big doors down the side there and you can
put it in the yard.'

I unhook my bags and dump them in the bar. I wheel
poor old Dobbin into the claustrophobic yard and leave
him contemplating the dustbins. I collect my bags and
follow madame up a dark narrow staircase. It smells of old

food and dirty carpet. She pushes open a door and hands me the key.

'This is your room.'

'And I can have dinner here tonight?'

'Yeah, yeah. Come down at half past seven.'

I tentatively approach the window. The view through the cobwebbed glass is that of the crossroads. I am in the attic of the shed. There is no number on the door but a staff timetable is nailed on the back where one would expect to see the tariff card. I remember my phone call to reserve a room and the *patronne's* confidence that there would be a space for me. Of course there would, she has simply turned out whoever would normally sleep here. The magenta patterned bedlinen is of what I would charitably describe as a 'cosy freshness'. I did not feel that I would be the first person to have slept in it.

I feel my way across the black landing to the toilet at the top of the stairs. The cabinet is lined with dark blue ruched cloth which is stained brown and peeling from the damp patches on the wall. Around the door handle it is grubby with the marks of groping hands. There is no toilet seat. Who needs one anyway?

Back in my room there is no soap. The water will not drain out of the cracked sink because the latter leans forward from the wall so I have to swish the water uphill to the plughole. I can find no functioning light in the room, there are no curtains and no shutters but luckily there hangs outside the window, an illuminated advertising sign. Might be a bit awkward should I want to sleep tonight.

I lie on the bed and watch the two flies dancing around the non-functioning light bulb. 'Will you walk into my parlour? said the spider to the fly'. I remember my nursery rhymes and suddenly I am full of an outrage of indignation. The rhyme is based on a patent deceit. Has anybody in the whole history of mankind ever seen a fly caught in a spider's web? I have not. Have you? In my house the spiders live on a diet of wood lice. In the garden the webs are full of dandelion seeds and bird feathers. On the road, spiders weave webs on my cap but I have never seen in real life the nursery book realisation of a fly in a web. It is an absolute fiction. It does not happen. And to prove it, the two flies continue their Viennese waltz around the ballroom of my ceiling whilst the dust-encrusted webs stretched across the windows and lodged in the corners of the walls, yawn with unassuaged hunger.

I go down to dinner. Standing at the bar are three men and a boy. The boy is bored and wants to go home but the men still have some drinking to do. The village people are coming in for dinner. I sit at a table in the dining end of the room. The décor here is tangerine and lime. And still the diners arrive. Two of them are on holiday and have been invited out by their locally resident friends. I do not know what they eat, but I have no choice. An unsmiling girl drops a plate onto my table. Stuck to its upper surface are one slice each of four different sausages. The bread is stale. The water I drink is tap water which was been poured into a plastic water bottle. This receptacle has been used so many times that the plastic shows white stress marks where one habitually grasps it to pour. My main course is a sausage and some rice in a tepid tomatoish sauce. The cheese board arrives straight from the fridge. The wood is clammy and cold and so slimy that I fail to make a purchase on it to move it nearer to me across the table. I have to cut the soft cheese at arm's length. Desert is a commercial ice cream cornet, still in its paper wrapper and served on a plate.

I return to my room and lie on the bed, waiting for the sign outside my window to extinguish so that I can sleep.

Saturday night at the Lion d'Or.

It's all MyMateMargaret's fault that I am here and I have not even got a telephone so that I can tell her.

That is probably fortuitous. She can be a mite touchy sometimes.

Hunting the Golden Lion

La Fresnaye – Home

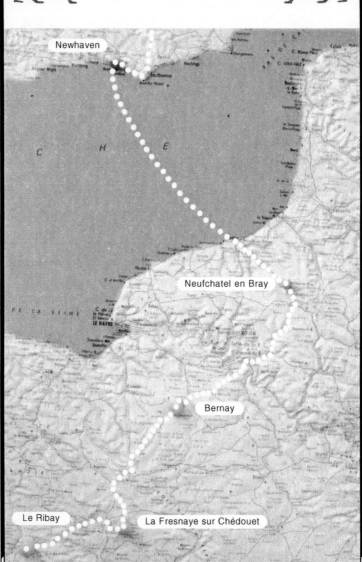

Newhaven

Neufchatel en Bray

Bernay

Le Ribay

La Fresnaye sur Chédouet

19 – Bernay

Iknow what Sundays are like in the French countryside. Hairy and I once stayed a Saturday night in an isolated hotel in the valley of the Somme. When we arose the next morning, nobody was up. We managed to find an unlocked door and loaded up our bikes and had put the money in an envelope and were in the act of pushing it under the front door when a bleary-eyed rustic dragged the door open and invited us in for the breakfast that we had thought we were having to forego.

So when the house had retired last night I had noted how the floorboards in my room had creaked and groaned as the residents had crammed themselves two to a bed next door and when I awoke on the Sunday morning, vibrant with the intention of leaving before midday, I walked back and forth, the length and breadth of my room until every board had protested and every joint had creaked; thus could I be sure that all the occupants of the Golden Lion would be awake.

I clattered down the dark staircase and spat my way through the flies towards the bar. In the ante-room a teenaged girl whom I assumed to be the daughter of the house was slumped sulkily on a chair against the wall. I greeted her with a sunny, 'bonjour' and received a sullen scowl in return, her insolent eyes tracking me as I crossed the room. I wondered whether it was she who had been evicted to provide my lodging for the night. I had to hope that she had not been obliged to spend the night in the chair.

I ate my breakfast, I paid up and I retrieved Dobbin from the rubbish bins. He heaved a sigh of relief but refused to speak to me until after lunch at which point he signalled his displeasure with a single *clang* on the clinkometer.

I had about fifty five miles before me, twenty of which would be in a dead straight line on the *nationale* but they would not be as monotonous as my early road through the Landes because here the terrain would be undulating to add variety.

The countryside around La Fresnaye was mixed pasture and arable. I crossed an insignificant stream and then realised that this was the perfidious river Sarthe on its way to try to seduce another county town. I crossed the main road to Mamers and entered a dark deciduous forest. It was deliciously silent on this Sunday morning. The only sounds were the tapping of the mist dropping from the trees and the whirring of my tyres on the road. But that was not the only thing on the road. There must have been a dispute running between the locals and a waste disposal company for the highway was now a billboard for their opinions which they had daubed in huge letters on the tarmac. *'No to the rubbish in the wood'* and *'No to the SITA'* the latter I deduced was the offending company. One blaze boldly claimed that the Office National des Forets was on their side but as none of the slogans was signed, you could choose whose side you believed the state forests commmission to be supporting.

I dawdled in the odour of damp woodland, in no hurry to reach the main road that I was looking for to take me to my next Golden Lion. Through the trees ran a railway line and right in the middle of the forest I found a railway station; a dark, damp, silent building cowering under the trees, hiding from the public gaze. Why was it there?

Nobody lived in the forest, there was no habitation of any sort, so why was a station built? Perhaps I should have stopped and asked somebody but I would have waited a long time to find a person from whom to enquire.

And making me wait a long time was what the traffic light at Essay had placed top of its agenda this Sunday morning. I sat astride my top tube under the red glare of its disapproval whilst I watched the traffic not pass on the other road. This was Sunday morning for heaven's sake, there is nobody on the road except me. I have seen only one car in the last forty minutes so be a good sport and change to green. After two minutes I realised that it would never change for me. Its apparatus had failed to detect my arrival. As far as the traffic light was concerned, I was a non-entity. It is galling to discover an inanimate object which demonstrates the ability to arrive at the same conclusion as had a large portion of contemporary society but I took the snub philosophically. I was still stuck with the red light though. Now, I am a law abiding soul, generally speaking, and I am not one of those cyclists who habitually jumps lights and rides on pavements so, in the middle of a deserted Sunday French village I dismounted and walked my bicycle through the red light. Before I had got my leg over the saddle to remount, the local gendarmes had driven past in the opposite direction. I tipped my head back and blew a kiss heavenwards.

This road was taking me to the town of Sées where I would join the *nationale*. The weather was now muggy as the sun was still failing to break through the mist. What breeze there was, blew from the south which suited me as I would be cycling northwards all day.

Sées was a bustling little town, teeming with French people jumping from cars to buy bread and flowers before everything shut at midday. The main street took a drunken stagger around the cathedral which had plonked itself down in the middle of the town, uncompromisingly astride the obvious through-route. I suppose that was one way of getting your beliefs noticed but it was a little unnecessary for it was impossible to escape the religious presence in the town; the place was stuffed full of churches, presbyteries, archbishops' palaces, monasteries and other miscellaneous religious institutions. Luckily they also had food shops.

Having stocked up for lunch I continued my journey northwards out of the town. By now I had crossed the geological divide. Ever since the Loire I had been trundling along on the igneous or metamorphic rocks – the granites and other products of ancient volcanic action but when I had cleared Alençon yesterday, I had passed onto the jolly old sedimentaries as represented by the limestones and chalks of Eastern Normandy. And now I was climbing to the Normandy watershed, just north east of Sées from which ten rivers disperse radially, draining to the Seine, the Loire and the coast of the Cotentin Peninsula. It was a *bocage* of fields hemmed in by hedges, a land of cider and horse breeding. To remind me of the importance of the latter, for the last hour I had been overtaken by numerous horse boxes carrying trotting horses. A few miles over to my left lay the famous French national horse stud called '*Le Haras du Pin*'. Do you remember the French minister Colbert who replanted that Forest of Tronçais so that the French navy would have oak for its ships? Well it was the very same chap who founded the *Haras du Pin* in 1665 to improve the horse stock of France. What a busy chap he must have been.

The southerly wind which had been whisking me along at a brisk pace suddenly switches around to the west and throws a cloudfull of rain at me. Shall I stop and put on my waterproof-that-isn't? If I had been wearing the cycling shirt that I had forgotten on my bed in England I would be able to just shrug off the light rain. I decide to pedal on through the drizzle in the hope that the heat produced by my effort would dry me off. As I cycle along I think of my safari and realise that I am now counting down from the other end.

I no longer remind myself that I am aiming for my seventeenth Golden Lion in a row but rather that I have only two more to go.

I leave the main road at Broglie and thunder down the winding hill into the small town. From here, according to MyMateMargaret, there is a railway cycle track to take me into Bernay and my Golden Lion.

I stop at the square and sit outside a café whilst the family inside finishes screaming and howling its way through its Sunday lunch. The adults are shouting their opinions at each other across the great table whilst on the periphery the shrimps wail, whine and cry for attention. I have great difficulty believing that this is a French family. In my experience, French children by the age of about three years have been taught how to conduct themselves at table. This family must have slipped through the net. Perhaps it is this cacophony that is preventing the waiter from taking my order. After ten minutes he pokes his head out of the doorway.

'Monsieur?'

'Coffee, please.'

He nods and disappears back inside. I sit for another ear-jangling five minutes then he walks out of the bar and crosses the road. In order to reassure me that, despite appearances, he has my every comfort in hand, he throws over his shoulder and vaguely in my direction, that superb French oxymoron, *'J'arrive. J'arrive pour le café.'* — 'I am arriving for the coffee.'

He bloody well was not; he was walking across the square with a cardboard box in his arms. How could that be categorised as 'arriving for the coffee'? I find dishonest this French use of the word 'arrive' to mean, 'I am leaving.' In the workplace, if you ask a Frenchman to stay there and perform a task for you when he has set his mind on doing something else, he will walk away from you, shouting *'j'arrive'* through the door which he slams behind him.

If you interrupt a Frenchwoman who is engrossed in an interesting operation and ask her to come over to you, she will call, *'j'arrive'* whilst she stands stock still and continues doing what she is doing until her satisfaction is fulfilled. When the French say, *'j'arrive'* in such circumstances, they actually mean, 'Shut up and wait. Can't you see that I have something far more interesting to do? I will get around to you eventually.'

I watched the waiter slide the empty wine bottles into the cavernous recycling skip. I counted them. There were fourteen. And the cardboard box could be crushed and put in the other skip. And then he could chat to the lady washing the step of the florist's. In his mind, he was still arriving. To his way of thinking, he was practically on the point of laying a steaming cup of coffee on the table before me. A task which he actually accomplished in a remarkably short span of time, once he had finished 'arriving.'

MyMateMargaret's cycle track was brilliant. The rain had stopped, the mist had dispersed and here I was, zinging along on smooth tarmac under dripping leafy trees. I was finishing the day's journey as I had started it: amongst the smells of damp woodland and the watery green light of foliage. I reached Bernay in the mid-afternoon and located my Lion d'Or quite easily but it was too early to retire. And in any case, I had work to do. I needed to decide my route out of Bernay to my final Lion d'Or at Neufchatel en Bray. In my own little understated way, I was quite excited. My safari was nearly over.

The cycle route led me, as one could imagine, to the railway station but according to the signs, the track had been extended by another ten kilometres. Those kilometres could be useful to me tomorrow. I cast about in an attempt to pick up the continuation; cycling up blind alleys and into people's driveways but I failed completely. This was bizarre. The signs were quite clear. It was the track which was inevident so I entered an office block opposite the station.

'Madame, could you tell me please how to get to the continuation of the cycle track from Broglie?'

'The cycle track from Broglie? You come in by the garden centre and you cross the road there. It used to be a level crossing.'

'Yes, I came that way from Broglie. I passed the garden centre and crossed the road.'

'Well, there you are then.' She smiled, satisfied at having joined up the circle for me.

'But I am looking for the extension from Bernay.'

'Well, you cross the road by the garden centre and follow it on and it takes you to Broglie.'

'Yes, I know that. I have just come from Broglie.'

'Well there you are then.' She contentedly completed another circle. Was she trying to construct the emblem for the Olympic Games? Thankfully for my sanity a colleague had been following the discussion from behind her computer screen.

'He's going in the other direction, Marie-T.'

'Yes, I am hoping to,' I said to the fringe of curls and the eyebrows which peered above the vdu screen like Chad on the garden wall. *'Wot no cycle track?'*

'You'll have to go by road,' the fringe told me.

'I was looking for the track. The signs say that it goes on out of Bernay.'

'Yes they do. They've put the signs up but the track has not been made yet. They had to put all the signs up at once you see.'

Perhaps the local authority should negotiate with Laval, for the latter town has a cycle track ready but only right-pointing signs whereas Bernay has the signs in place but not the track. I cycled off down the road to the junction and stopped short of the roundabout to read the signs. As I stood there, comparing names with those on my map, another cyclist rolled up. He was bearded and his bicycle was weighed down by camping equipment.

'Is this the good way to Le Neubourg?' he enquired in thick Germanic tones.

'That is exactly what I am trying to decide. Are you going to Le Neubourg?'

'Ya.'

'So am I, but not until tomorrow. I am staying in a hotel here. Are you camping?'

'Ya.'

I looked up at the sign.

'That is the road you want. The one marked "*Serquigny*".' I showed him my map.

'Ya, that is good. You have more names on your map.'

This was not surprising. His map covered a vaste swathe of North West Europe. Ideal if you are leading a Panzer division to the Caucasus but not much use to a cyclist.

'Are you on your way home now?'

'Ya, to Germany.'

I thought of the plains of Northern France and the flatness of Belgium and Holland and compared them to what I had covered from the Pyrenees.

'Well you will have a nice easy ride now. It's flat all the way to Germany.'

'No, it is not.' His contradiction was adamant.

'Well, you go up through Belgium and Holland.'

'No, no. Germans, we go through the Ardennes.'

'Ah yes, of course, Germans go through the Ardennes. I had forgotten the Ardennes,' I admitted, tactfully trying to expunge the curving arrowheads of the Schlieffen Plan and the Battle of the Bulge from the history text book of my mind.

Since I had last visited, several years earlier, the Lion d'Or at Bernay had leased part of its ground floor to a Chinese restaurant. I pushed my bicycle through the archway and parked it in the courtyard. There I found a new entrance door. The girl at the reception desk had my key ready and assured me that the bicycle would be safe where I had locked it. I recalled from my previous visit and, more recently, from MyMateMargaret's database that the hotel restaurant closed one evening a week and I was pretty sure that it was Monday evening which suited me, this being Sunday. But I needed to check.

'Can I dine here in the hotel tonight?'

'Oh yes, if you want to.'

'You are not closed this evening? Only, you do close one evening don't you?' The girl shrugged. 'What time shall I come down for dinner?'

She shrugged again. 'It's up to you.'

'Half past seven?'

'Yes that should be OK.'

'Right, so dinner down here at half past seven then,' I confirmed, although I was not yet convinced. Perhaps I was distracted by her relaxed responses to my enquiries. I looked through the doorway into the dining area. 'I eat just in there, do I?'

The girl waved vaguely at the chairs and tables. 'Yes around there.' She flapped her hand at the lounge area on the street side of the hotel, 'or just around there.'

She did not seem at all engaged in providing for my stay. It was probably just the manner of the youth of today.

I came down to dinner, right on the spot of half past seven. 'OK,' I said, rubbing my hands together, 'where's dinner?'

'Oh, where you like, really, it's your choice. Anywhere there.' She waggled her hand towards the front door.

I wandered uncertainly into the lounge and bar area and stood looking at the low sofas and ankle-high coffee tables. How did she expect me to eat here? I returned to her reception desk.

'Um... can you show me where I should eat please?'

'Well, where you like, really.' She walked with me to the front door. 'There's a pizza restaurant across the little square there, I think that is open on Sundays. There's a sort of grill place down that way.' She pointed down the street in the opposite direction. 'You'll find somewhere to eat,' she reassured me.

But obviously not in the hotel. As I sat on a wobbly wooden chair in the poky little restaurant, decorated in the rustic style, I tried to fathom out where our communication had broken down. I had clearly asked if I could dine in the hotel tonight. My French may be old fashioned but it is correct and clear. All the subsequent obfuscation had been caused by my thinking that she was telling me where the dining room in the hotel could be found whilst she was directing me to various restaurants in the town.

The man behind me begins to grumble to the waitress about the table decorations.

'But I don't like those things there,' he complains. She takes no notice and serves him his next course.

I read the label on the bottle of water from source *Sergentale* in the Auvergne which admits that the low output of the spring does not permit them to advertise. The man behind me is talking to himself now. I think of the girl in the hotel at Aubusson who gave me weird directions which brought me back to my starting point. Had I really lost my ability to make myself understood in French? It appeared so.

I eat some smoked salmon and follow it with a steak accompanied by floury chips of the sort that you can throw straight from the freezer into the frier. Some things are crawling up my trouser legs. I think they are ants. The keyring on my sandal hooks itself onto an invisible projection on the table leg. It is a distraction but I am still pondering the problem of the failure of communication. I reason that what these young people no longer do, is to talk or think in sentences and so when I address them in grammatical phrases they save themselves the bother of trying to sort out exactly what I have said by 'googling' my sentence. She just threw my question into her mental search engine and it came up with the words, 'dinner' and 'tonight' and 'where' and she formed an answer based on a possible enquiry which might have used all of these words. The precise nature of the enquiry was not important.

The man behind me is now smoking a perfumed cigar.

Back at the hotel, I clock in to Mission Control.

'You've not rung for two days. Where have you been?'

'I'm still in France, if that is the nature of your enquiry.'

'Why no phone call?'

'Well, the Golden Lion's mother did not have a phone and the ghastly place I stayed in last night didn't even have a toilet seat. I need to talk to you about that.'

'Don't be vulgar. Continental sanitary ware is not a topic for genteel conversation. Now pay attention, this could be important. The BBC left a message on your answerphone.'

'Oh yes? Which part of the BBC?'

'Radio 4.'

'What do they want? Not another ratings-busting appearance on *You and Yours?* They enjoyed it last time didn't they?'

'Will you be quiet for a moment? Thank you. They want to do a programme on the history of the passport and thought you would like to take part.'

'They would have great difficulty doing it without me.'

'Don't be so arrogant.'

'What is the programme?'

'*The Archive Hour.*'

'Never heard of it. They don't play it on the World Service. What's the format?'

'It's an hour long programme where they dig out old recordings from their sound archive.' MyMateMargaret's voice was brimming with enthusiasm and energy and the promise of a new hat and outfit for London.

'Sounds daft to me.'

'Why?'

'Well, what noise does a passport make?'

Out went the hat.

'That's not the point. They find recordings of people talking about passports.' I could detect a soupçon of petulance creeping into her voice.

'It's a crackpot idea. I've traced passports back three and a half thousand years, their sound archive cannot go back much further than a hundred years.'

Out went the suit.

'So what will you tell them?' Her voice was rather small.

'It can wait till I get home.' Got to leave her with some hope, after all, she is still my lifeline. 'Only a couple more days.'

20 – Neufchatel en Bray

I am sure that the mediaeval timbered buildings of Bernay, whatever their authenticity, are much admired by tourists but they have one disadvantage – they provide roosts for pigeons and Bernay has pigeons in squadrons. The lads perched by my window must have finished ops for the day and had decided to do some carousing outside the mess. They got up to all the usual stuff: dancing on the piano, playing rugby over the sofas, trying to drink the wingco under the table. I don't mind good clean high spirits and I can understand why they act as they do, never knowing from one day to the next whether it will be their name that will be rubbed from the blackboard but I admit that I am a bit of a nimby in this respect. Why could they not have celebrated outside a window further along?

But when I came down to breakfast and saw the faces of the other guests I drew the conclusion that between us we must have entertained the entire air force. No matter. Breakfast, we all knew from the information supplied by the hotel, was served from seven o'clock and I had eighty miles to do to reach my last Golden Lion so I needed to get cracking, which was why I was standing in reception scrutinising the faces of the other guests. But it is a quarter past seven, should I not be tucking into croissants and steaming black coffee? How perceptive you are and this thought had occurred to the others who milled around looking at their watches and wondering whether Normandy time was different from the rest of France. One couple even started to count out their cash on the desk to see if they could leave their payment and depart. All the cars had been loaded, maps had been folded and re-folded to the day's route and windscreens had been cleaned. What was needed now was the breakfast that we had been promised would be available from seven o'clock.

At twenty minutes to eight a lady turned up and busied herself with tidying the newspapers at the reception desk and collecting money from departing guests. Any timid requests for sustenance she met by declaring that breakfast was available from eight o' clock. Remonstrance that every notice in the hotel indicated an earlier start was parried with a bare faced denial of the facts and the declaration that as it was she who was going to serve breakfast, and she would not do it before eight o' clock, then she was patently right. She had blue eyes which suggested that she had Norman antecedents and yet, for reasons too obscure to explain, I was convinced that she was a Liverpudlian pretending to be French.

Today was the day! If it went as it should I would be sleeping tonight in my eighteenth and final Lion d'Or before taking the ferry home from Dieppe. And I would have succeeded in my safari but I should not count my chickens; there remained still quite a distance to cover. Today I would have to keep moving as much as I could. The stops would have to be short. I could foresee eight hours in the saddle.

The sky was clear and the sun already strong as I followed in the train of the German cyclist of yesterday and took the road to Serquigny. It was a broad smooth swathe of tarmac which clung lovingly to the curves of the wooded valley side. The traffic was light, the gradients were slight and I fairly flew along it. The only flint in my muesli was an annoying clicking which had started up on my left pedal.

I invoked the ostrich defence and tried to ignore it because I knew what it meant. Eventually I had to stop and empty the sand from my ears. My left pedal bearing was seizing up and I could do little about it. No cyclist carries a pedal spanner with him; it is a foot long and rarely used outside a workshop. But if I did not find a solution, the bearings would weld the pedal solidly to its axle and jam it in one position so that my foot would be thrown off it with each revolution of the crank. I had cycled nine hundred miles and was only eighty miles from my goal, I could not fail now.

I stopped to buy some almond-coated croissants and I examined the damage. When I turned the pedal, it grated and cracked like a coffee grinder. Incidentally, did you know that Peugeot, who made bicycles before they made cars, actually started by manufacturing coffee grinders? But I am only trying to distract you from drawing the conclusion that I had not maintained my bicycle as I should have done. Such an inference would be as unkind as it were ill-informed. To return to the pedal, I prised off the cap and peered in at the bearings. I could see two or three small silver balls and a lot of stuff which looked like steel wool. That would be the remains of the other ball bearings. It was not good news. Would it last until tonight? I had to hope so. There was no way of knowing. I decided to carry on to the first big town and purchase some grease. In the interim, I proceeded with the subtle manipulation that had worked in the past: I stood back and gave the end of the pedal a hefty kick with the heel of my shoe. And when I started off again, it ran as smoothly as silk.

I climbed up through the wooded hillside to reach the plain of Le Neubourg. It had not changed much since I had first cycled on it forty years earlier. The entrance to the town was dominated by the statue of Jacques Charles Dupont de l'Eure who had been born there and gone on to become the president of France during the provisional revolutionary government of 1848. More relevant to my history was a new sign pointing the way to the Museum of Anatomical Models. My very first visit to France had been as an exchange student. The family owned a country house nearby and it was in their works that these models were built up. I remembered the papier maché and the red and blue sleeved wires which were twisted to make the arteries. I would have to wait for a return visit to visit this museum; I had more important tasks to attend to.

The old railway station had been converted into the tourist office and the line into a superb cycle track. Unfortunately it did not go in the direction that I needed. I did accost a couple of cyclists to ask whether they had a tube of grease with them. He looked at her and she looked at him and they exchanged glances which clearly showed that they believed that I belonged to a clandestine organisation and had uttered some sort of secret password to which they were expected to respond. Whatever the ramifications of their misunderstanding the result was the same. No grease.

But why did I need grease? Was not my pedal behaving perfectly? And was I not maintaining a good speed? I could see no advantage in seeking complications. I pressed on towards the Seine. The fields were dotted with roly-poly bales and the edges of the road were sprinkled with grain. In the village of Tostes I stopped to eat a croissant and noticed that the village sign declared that it was part of the 'communes north of the Seine'. This confused me. I felt certain that had I crossed the Seine I would have noticed. It was not a puddle that you could jump over. My map was emphatic. I was still south of the Seine. I can offer no explanation for the sign; local aspirations, perhaps?

With the loose bolt of the clinkometer rattling in the tube, I hurtled down the long descent into the valley of the Seine. Pont de l'Arche was to be my crossing point – where the river Eure flows into the Seine. In fact, the rivers join under the bridge. There has been a bridge here since

Roman times, it being a natural defensive site. The town still has a few ramparts scattered about and the old main street winds down to the bank from which the 1858 stone arched bridge stretched across to the north bank. Now, its replacement strides across, boldly claiming that, as at the 29th January 1955 when it was opened, it held the record for the longest welded girder bridge in Europe. In 1955 when a heavy goods vehicle was one which carried 10 tons, could they have imagined that within fifty years, forty four ton lorries would be snorting across the bridge, nose to tail in both directions? I eyed them with distaste and misgiving. I did not want to share my space with such monsters, however, when I approached closer I found that the cyclists were directed onto the sidewalk. It was not a pleasant crossing; with lorries rumbling by on one side and a fifty foot drop into the water on the other, the consequences of an inadvertent deflection to the right or left looked very unappealing.

Historically, the industries of Normandy have leaned towards the extractive: stone and gravel for construction, chalk for cement, peat for fuel and sand for the excuse to dig up the road which I have taken from the other end of the bridge as a short cut to the main road. How do they get away with it? They have simply erected a fence across the highway and converted it into a quarry. I retraced my route to the bridge and joined the traffic running eastwards. Well, it was worth a try. Nothing ventured, nothing gained, as the world's non-achievers proclaim in the smugness of their defeat.

My aim was to cycle up the valley of the river Andelle which would take me to Forges les Eaux. From there ran a railway cycle track straight to Neufchatel en Bray and my victorious final Golden Lion. After a few miles of main road I recognised a village through which I had passed once on my way to Spain. Its importance was that here, you could take a minor road which ran along the quiet side of the

valley and leave the main road for the busy traffic yet I
hesitated before I turned. Was there not something else I
had to remember about this road? Nothing came to mind,
it was only a vague feeling so I took the plunge. The lane
ran under a line of majestic trees alongside a ruined abbey,
over the weirs of whose mill the Andelle sparkled gaily as it
tumbled. I remembered the ruins. And now I remembered
the hill. It was 1 in 8 and utterly pointless. You climbed up
the side of the valley and then came straight down again.
But it was prettier and quieter than the main road so who
cares?

I would have called the Andelle a trout stream. It ran
clear over a brown pebbled bed and in some places flowed
quite swiftly under leaning trees. What astonished me was
that the valley was highly industrialised. Every turn of the
road revealed another factory. Whether these were the
children of forges or spinning mills, both of which had
been very important in this area in the nineteenth century,
I never found out.

As the day wore on and I wore out, the factories became
sparser in the upper reaches of the valley. I stopped in a
hamlet and enjoyed their garden by the river. The croissant
dusted with almonds which I had bought that morning, I
found to be too sweet for my taste so I wrapped it up in its
paper and thrust it back into my cycle bag. Three days later
I rediscovered it tucked into a corner of my bag and so I
presented it to MyMateMargaret. For the moment, I walked
to the shop and bought myself some bread and cheese.

My computer showed that I had cycled nearly sixty miles
and it was still the early afternoon. My policy of taking
frequent but short stops had paid off. Also, the wind was still
vaguely behind me, a factor not to be ignored. I only had
about twenty more miles to cover. Now that success was
within my grasp, I should have felt a sort of elation and I
suppose I did, somewhere within my psyche, but I had to
concentrate on the task in hand. This did not stop me from

dreaming of fame as the man who pedalled across France in his pyjamas and stayed only in Lion d'Ors.

Further up the valley I saw a terrace of Norman timbered workers' cottages which had been built alongside the road. They looked quite bizarre – an emblem of industrialisation in the middle of rusticana

Click, click, click. Oh dear. That pedal is reasserting itself. I try pushing with my right leg only but the extra effort hurts my hip and knee and I cannot generate enough momentum to swing the left pedal over without having to press on it. And when I press on it, it clicks.

Click crack, click crack, click crack. Only eighteen miles more, surely it will hold out? I freewheel down every slope.

Click crack bonk, click crack bonk, click crack bonk. I am not going to make it. These noises signal the final collapse of my bearings. I stop on a patch of tarmac outside a church and lean my bicycle against the wall. I take a drink of water and think. What have I got in my tool kit that could help? I lay it out on the ground but I already know that I do not have a socket spanner long enough to reach the nut on the bearing race. Eighteen miles, that's all I need, eighteen miles.

I pull out some bread and cheese and have another think. As if in a dream I take out MyMateMargaret's survival pack. I had discarded everything except the Savlon. I only need grease. Well surely Savlon is greasy? I unscrew the cap from the tube to reveal a long snout like an ant-eater. The kind of snout that will reach right down the inside of my pedal to the shredded bearings. The cars wander past, unheeding, as an Englishman kneels piously before a church and pumps antiseptic cream into his bicycle pedal. I did not hear another complaint from that pedal for two months.

I reached Forges les Eaux at half past four and rolled onto the cycle track. Around the town we curved until I finally hit the old railway line that would lead me home.

This Monday afternoon of the 13th August, people were strolling, children were skipping and roller skating, families were gossiping five abreast and cyclists were passing in both directions. Unknown to them all, history was being made. Martin Lloyd was less than ten miles from his final Golden Lion.

I stopped at a wooden cabin before which a tangle of bicycles was leaning. The terrace around the chalet had been laid with gravel and sown with tables and chairs. *Chez Dominique* was obviously a popular refreshment stop for all. I sat chatting to a group of French cyclists, husbands and wives, who went on an annual cycle ride together. This year they had cycled around the Dieppe region and were now returning homewards via the *voie verte*. Where would they go next year, they wondered?

'I would like to try the Forest of Compiègne,' said one of the ladies.

'It's very green and shaded,' I said.

'That would be good. You can have too much sun.'

'You can in France. Not in England.' And then it occurred to me. 'Why don't you try the other end of this track in England? It's called the Cuckoo Trail. You could all get the ferry from Dieppe to Newhaven and then cycle along to Eastbourne and up the Trail, just as I will be doing tomorrow.'

'Yes, we've seen the notices about it. Is it like this?'

'Well, it is an old railway line but it is much prettier. The landscape is more varied and we do not spray weed killer along the track like you do. It is fringed with wild flowers and all kinds of animals and birds.'

'And the surface is like this?'

'Ah no, that is where you beat us. The surface is rougher; gravel, tarmac, loose shingle, but you can ride it on an ordinary bicycle, you don't need thick tyres.'

I left them pondering. I had a Golden Lion to bag. For the last eight miles I put my head down and steamed along at fifteen miles per hour. It was a pointless demonstration but I was impressed by my ability to achieve such a feat after more than seventy miles pedalled.

At half past six, glowing with effort and pride, I rode majestically up the main street of Neufchatel en Bray towards the beckoning sign of the Lion d'Or.

I had dined on a *croustillant de Neufchatel*, which turned out to be cheese on toast and a *magret de canard* which always suggests to me the literary character of a French duck detective. To complete this bizarre sounding but palatable meal, I had consumed a *soupe de fruits* which was exactly what it said it was. I was now in my room, toying with the telephone. MyMateMargaret would be waiting for me to clock in. I dialled her number. You know what her first question was, don't you?

'Where are you?'

'At Neufchatel en Bray where I am supposed to be.'

'Well done!'

'I did eighty miles today in seven hours of cycling. I simply flew along.'

'Brilliant. What time will you get back tomorrow? The ferries from Dieppe are at 08.30 and 13.30.'

'I'll take the half past one. That will get me in to Newhaven by about half past four. Say a couple of hours to Eastbourne then up the hill to Polegate and onto the Cuckoo Trail.'

'I'll meet you at Horam then. In the car park.'

'Thanks. I'll look forward to that.' You have to say things like that to keep them sweet. 'It's a good job I thought to do the tour this way around, I see in the paper that there are thirty thousand pilgrims in Lourdes today. That is where I would have been.'

'A good job WHO thought to do the tour this way around?

'Well, it was a joint decision.'

'But my idea.' I didn't rise to the bait. It is not worth the anguish. 'So what is the Lion d'Or at Neufchatel like?'

Decision time. Do I tell her the truth?

'Um... well... I don't really know.'

'Why not?'

'I'm not in it. It closed down some years ago. Apparently. Funny isn't it? I'm in a hotel up the road.'

There are some aspects of a relationship which should always remain special. And secret. I would not want to burden you with an account of what was said. I am sure you can imagine it perfectly. And of course, my feelings were a matter of trifling consequence in the discussion. The Golden Lion sign which had welcomed me to Neufchatel had been swinging above an insurance office. I had not booked the hotel in advance because I had stayed in it twice before and there had never been any problems finding accommodation; it had always had rooms available. That, I realised in retrospect, was an appetiser of the dish that the devil's chef was preparing for me in the Kitchen of Fate. The Lion d'Or was now a block of flats.

As I lay in bed with my ears stinging, my brain ran over the fantastic journey that I had nearly brought to a close. Before my mind's eye paraded the Golden Lions, good and bad; the sumptuous meals and the simple; the changing countryside and the extraordinary encounters; and as my limbs and mind thankfully surrendered to sleep it occurred to me that, if I were to align myself with the promoters of the oft-heard conceit, then I had surely succeeded in my quest to cross France staying only in Lions d'Ors. I pulled the bed clothes up closer around my ears. After all, was I not in my very own *'lit on dort'*?

21 – CLEARING UP

The morrow awoke with a breeze. The direction of the wind was of minor import compared to its magnitude. This afternoon I was to cross the Channel and not on the very narrow bit. In over forty years of such maritime reciprocation I had never been sick. By divulging this statistic I am not courting your admiration; I am seeking your sympathy. On several occasions I have wished to be sick; my co-travellers, who turn all shades of the spectrum, successfully achieve this simple gastro-convulsive operation but I always remain tight-lipped and jealously possessive of all my emanations. And it makes me feel awful. Whilst the erstwhile sufferers of *mal de mer* leap gleefully about the foc'sle, lighter in spirit and, perforce, body, I slop around the deck moaning and sweating, praying for release.

However, to continue this peroration would only leave a bad taste in one's mouth. The track coastwards was smooth and flat and, dare I say it, just a little bit boring? Passing through villages I occasionally met a person dragging along a reluctant hound. In one village the activity was the other way around; the dog was walking ahead and then turning in exasperation to wait for its owner to catch up.

Before leaving Neufchatel I had managed to purchase some savoury pastries and fruit to feed me on this, my final day. It was a welcome change from the inescapable sweet pastries of Normandy. The track ended a few miles short of Dieppe and I stopped there for my elevenses. I leaned my bicycle up against the sign which foretold the imminent end of the track. It wobbled. Alarm bells began to ring in my head. Instead of being implanted firmly in the ground the sign sat on the gravel, weighed down by a broad heavy base. It looked like a giant toy. The Ignominy of Poitiers sprang to mind and I moved my bicycle across the track and leaned it against a tree.

You see, one day, I was coming back from a wedding in Poitiers; my bicycle was loaded with bags front and back and I was looking forward to a relaxed five or six day ride to the coast. At lunchtime on the first day I stopped in the square in a small town whose name now escapes me. My inability to recall the name is probably evidence of a neurological safeguard denying me access to the trauma caused by the incident. I cycled slowly around the square, which was rectangular. I noted the several brasseries and cafés with terraces set out attractively; I remarked upon the statue in the middle of the square and of the greenness of the lawns surrounding it but I did not find a bench to sit upon. At my second circuit I noticed that several of the locals had sat themselves on the grass. There was no sign forbidding such activity so I joined them.

Speared into the lawn stood a road sign. Its purpose was to forbid drivers from parking on that side of the square and it looked like a giant lollipop. It was inviting me to lean my bicycle against it, which I accordingly did. But this sign had the potential to furnish me with further comforts for I noticed that it cast an elliptical shadow on the grass behind. I took my picnic from my cycle and installed myself in the shadow rather as if I were sitting on a picnic rug.

The commerces of the square began to liven up. The terraces filled with diners and soon the orchestration of plates, glasses and cutlery was noised abroad, titivated by the chorale of waiters shouting orders to the bar. I had apparently stumbled upon a very popular lunchtime eating place. Over to my left, a young couple were canoodling on the grass and to my right a mother was entertaining two children. We sat and looked at the diners; they sat and looked at us.

As the sun moved higher in the sky, my adumbral picnic rug migrated across the grass towards the sign and I was obliged to shuffle myself with it if I wanted to remain in the shade, which, given the intensity of the heat, was my desire. By the time that I had finished, I was sitting close against the sign and the picnic rug was the width of a football sock. But I could not sit here all day. I dusted the crumbs from my fingers, leaned forwards and grasped the pole of the sign to pull myself up. The sequence of events which then occurred confused me somewhat. I had performed the manoeuvre with success, that I was sure of, for success would result in the pole being in closer proximity to my body than it had been before. The pole was definitely closer to me, but I was not standing. I was lying on my back looking up at a dazzling sun. On top of me lay the road sign and across that lounged my bicycle. Can you imagine the possible embarrassment that could be felt by any person of a sensitive nature should he find himself in the middle of a town square in full view of a hundred diners, having just uprooted a road sign which had reacted by laying him out flat?

I do not consider myself to be unusually sensitive but I did experience a few thrills of anguish as I flailed and struggled beneath the combined weight of sign and bicycle. I was pinned down like a specimen on a dissection board. I tried to heave the sign up but it was in consort with my bicycle. Both were determined to ridicule me. My plight had excited the interest of many but not sufficiently for any of them to proffer assistance so I squeezed and wriggled, heaved and squirmed until I reached free lawn. I stood up and pulled my bicycle from its intimate embrace with the street furniture. Now, of course, I had nowhere to lean it so I had to lay it down on the grass. I was then confronted with the supine sign. I was surrounded by goggling eyes, I could not ignore the results of my vandalism, I would have to make reparations.

The concrete base in which the pole had been cast had ripped up through the grass as I had pulled the sign over. This movement had been treacherously promoted by my heavy bicycle jeering as it had pushed from the other side. I stood the sign up and coaxed the concrete plug back into the crater. I tentatively released the pole and as my bicycle insolently shouted, 'timber!' the giant lollipop measured its length on the grass.

By now, all around the square, main courses were going cold and diners were rushing off to get their video cameras. I usually perform well before an audience but that day I could not raise the enthusiasm. I unceremoniously stood the sign up and ran for my bicycle. Before I had reached it the umpire's whistle had blown and the hated pole was already leaning as if foraging in the grass for worms. Subterfuge and disguised speed were what was needed. I grasped the pole in a confident manner and stood it upright in its crater. I twisted it to bed it in and then I stamped around it, rather as if I were planting a tree. When I was certain that it was absolutely vertical, I released it and dusted off my hands with a job well done. I just hoped that a sparrow was not going to land on it before I got out of town, for the distant audience could not see, but I knew that it was teetering.

I hauled up my bicycle from its sunbathing and kicked it up to a rapid fifteen mph as I tore out of the square and up the road towards home. After a hundred yards, when I was certain that I was out of sight of the diners, I stopped and looked back. The lollipop was slowly inclining to the horizontal. Not my problem now.

Now you know why I leaned my bicycle against a tree.

I had not passed through Dieppe for several decades. I was expecting there to have been some changes but the obvious one I had not thought of – the ferries no longer come into the town centre. Dieppe used to be one of those picturesque working ports where the ships tied up at a cobbled quayside laced with railway lines and planted with cranes and across the road one could espy the population shopping and visiting the bars. You were right in the middle of activity. But of course, ships had grown larger and so to accommodate them a brand new port had been built under the cliff, outside the entrance to the old port. Once I had realised this, I ignored the signs entreating me to make a wide diversion around the town on a fast road and instead I navigated myself through the centre of town on quieter, safer roads. Marginally safer, that is, for I discovered that I had acquired an unusual quality: I had become invisible. Buses pulled away from the kerb before me and pedestrians stepped off the pavement and continued across the highway, unheedingly closing the acute angles of an obvious collision course. It was bizarre and unnerving.

The port might have been brand new but it was comforting to see that the Dieppe Chamber of Commerce could still do 'retro' when it tried. The outside was designed in the contemporary Municipal this-will-get-us-EC-funding style but the interior conformed to the homely French architectural ethos of shall-we-put-a-door-here? design. I thought I had stepped back into the 1960s; a time when you could see the '*Join the Foreign Legion*' posters in all the French channel port terminals. The poster was the only artefact missing. This is a terminal from a time-warp. It has tiled floors and cream paint. People are queuing through wooden doorways; papers are handed through hatchways like hot dinners and the air is uncluttered with tannoy announcements. Whilst I am buying my ticket, what I took to be a wooden cupboard door at the side of me opens and disembarking travellers poke enquiring heads through.

'Where is our baggage?' they want to know. With a flick of her pen, the hostess directs them back into the café, where the baggage x-ray machine is spewing out cases.

I buy my ticket and sit outside, enjoying sunshine from a stationary position. I had not done much of that over the last three weeks. The departing foot passengers deposit their suitcases in a trailer parked on the patio. They have every confidence that this apparently ad-hoc approach to loading the ship would function perfectly, and so had I.

And then Sententious Twit arrives. He is accompanied by two boys. He chooses a table near me and validates his choice with the observation, 'sit here boys because I don't think that gentleman there is going to smoke.' This manner of speaking about people in a loud voice in public, I find irritatingly presumptious. Had I been intending to smoke, I now feel obliged to desist for the sake of his children. The phraseology is an insidious affectation which isolates the perpetrator from the victim by making it clear to everybody that, as one is of a different class to the other man, then one would not envisage talking to him, only about him.

'You might pass the salt' was once inflicted upon me by a hoity-toity aspirant aristocrat. Was he making a risk assessment? I might pass the salt, on the other hand, I might not. And if I did pass the salt, what would ensue? It took me some time to realise that what he meant was, 'please pass the salt'. He could not have said that, of course, because he would have been begging for a favour instead of reminding me of my feudal duty.

I was in MyMateJohn's bookshop one day, before it became a sandwich bar, and I was browsing along the shelves when I became aware of a sports jacket and rimless spectacles at the side of me. He turned back to a wigwam eyebrows and blue rinse.

'I am trying to my dear,' he said to her and all the shop in a loud voice, shifting plums from one cheek to the other as he did so, 'but that man is in the way and he won't move.'

That was news to me. He had not asked me to move. Probably because he feared that my response would have been to ask why. The answer, we all knew, was that I was looking at the shelf that he wanted to look at and he could not see why I had not evaporated the moment that he had walked into the shop. He should have got up earlier in the morning and then he would have been standing where I was. Everybody has to be somewhere. I never did learn what he was looking for. Instead I developed a sudden and all-consuming interest in jam making and preserves, which just happened to feature in the nearest book to hand and the shock of discovering this passion afflicted me with a profound deafness.

I could benefit from that deafness now. The two boys have started to whoop like locomotives, each one trying to outdo the other. They are not playing a game, they are just being obnoxious. Now the man is whistling the same five notes of a popular tune over and over again. It is not a popular tune with me. I wish I smoked.

The boys spend the next ten minutes fighting and screaming on the patch of grass in front of me. They are biting each other, and yelling and grunting and punching. He is obviously bringing them up to be louts. Now they are crying.

'Come here boys. Sit there. Now tell me why are you both crying?'

'He punched me.'

'Well you bit me.'

'So you both got hurt did you? That is why you are crying. And do you know why you both got hurt? It was because you were fighting. So, the answer is simple, isn't it? If you don't want to get hurt, don't fight.'

Sententious twit.

'Why are the cliffs white?' one of the lachrymose louts splutters. He obviously knows the vanity of his target. Responding majestically to the invitation, the man declares,

'Because they are chalk.'

'Can we write with it?'

'If you took a hammer and chisel and chipped off a piece you could draw on the pavement with it.' Just as I suspected – they have not yet learned the alphabet. 'Do you know where it came from?' he continues, 'it was all pushed up by volcanoes.'

I somehow think he has missed the point about isostatic recovery, and I winced at his inability to distinguish between igneous and sedimentary rock. He probably thinks that sedimentary rocks are stones that sit down all day long.

At last I board the ship and find myself assisting a young lady to attach her bicycle to the ship's side to prevent it from flailing about the car deck. I am not a person to push my company on strangers. I rarely have the chance, they usually run away but Abby, as the young lady tells me her name is, seems quite unconcerned that we should sit together and chat to pass the time on the crossing. It was the best investment I made. The crossing should have taken four hours, it took over five. All around the coast of Britain, ships were holed up in ports or running for cover. Storm warnings went out. MyMateMargaret was glued to the internet trying to work out what was going to happen to me and all this time, Abby and I were chatting quite unconcernedly, about her life in China and Russia and her immediate intention to move to France to teach English as a foreign language. I did not see the time passing.

Abby had a super story to tell and wanted to write it up. I hope I enthused her and guided her with my advice and obervations and opened her eyes also, to the hard graft that would be coming her way. And when we got to Newhaven she lent me her mobile phone (after dialling the number for me) so that I could announce my safe arrival to Mission Control.

Then it was onto the Seaford road in the rush hour – a car passing every two seconds, the rain howling down, the south westerly gale blowing me off the road twice as I climb Beachy Head. I am out of breath for the first time in three weeks and I am going to be late for the rendezvous at Horam. Always conscious of MyMateMargaret's searing intransigence, I struggle into a telephone kiosk, my water-proofs-that-aren't flapping in the gale, the water pouring down my neck. I have carried those two twenty pence pieces all around France, from Golden Lion to Golden Lion. They had asked each other what they were doing there but now their moment of glory has come. I leave a message on her answering machine giving my progress and revised ETA. She is the one who is IT-savvy. I know she can pick it up on her mobile phone and adjust her activity accordingly.

Water is collecting in my shoes, sloshing from heel to toe and back again as I pedal. At Polegate I squeeze into a bus shelter and eat a *pain au chocolat*. I now have my lights on. I find the Cuckoo Trail and start a mad and manic high speed pedal up the trail in the pitch dark, thin branches of sopping leaves slap my face as I veer around the various gates and posts; cats, badgers, rats and other fauna scurry away into the undergrowth.

I can see my van sitting in the car park. MyMateMargaret is there.

'You're late.'

How can you possibly be late after three weeks and a thousand miles?

'I left you a message on your answerphone. Didn't you get it?'

She has the grace to look a little abashed. 'My mobile phone doesn't work here. There is no coverage.'

'That's why I didn't take one with me,' I lied. 'You just can't rely upon them.'

I emptied the water from my shoes and climbed into the van.

Home.

And here I am finishing the last chapter. The watch is back in my drawer, never to be needed again; the Savlon is still in the pedal and my sandals are still held together with a keyring. I fixed my handlebars but the saddle was not such an easy proposition so I had it entirely rebuilt by Tony Colegrave to a standard and specification higher than the original. It is bliss under the bum.

MyMateJohn pretends to fuss about his being mentioned in the book but he likes the idea really. He does not try to discourage me and when, in the middle of my writing chapter six, he drilled his electric screwdriver through the end of my right index finger, putting me out of action for a fortnight, I did not take this as evidence of disapprobation but rather as a bonding ritual, binding us forever in blood. Only my blood, as it transpired but I suppose that is the way of the world.

At Christmas I received a postcard from France. Abby was having a great time in Rouen and any time that I was passing, I would be welcome to visit her. Well, I say the card was from Abby but it was difficult to be sure. If it was you, Abby, and you do succeed in writing the book that you have in you, take a tip from a successful writer. Make sure you put your address on your typescript when you send it to your publisher; it will enable them to correspond with you.

And if you sign it with your name, they will even know who sent it to them.

Every Picture

Martin Lloyd

"... *a tender and engaging love story...*"

When Jennifer Pye bumped into Richard Ennessy on his first day at art college she did not know that he was a viscount and he did not tell her. Why should he? How was he to know that their paths would cross and recross and that he would end up falling in love with her?

And once that had happened, he then found it impossible to tell her the truth for fear of losing her. At the very moment that they finally admit their feelings for one another, the relationship is abruptly wrenched asunder as their lives take a violent and unpredictable turn, casting their two destinies onto divergent courses.

Would they ever meet again?

Published by Queen Anne's Fan ISBN: 9780 9547 1505 2

The Trouble with France

Martin Lloyd's new international
number one blockbusting
bestseller

"…makes Baedeker's look like a guidebook…"

When Martin Lloyd set out on his holiday to Suffolk why
did he end up in Boulogne? What caused Max the Mad
Alsatian to steal his map and what did the knitted
grandma really think of his display of hot plate juggling?
The answers to these and many more mysteries are to be
found in THE TROUBLE WITH FRANCE

THE TROUBLE WITH FRANCE contains no recipes and
no hand drawn maps. It does not recount how somebody
richer than you went to a part of France that you have
never heard of, bought a stone ruin for a song and
converted it into a luxurious retreat which they expect
you to finance by buying their book.

Nor is it the self satisfied account of another ultra fit
expedition cyclist abseiling down Everest on a penny
farthing but Martin Lloyd attempting an uneventful ride
on a mundane bicycle through an uninteresting part
of France… and failing with outstanding success.

THE TROUBLE WITH FRANCE is destined to be a worldwide
success now that Margaret's Mum has been down the
road and told her friend Pat about it.

Published by Queen Anne's Fan ISBN: 9780 9547 1500 7

NOW IN ITS FIFTH IMPRESSION

...also available as an audiobook

Listen at your leisure whilst
Martin Lloyd reads

The Trouble with France

complete and unabridged.

More than five hours of
entertainment on five CDs.

Published by Queen Anne's Fan ISBN: 9780 9547 1504 5

*Martin Lloyd has recorded THE TROUBLE WITH FRANCE as
a talking book for the blind. RNIB catalogue no: TB 15323*

The Trouble with Spain

MARTIN LLOYD

FROM THE BESTSELLING AUTHOR OF
THE TROUBLE WITH FRANCE *COMES*
THIS EAGERLY AWAITED SEQUEL

"...makes Munchausen look like a liar..."

Still smarting from his brutal encounter with Gaul as
detailed in his much acclaimed book, THE TROUBLE WITH
FRANCE, Martin Lloyd drags his bicycle over the Pyrenees
to pursue the twin delights of sun and breakfast.

What factor will defeat his proposed headlong plunge
into raw hedonism? Will it be his profound and extensive
ignorance of Spanish history or perhaps his coarse
insensitivity to the culture of the peninsula?
Or would it be the damning condemnation that
he is just too lazy to learn the language?

Read THE TROUBLE WITH SPAIN and you will discover
nothing about bull fights and enjoy no colourful
descriptions of sensual flamenco dancing but you will
learn why you cannot train goldfish to be guard dogs
and you will clearly understand why even
Martin Lloyd's trousers ran away from him.

CAUTION
This book contains moderate use of humour, some
expressions in foreign language and a short but ultimately
frustrating scene in a lady's bedroom.

Published by Queen Anne's Fan ISBN: 9780 9547 1501 4

The
Chinese
Transfer

Martin Lloyd

The

Chinese Transfer

a thriller romance that you will not
want to put down

"...this is storytelling as it used to be..."

Paris in the 1970s – student demonstrations, union strikes
and oppressive heat. Coach driver Simon Laperche is sent
to Orly Airport to pick up a Chinese group and take them
to their hotel in the city. A run of the mill job. He could
do it with his eyes shut. It was a pity about the guide,
but then, he could not expect to please everybody.

Abruptly, things go wrong. The plane is diverted to Lyons
and Laperche is ordered to drive his coach south to
meet it... and he has to take that infuriating guide
with him. Unknown to them both, a terrorist unit has
targeted their group and is intent upon its destruction.

Stalked by the terrorists, the driver and guide continue
to bicker as they struggle to bring their group safely to
Paris. Will the mutual respect which eventually begins
to grow between them prove strong enough
when the test comes?

Published by Queen Anne's Fan ISBN: 9780 9547 1502 1

Martin Lloyd's books are available in all good
bookshops or can be purchased direct from:

Queen Anne's Fan PO Box 883, Canterbury, CT1 3WJ

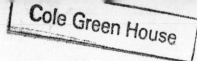

Cole Green House

THE PASSPORT

The History of Man's Most Travelled Document

*SECOND EDITION, REVISED
AND ENLARGED*
with 246 pages and 80 illustrations

The passport is a document familiar to many, used and recognised worldwide and yet it has no basis in law: one country cannot oblige another to admit its subjects simply by issuing a document. But the state, by insisting on the requirement to hold a passport, provides for itself a neat, self-financing data collection and surveillance system.

This well illustrated book tells for the first time the story of the passport from its earliest origins to its latest high-tech developments. Handwritten documents adorned with wax seals, modern versions in plastic covers, diplomatic passports and wartime safe conducts, all drawn from the author's collection, complement the exciting exploits of spies and criminals and the tragic real life experiences of refugees.

Whether recounting the birth of the British blue passport of the 1920s or divulging the secrets of today's machine readable passport, Martin Lloyd has written an informative and engrossing history book which is accessible to everyone.

"...a lively and thoughtful book..."
SUNDAY TELEGRAPH

Published by Queen Anne's Fan ISBN: 9780 9547 1503 8

Martin Lloyd has recorded THE PASSPORT *as a talking book for the blind. RNIB catalogue no: TB 14107*